D0725713

PRAYERS
for
TODAY

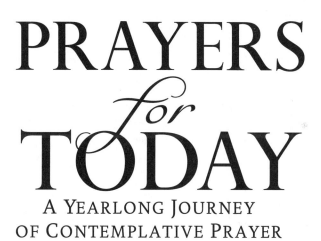

PRAYERS *for* TODAY

A YEARLONG JOURNEY OF CONTEMPLATIVE PRAYER

KURT BJORKLUND

MOODY PUBLISHERS
CHICAGO

© 2011 by
KURT BJORKLUND

All rights reserved. No part of this book may be reproduced in any form without permission in writing from the publisher, except in the case of brief quotations embodied in critical articles or reviews.

All Scripture, unless otherwise indicated, are a paraphrase by the author based on *The Holy Bible, English Standard Version.* Copyright © 2000, 2001 by Crossway Bibles, a division of Good News Publishers.

Scripture paraphrase marked MSG are based on *The Message,* copyright © by Eugene H. Peterson 1993, 1994, 1995.

Scripture quotations marked NASB are taken from the *New American Standard Bible*®, Copyright © 1960, 1962, 1963, 1968, 1971, 1972, 1973, 1975, 1977, 1995 by The Lockman Foundation. Used by permission. (www.Lockman.org)

Scripture quotations marked NIV are taken from the *Holy Bible, New International Version*®, NIV®. Copyright © 1973, 1978, 1984 by Biblica, Inc.™ Used by permission of Zondervan. All rights reserved worldwide. www.zondervan.com

Edited by Jim Vincent
Interior design: Smartt Guys design
Cover design: Dugan Design Group
Cover image: Fotolia, 8209008

Library of Congress Cataloging-in-Publication Data

Prayers for today : a yearlong journey of contemplative prayer / [compiled by] Kurt Bjorklund.
    p. cm.
Includes bibliographical references.
ISBN 978-0-8024-6350-0
1. Prayers. 2. Devotional calendars. I. Bjorklund, Kurt.
BV245.P849 2011
242'.2—dc23

2011027085

We hope you enjoy this book from Moody Publishers. Our goal is to provide high-quality, thought-provoking books and products that connect truth to your real needs and challenges. For more information on other books and products written and produced from a biblical perspective, go to www.moodypublishers.com or write to:

Moody Publishers
820 N. LaSalle Boulevard
Chicago, IL 60610

3 5 7 9 10 8 6 4

Printed in the United States of America

To my wife, Faith
"A wife of noble character is her husband's crown" (Proverbs 12:4 NIV).
You are my crown, my joy, and my best friend.

And to my four sons, Drew, David, Ben, and Nathan
"Sons are a heritage from the Lord, . . .
Like arrows in the hands of a warrior are sons born in one's youth.
Blessed is the man whose quiver is full of them" (Psalm 127:3–5 NIV).

CONTENTS

ACKNOWLEDGMENTS

I am grateful to Brian Shivler, Jackie Wick, Meg Tomko, Shannon Miller, Shirley Bjorklund, and Faith Bjorklund for their support, encouragement, and editing throughout this project. I am also thankful to Leighton Ford for his spiritual mentoring in my life and for pointing me to resources that renewed my spirit. My thanks as well to Hutz Hertzberg for his belief in me and in this project from the early stages.

I want to thank the entire staff team and congregation of Orchard Hill Church for their consistent support and encouragement.

I am grateful for the work of many compilers of prayers, creeds, and liturgies that have reprinted classic works both old and ancient. Most of the works themselves are in public domain, but the compilers and their publishers have made access to these prayers much easier for the authors. In addition to the prayers that are reprinted with permission (see "Permissions"), I wish to acknowledge the following compilations that were helpful in gathering the more than five hundred classic and ancient prayers:

1. *Between Heaven and Earth,* by Ken Gire. New York: HarperOne, 1997.
2. *The Book of Common Prayer*, by the Episcopal Church. New York: The Church Hymnal Corp., 1979.
3. *The Book of a Thousand Prayers*, compiled by Angela Ashwin. Grand Rapids: Zondervan, 1996.
4. *The Catholic Prayer Book.* Cincinnati: St. Anthony Messenger, 1986.
5. *Celtic Daily Prayer: Prayers and Readings from the Northrumbria Community.* New York: Harper Collins, 2002.
6. *The Complete Book of Christian Prayer*. New York: Continuum, 2000.
7. *The Encyclopedia of Prayer and Praise*, edited by Mark Water. Peabody, MA: Hendrickson, 2004.
8. *The Oxford Book of Prayer*, edited by George Appleton. New York: Oxford, 1985.

PERMISSIONS

Grateful acknowledgment is expressed to the following who have granted permission to include copyrighted materials in this book. Every effort has been made to contact those whose material exceeds fair use limits. Any inadvertent omission of credit will be gladly corrected in future editions.

Days 1, 48, 59, 218: Taken from *Pierced by the Word* by John Piper, © 2007, pp. 53, 111, 14, 129, respectively. Used by permission of Crossway, a publishing ministry of Good News Publishers, Wheaton, IL 60187, www.crossway.org.

Days 23, 75, 109, 233: Taken from *A Passion for God* by Raymond C. Ortlund Jr., © 1994, pp. 31, 143–44, 192–93, and 32, respectively. Used by permission of Crossway, a publishing ministry of Good News Publishers, Wheaton, IL 60187, www.crossway.org.

Day 65: Taken from *The Valley of Vision* by Arthur Bennett, © 1975, p. 1. Used by permission of The Banner of Truth, Carlisle, PA 17013, printed edition 2001.

Day 101: "Prayer While Scrubbing a Floor" originally appeared in *I've Got to Talk to Somebody, God* by Marjorie Williams (Garden City, NY: Doubleday, 1969), 30–31. Reprinted with permission from the Estate of Marjorie Holmes. As quoted in *Between Heaven and Earth* by Ken Gire.

Day 134: Taken from *Leadership Prayers* by Richard Kriegbaum, copyright © 1998. Used by permission of Tyndale House Publishers, Inc. All rights reserved.

Day 149: Taken from *Developing a Prayer-Care-Share Lifestyle* by Alvin Vander Griend, published by Hope Ministries, copyright 1999. Used by permission of Mission India. All rights reserved.

Day 155: Taken from *The Face of Love* by Gilbert Shaw, published by SLG Press, Oxford, England, as reprinted in The Oxford Book of Prayer, edited by George Appleton. Used by permission.

Days 163 and 249: Taken from *Prayers for the Christian Year* by William Barclay. Published by SCM Press 1989. © William Barclay. Used by permission of Hymns Ancient & Modern Ltd.

Days 222 and 253: Taken from *Seeing and Savoring Jesus Christ* by John Piper, © 2001, pp. 96–97, 69–70, respectively. Used by permission of Crossway, a publishing ministry of Good News Publishers, Wheaton, IL 60187, www. crossway.org.

INTRODUCTION:
A JOURNEY TO VITAL PRAYERS

As a young Christian, I was drawn to and inspired by the possibilities of prayer. I was drawn to the bold promise of Scripture that God would do anything I asked (John 14:13). This belief was bolstered as I read great books on prayer, like E. M. Bounds' book *The Possibilities of Prayer* and O. Hallesby's *Prayer*. Anytime I heard a compelling quote on prayer I would jot it down. Two of my favorites are:

"Where there is much prayer, there is much power. Where there is little prayer there is little power. And where there is no prayer, there is no power."

"When we work, we work, but when we pray, God works."

My excitement was further enhanced as I prayed and saw God do some truly miraculous things. I was inspired by the possibilities of communicating with the very Creator and Ruler of the entire Universe.

Yet, I was not only drawn to prayer, I was disappointed in prayer. For every miraculous answer, there were dozens of prayers that seemed to garner no response. For every moment of intimacy with God, there were numerous moments characterized by distance. Slowly over the years, my prayers became more a vague "should" than a pathway to the heart of God. Certainly, there were moments of intimacy, but the overriding experience was one of frustration.

To complicate matters, my profession is that of a minister. I preach, counsel, and lead in the spiritual arena constantly. I could not help but feel that there "should" be more to my prayers.

To further compound this disappointment, the tradition of my early faith experience emphasized extemporaneous prayer and viewed the classic practice of liturgy and written prayers with suspicion. On the recommendation of a friend, I tried a prepared book of prayers using Scripture. I began to find renewal in my prayers.

A JOURNEY INTO INTIMACY WITH GOD

Later, I found prayer books written by a variety of people from a range of backgrounds to be helpful in facilitating my own language and experience of prayer. I discovered that as I prayed along with the words others had penned, it gave a voice to my own feelings, longings, and struggles. I also realized I was not alone but shared the company of many who had gone before me. By allowing structure to shape my prayers, I prayed about things I had not prayed about before, and I was connecting with God around the great themes of the Bible. The result? This discipline produced greater intimacy in my prayers—and I found that I learned about myself. For example, I learned that there were areas that I thought I had surrendered to God that I could not easily give to Him in prayer.

I also learned that prayer is not as much about getting God to act in certain ways as it is about getting to the heart of God and getting my heart to reflect His heart. And I learned that the struggles of Christians through the centuries aren't that different from our struggles today.

I still find great value in spontaneous prayer, but often I find value in being prompted by the prayers of others and by Scripture about what and how to pray.

From my personal journey with prayer was born this daily compilation of prayers from classic and contemporary sources, from poems, hymns, and spiritual songs, a fresh translation/paraphrase of Scriptures, and a final prayer called "A Prayer for Today." I invite you to use these prayers daily to discover anew the intimacy with our Father promised through prayer.

ABOUT PRAYING THE SCRIPTURES

Prayers for Today contains three kinds of prayers, described in the next section. None is more valuable than the others, but we begin intentionally with Scripture prayers. By utilizing Scripture to form prayers, we begin to think as God thinks and we pray in a way that is pleasing to God. I believe God loves to hear about our needs, but I also believe that He loves for us to pray back His promises, to pray praise, to pray commitments, and to surrender to Him. Often our prayers can degenerate into a list of needs presented to God. With Scripture as our guide, we can have balance in our prayers.

In addition, by praying the Scriptures, we can personalize the message of the Bible and internalize the truths that we read.

HOW TO USE THIS BOOK

This book is primarily intended to be used as a means for personal prompting for prayer and reflection. There are 260 days of prayers and promptings for prayer. Two hundred and sixty were selected to comprise five a week for fifty-two weeks. Obviously, work through these prayers at whatever pace facilitates prayer for you. They are not dated, but numbered so that you can start anytime, and take breaks anytime. Since they are not dated, you may want to return to the same day many times until you feel a sense of being able to pray with conviction what is written and prompted. Coupled with Bible reading—perhaps with reading the Bible passage associated with the Scripture prayer(s)—these prayers can form the foundation for your personal time with God each day.

Worship leaders, pastors, youth leaders, and small group leaders will also find that this material can be used to lead their congregations or groups in times of prayer and worship.

Each day contains three types of headings. As mentioned earlier, there are Scripture prayers—verses of Scripture translated/paraphrased so that they read as prayers. I worked directly with the Hebrew and Greek to create these translations and found ideas from writers who did similar things in devotional works such as Lancelot Andrewes' *Private Devotions*, Matthew Henry's *Bible Prayers*, and Kenneth Boa's *Face to Face.*

Second, there are written or recited prayers from a variety of sources—some ancient, some in the past one hundred years—that are meant to be read and prayed. You may even find contemporary songwriters next to the early church fathers, reminding us of our need for intimacy and humility and praise before our Father God.

Third, there is a section called "A Prayer for Today." This section is meant to prompt you to pray. While it can simply be read, the use of the ellipses [. . .] indicates a place for you to take some time to reflect and pray through the issue raised. This guide is meant to prompt prayer, not to restrict where God may lead you as you pray and reflect on the theme of each day.

One suggestion is to try praying these prayers out loud. Obviously, pray in whatever way works best for you, but often vocalizing these prayers will help you to not quickly glance over the words. By saying them out loud, and particularly by reading the "Prayer for Today" aloud while filing in your own thoughts and words [where the ellipses appears], you may better internalize the thoughts and prayers of each day.

TYPES OF PRAYERS

The default mode in prayer for many people is coming to God and asking God to do things in their lives. Surely, God invites and values the requests of His people, but this approach to God can quickly erode to coming to God with a grocery list of requests. Yet, there are more than twenty types of prayers that are identifiable in Scripture. Using the teaching of Jesus on prayer (Matthew 6:1–15), ten primary types of prayer have been chosen as the basis for the days of prayer. These ten themes rotate systematically, serving to prompt you to pray in ways that may not be as natural for you to pray. Certainly, in addition to the prompts that are given, pray in whatever way you sense God is leading you.

- *Prayers of Thanksgiving*. While there is no direct indication of this in the Lord's Prayer, it is hinted at with the phrase, "hallowed be thy name," and the concept of praying prayers of thanksgiving is clearly taught in other places in the Bible (Psalm 100:4; 1 Thessalonians 5:18).
- *Prayers of Confession*. This is seen in the phrase "forgive us our debts." Confession is acknowledging our sin to God and asking for forgiveness.
- *Prayers of Affirmation*. This is seen in the phrase "thy kingdom come." Affirmation is agreeing with God and longing for what is best.
- *Prayers of Petition*. This is seen in the phrase "give us this day our daily bread." Petition is asking God for things for personal requests, including our practical and physical needs.
- *Prayers for Renewal*. This is seen in the phrase "but deliver us from evil." A prayer of renewal is asking God to work in and through us in the circumstances and difficulties we face.

- *Prayers of Praise/Adoration*. This is seen in the phrase "Our father, who is in heaven, hallowed be thy name." Adoration is praising God for who He is. Praise is affirming God.
- *Prayers for Christlike Character*. This is seen in the phrase "as we forgive our debtors." Praying for Christlike character is a prayer asking God to mold our lives to Christ's life.
- *Prayers for Wisdom/Guidance*. This is seen in the phrase "lead us not into temptation." Praying for wisdom is asking God to direct and guide us to what is right and best.
- *Prayers of Intercession*. This is seen in the phrase "give us this day our daily bread." The plural aspect of the "us" indicates that there is request being made for more than just the one praying. Intercession is asking God for things for others.
- *Prayers of Surrender*. This is seen in the phrase "thy will be done, on earth as it is in heaven." Surrender is personally coming under the leadership and Lordship of Christ.

SPECIAL MARKINGS

Works Cited (BCP, 25). Instead of footnoting the sources used in this book, a two or three letter abbreviation is noted at the end of the quote to indicate the source, followed by a comma and then the page number. A list of works cited is available in the back of the book. The description of each author is chosen as the most recognizable aspect of his or her life work.

Words in Italics. When italics appear in a prayer from someone, they indicate that the original was changed and the new word in italics was inserted. Greek and Hebrew notes are also in italics. Occasionally there is a line of explanation or context provided under the name of the person who scripted the prayer. Italics that appear in the "A Prayer for Today" section indicate that there is a note of further instruction or clarification. Usually this is a direct address to you as the reader with a suggested way to pray.

The Ellipses (…). In the prayers from people and Scripture, ellipses are used in the traditional sense of meaning a break in the quote. In the "A Prayer for Today" section, ellipses marks connote a place for greater thought and personal reflection.

Sentences in Boldface. Certain prayers include bold lettering to indicate the particular prayer could be treated as a responsive reading or public prayer. So a prayer leader could read/pray the normal print, and the assembled congregation or group could read/pray the boldface print.

(Heb. or Gk.=) Heb. or Gk. notes a definition or explanation from the original language. Hebrew underlies most of our current Old Testament, and Greek, underlies our New Testament.

A FEW DISCLAIMERS

As you read *Prayers for Today*, some questions may arise about the prayers themselves, their writers, and even the adapted Scriptures. So here are five disclaimers that should clarify the purpose and intent of this book:

- This book is written from a decidedly Christian perspective. While I believe that non-Christians will benefit from the book, *Prayers for Today* assumes a Christian God and that Jesus Christ is God serving as the Savior and Redeemer of humanity. It accepts the biblical concept that the Holy Spirit, part of the Triune God, acts as God's presence and power in the lives of people today (see John 16:7–14; Romans 8:26–27; Galatians 5:16, 22–25).
- Use of a person or source is not an endorsement of all that this person teaches or has written. Each prayer is simply taken for what it is.
- The use of the title "Saint" for people commonly referred to as saints was avoided because the Bible indicates that all followers of Jesus Christ are saints (Philippians 1:1).
- Generally, the spelling, punctuation, and capitalization of the authors of the prayers are followed. No attempt is made to standardize the uses. When changes in the original quotes have been made, they are noted by italics in the quoted sections. When changes are made, they appear for clarity, for modernization, or for stylistic reasons. Often older English forms are retained.
- The Scripture quotations that are utilized do not follow any one translation (unless specially noted) but are a fresh paraphrase of the original languages. Greater liberties were taken than would be acceptable in a literal translation, in order to phrase the words into prayers.

Through these prayers, I hope your experience of prayer will be enriched, your relationship with God will be deepened, and your desire to serve God and the needs of the world will be expanded.

PRAYERS *of* THANKSGIVING

Hear my cry, O God: Give heed to my prayer.
From the ends of the earth I will call to Thee, when my heart is faint;
Lead me to the rock that is higher than I.   **PSALM 61:1–2**

By trusting in You, I will be empowered to do greater things than have been done. Whatever I request along the lines of who You are and what You are doing, You will do.   **JOHN 14:12–14**

Eternal Father of my soul, let my first thought today be of Thee . . .
let my first action be to kneel before Thee in prayer.
For Thy perfect wisdom and perfect goodness:
For the love wherewith Thou lovest *humanity*:
For the love wherewith Thou lovest me: . . .
For the *many wonderful* gifts of Thy Spirit:
   I praise and worship Thee, O Lord.
JOHN BAILLIE, *Scottish theologian (1886–1960) [DPP, 9]*

Lord of all creation, You made us for Yourself, and You always take pleasure in granting us every good and perfect gift. Your Word is trustworthy and Your promises are sure. In spite of this, . . . I often succumb to my own devices and desires, foolishly hoping that I can successfully order my life without conscious dependence on You. . . . Give me the grace to believe that You really do know what is best for me and that I do not. May I cling to Your character and rejoice in Your pursuit of me.
KENNETH BOA, JOHN ALAN TURNER, *American authors (twenty-first century) [GSB, 31]*

Merciful Father, thank You for being a prayer-hearing God. . . .
It is an overwhelming thought that *You* the Creator and Sustainer of all things gives heed to our prayers and meets our needs. . . .
Increase our faith in the truth that by prayer we have an influence in the world all out of proportion with how small we are. In Jesus' name we pray. Amen.
JOHN PIPER, *American pastor (1946–present day) [PBW, 53]*

Thank You that I am not alone in this world and for hearing my prayers. Thank You that You promise to not only hear my prayers, but to work in response to my prayer. You will not simply give me what I want, but You will give me what is best and most needed. Today I bring the following prayers to You . . .
I am confident that You will hear and act.
Pause to add your own prayers of thankfulness for who God is and what He has done . . .

PRAYERS *of* CONFESSION

From within, out of my heart proceed
> evil, sexual immorality, thefts, murders, adulteries,
> greed, wickedness, deceit, lewdness,
> envy, slander, arrogance, and folly.

All these evil things come from within my heart and defile me.
> **MARK 7:21–23**

Father—the truth about me is that often I choose sin:
> Sometimes I choose hatred. Sometimes I choose slander.
> Sometimes I choose envy. Sometimes I choose greed.
> Sometimes I choose pettiness. Sometimes I choose lust.
> Sometimes I choose gossip. Sometimes I choose pride.
> Sometimes I choose self-reliance.
> Sometimes I choose self-righteousness.
> Sometimes I choose self-aggrandizement.
> Sometimes I choose dishonesty.
> Sometimes I choose unkind words.
> Sometimes I choose to ignore the obvious needs around me.
> Sometimes I choose to hoard my resources.
> Sometimes I choose to neglect Your command to share the gospel.

The list of things I wrongly choose could go on and on. And sometimes
I act on these things in ways that are darker than I even care to state.
Each time I make such a choice, I choose death (Romans 6:23).
Today, I ask that You would breathe life into my soul afresh
And enable me to choose life—to choose You and Your ways.
> **KURT BJORKLUND**, *American minister (1968–present day)*

For You, my Lord God, have proclaimed:
"I, even I, am the one who blots out your transgressions—for my own sake.
And I will remember your sins no more." **ISAIAH 43:25**

A PRAYER FOR TODAY

Father I confess these sins to You . . .
Today I identify the following areas that I have not surrendered to You . . .
And I confess them—and turn from them.
I accept Your blotting out of my transgressions.
I thank You that You will remember them no more. Amen
You may want to write down some of these things and then symbolically burn, shred, or throw away the paper to represent those sins being blotted out.

PRAYERS *of* AFFIRMATION

What then shall I say? If You, O God, are for me, who can be against me? You who did not spare Your own Son, but gave Him up for us all— how will You not also graciously give us all things?
Who will bring a charge against those whom You, O God, have chosen? You alone declare us justified.
Who can condemn? No one. Christ Jesus who died—more than that, who was raised to life—is at Your right hand, O God, and is also interceding for us.
Who shall separate me from the love of Christ? Shall trouble or hardship or persecution or famine or nakedness or danger or sword? . . .
No, in all these things we are more than conquerors through Him who loved us. **ROMANS 8:31–35, 37**

O God, I believe that You are, and that You are the Father Almighty, Maker of Heaven and Earth.
I believe in Jesus Christ, Your only Son, my Lord;
> Who was conceived by the Holy Spirit,
> Born of the Virgin Mary,
> Suffered under Pontius Pilate,
> Was crucified, dead, and buried, . . .
> And bore the punishment for sin.
> The third day he rose again from the dead,
> Ascended into heaven,
> And now sits at Your right hand, You the Almighty Father. And from thence he shall come to judge the quick and the dead.
I believe in the Holy Spirit.
> The holy catholic *(universal)* church,
> The communion of saints,
> The forgiveness of sins,
> The resurrection of the body, and life everlasting. Amen.
> **THE APOSTLES' CREED** *(first appeared around 390)* [PD]

A PRAYER FOR TODAY

Consider the time-honored words of the Apostles' Creed, carefully affirming the truth of every line. . . .
Then reread Romans 8:31–37, pausing for any words or phrases that affirm God's love for you. . . .
Sit in silence and let the facts of the Christian faith and the affirmation of God's love settle into the depths of your soul. If your mind wanders, say aloud the words, "Nothing can separate me from the love of Christ."

PRAYERS *of* PETITION

Hear, O Lord, and be merciful to me;
O Lord, be my helper. (Heb.=*azar: to help, support, give military assistance*)
You turn my mourning into dancing;
You remove my sackcloth and clothe me with gladness,
That my heart may sing praise to You and not be silent.
O Lord my God, I will give thanks to You forever.   PSALM 30:10–12

O God, early in the morning do I cry unto Thee.
Help me to pray, and to think only of Thee.
I cannot pray alone. In me there is darkness. But with Thee there is light.
I am lonely, but Thou leavest me not.
I am feeble in heart, but Thou leavest me not.
I am restless, but with Thee there is peace.
In me there is bitterness, but with Thee there is patience.
Thy ways are past understanding, but Thou knowest the way for me.
Lord Jesus, Thou was poor and in misery, a captive and forsaken as I am.
Thou knowest all man's distress;
Thou abidest with me when all others have deserted me.

I would remember before Thee all my loved ones, my fellow prisoners,
And all who in this house perform their hard service.
Lord, have mercy.
Restore my liberty and enable me so to live that I may answer before Thee
and before the World.

Lord, whatsoever this day may bring, Thy name be praised.
Be gracious unto me and help me.
Grant me strength to bear whatsoever Thou dost send,
And let not fear overrule me.
I trust Thy grace, and commit my life wholly into Thy Hands.
Whether I live or whether I die, I am with Thee and Thou are with me. . . .
Lord, I wait for Thy salvation, and for the coming of Thy Kingdom. Amen.

> DIETRICH BONHOEFFER, *German pastor (1906–1945)* [BHE, 253–54]
> *Written on Christmas Day 1943 while in a Nazi concentration camp*

PRAYER FOR TODAY

Lord, here are my concerns for this week . . .
I ask that You would work in all of the activities that I am engaged in by . . .
I ask that You would grant me the perspective that desires character over
comfort. Amen.

PRAYERS *for* RENEWAL

When I rest, dwell in Your shelter, Most High God,
then I will rest in Your shadow, Almighty God.
(Hebrew for *dwell* is *seter*: *a hidden safe place, a place of refuge*)
PSALM 91:1

Your name, Lord, is a strong tower,
the righteous run into it and they are safe.   **PROVERBS 18:10**

O God, I will put on Your full armor so that I am able to withstand the evil
schemes of the devil.   **EPHESIANS 6:11**

Be Thou my Vision, O Lord of my heart;
Naught be all else to me, save that Thou art;
Thou my best thought, by day or by night, waking or sleeping, Thy
   presence my light.

Be Thou my wisdom, and Thou my true Word; I ever with Thee and Thou
   with me, Lord;
Thou my great Father, I Thy true son; Thou in me dwelling, and I with
   Thee one.

Be Thou my battle shield, sword for the fight;
Be Thou my dignity, Thou my delight; Thou my soul's shelter, Thou my
   high tower: Raise Thou me heavenward, O power of my power. . . .
Thou and Thou only, first in my heart; High King of Heaven, my Treasure
   Thou art.
   "BE THOU MY VISION," *Traditional Irish hymn* [PD]

A PRAYER FOR TODAY

Father, may I see Your vision for my life.
   (What unique leading is God stirring in me today?) . . .
May I see where evil is intended and run to Your shelter.
   (Where is evil showing itself in my circumstances?) . . .
May I see where I have been seduced by riches.
   (Am I looking for fulfillment through the acquisition of things?) . . .
May I see where I have sought people's approval.
   (From where have I longed for approval other than from God?) . . .
Lord, seeing the places that I need renewal, become my vision once again.
Amen.

PRAYERS *of* PRAISE/ADORATION

You are great, Lord, and most worthy of my praise;
You are to be revered above all gods.
For all the gods of the nations are but idols, but You made the heavens.
Splendor and majesty are before You;
Strength and beauty are in Your sanctuary.
I will ascribe to You, O Lord, glory and strength.
I will ascribe to You the glory due Your name and worship You in the
beauty of Your holiness. **PSALM 96:4–9**

We give *praise* to you, O God of holiness, and truth, wisdom and goodness, justice and mercy, purity and lovingkindness, for with goodness and
wisdom unmatched you revealed yourself to us, sending your Son into the
world, destined to assume human nature and to become a sacrifice for us.
PHILIP MELANCHTHON, *German reformer (1497–1560)* [*EPP, 57* PD]

Lord, I know Who You are and I am so grateful that Your majesty is
displayed in heaven and in the entire universe.
I know that You see from Your vantage point all of the issues in my life and
all of the matters of this world.
You have a view that no one here has.
You see the beginning of the parade and the end of it all at the same time.
Lord, You are in heaven and I am on earth.
I worship Your majesty this day.
And yet at the same time, God, You are my Father. I cannot completely
understand all of that, and I know that I never will. But to know that
You are my Father is such a comfort to me. . . .
You are gracious and kind. You remember that we are dust. You forgive and
You encourage, and I want that to be true of me as well.
Dear God, thank You for being my Father.
DAVID JEREMIAH, *American pastor (1946–present day)* [*PGA, 89*]

A PRAYER FOR TODAY

Lord, sometimes I see things more from my perspective than Yours.
Help me today to see beyond my natural perspective and adopt Your
perspective.
I praise You for Your greatness and power seen in these ways . . .
I praise You for Your nearness and tenderness seen in these ways . . .
I pause to meditate on the following quality noted above . . .
and how that quality of Yours encourages me. . . .
I give You all my worship and praise today. Amen.

PRAYERS *for* CHRISTLIKE CHARACTER

May I live as an obedient child, not conforming myself to the former desires that drove me when I lived in ignorance, but as You who called me are holy, may I also be holy in all my conduct, because it is written, "You shall be holy, for I am holy." **1 PETER 1:14–16**

Lord, help me to do great things as though they were little since I do them with your power;
and little things as though they were great since I do them in your name.
BLAISE PASCAL, *French philosopher (1623–1662)* [PD]

Lord, make me an instrument of thy peace,
That where there is hatred, may I bring love;
That where there is wrong, may I bring a spirit of forgiveness;
That where there is discord, may I bring harmony;
That where there is error, may I bring truth;
That where there is doubt, may I bring faith;
That where there is despair, may I bring hope;
That where there are shadows, may I bring light;
That where there is sadness, may I bring joy.
Lord, grant that I may seek to comfort, rather than to be comforted;
To understand rather than to be understood;
To love rather than to be loved;
For it is in giving that we are received;
It is by forgiving that we are forgiven,
And it is by dying that we awaken to eternal life.
Attributed to **FRANCIS OF ASSISI**, *Italian monk (1181–1226), and others* [PD]

A PRAYER FOR TODAY

Consider the things that seem too difficult in your life today—ask God for power. . . .
Consider the things that seem menial in your life today—ask God for perspective. . . .
Consider the opportunities to bring restoration in your sphere of influence—ask God for courage. . . .
Consider the alternatives to serving God—affirm your desire to serve Him above all other gods. . . .
Reread the prayer by Francis of Assisi thinking about each situation in your life where you can live out the reality of the prayer.
Lord, please develop in me the kind of character that You order. Amen.

PRAYERS *for* WISDOM/GUIDANCE

🌿 Whoever drinks of the water that You give will never thirst again. Your
water will become a fountain of water springing up into everlasting life.
   JOHN 4:14

🌿 You are the bread of life. Whoever comes to You will never hunger again.
   JOHN 6:35

🌿 Most merciful God, order my day so that I may know what you want me to
do, and then help me to do it. Let me not be elated by success or depressed
by failure. I want only to take pleasure in what pleases you, and only to
grieve at what displeases you.
For the sake of your love I would willingly forgo all temporal comforts.
May all the joys in which you have no part weary me.
May all the work which you do not prompt be tedious to me.
Let my thoughts frequently turn to you, that I may be
   obedient to you without complaint,
   patient without grumbling,
   cheerful without self-indulgence,
   contrite without dejections,
   and serious without solemnity.
Let me hold you in awe without feeling terrified of you, and let me be an
example to others without any trace of pride.
   THOMAS AQUINAS, *Italian theologian (1225–1274)* [*BHE, 72* PD]

🌿 Lord, help me now to unclutter my life, to organize myself in the direction
of simplicity. Lord, teach me to . . . welcome change, instead of fearing it.
Lord, I give You these stirrings inside me,
   I give You my discontent, I give You my restlessness,
   I give You my doubt, I give You my despair,
   I give You all the longings I hold inside.
Help me to listen to these signs of change, of growth;
To listen seriously and follow where they lead.
   ANONYMOUS [*CDP, 220–21*]

A PRAYER FOR TODAY

Father, I give You the places of my life where I am not satisfied. . . .
I ask to be fully satisfied in You and the direction You are leading my life.
Show me what changes I could make in my life that would be most pleasing to
You. . . . Amen.

PRAYERS *of* INTERCESSION

I am blessed when I consider (Heb.=*sakal: regard, careful thought, not a per-functory glance*) the weak; for then You will deliver me in times of trouble.
PSALM 41:1

O Lord, baptize our hearts into a sense of the needs and conditions of all.
GEORGE FOX, *founder of the Quakers (1624–1691)* [*OBP, 134* PD]

O God, our Father,
We ask you to bless those for whom there will be no sleep tonight;
those who must work throughout the night to maintain the public services,
doctors who must wake to usher new life into the world,
   to close the eyes of those for whom this life is passing away,
   to ease the sufferer's pain;
nurses and all who watch by the bedside of those who are ill;
those who this night will not sleep because of the pain of their body or the distress of their mind;
those in misfortune, who will lie down in hunger and in cold;
those who are far from home and far from friends,
and who are lonely as the shadows fall.
Grant that in our own happiness and comfort we may never forget the sorrow and the pain, the loneliness and the need of others in the slow, dark hours. This we ask for your love's sake.
WILLIAM BARCLAY, *Scottish Bible professor (1907–1978)* [*CPB, 162*]

Lord Jesus Christ, in everything I do, I want to be like Paul, who showed by his hard work a calling to help the weak, remembering Your words, "It is more blessed to give than to receive." **ACTS 20:35**

A PRAYER FOR TODAY

Think about the plight of those who are struggling with the bare essentials of life....
If possible, go and see someone or an area where this struggle is evident; allow yourself to feel it and "regard" it.
Lord, I ask You to provide for and care for those whose lives I have thought about today....
I ask what You would direct me to do to "regard" those who are in these struggles....
If you are already regularly doing something for those in need, what can you do to help others "regard" their situation?... Amen.

PRAYERS *of* SURRENDER

I will not seek to commend myself in other people's eyes;
You, O God, know my heart, and what is highly esteemed among people is
detestable in Your sight.   LUKE 16:15

My Father, I commend myself to You;
I give myself to You; I leave myself in Your hands.
My Father, do with me as You wish.
Whatever You do with me, I thank You. I accept everything.
I am ready for anything. I thank You always.
So long as Your will is done in me and in all creatures,
I have no other wish, my God.
I put my soul into Your hands . . .
Without reserve, with utter confidence, for are You not my Father?
    CELTIC PRAYER [*CDP, 650–51* PD]

Lord, I will provide bags for myself that will not wear out, a treasure in
heaven that will not be exhausted, where . . . no moth destroys. For where
my treasure is there my heart will be also.   LUKE 12:33–34

Into Thy hands, O Lord, I commend myself, my spirit, soul and body:
Thou didst make, and didst redeem them:
O Lord, Thou God of truth.
And together with me, all my friends and all that belongs to me.
Thou hast secured them to me Lord, in Thy goodness.
Guard my lying down and my rising up, from this time forth and even
forevermore. . . .
I will lay me down in peace, and take my rest:
for it is Thou, Lord, only, that makest me dwell in safety.
    LANCELOT ANDREWES, *English minister, translator of KJV (1555–1626)*
    [*PDL, 20–21* PD]

A PRAYER FOR TODAY

Father, I commend myself and my life to You. To commend means to entrust
    to someone or something. So I entrust myself to You.
At this moment that means . . .
"Do with me whatever You wish" can be prayed only when I am confident in
    Your power and goodness. So based on my belief in Your power and
    goodness, I entrust _____ to You. *(Name your reservations and
    give them to God.)* Amen.

PRAYERS *of* THANKSGIVING

Father, we look for the time when the Holy City, the New Jerusalem, will
come down out of heaven, prepared as a bride adorned for her husband.
A loud voice from the throne will say, "Behold, God makes His home with
people. And He will dwell with them, and they will be His people, and God
Himself will be with them, and be their God, and He will wipe every tear
from their eyes.
There will be no more death or mourning or crying or pain,
for the former things will pass away."
You . . . will say, "Behold, I make all things new." **REVELATION 21:2–5**

Lord, You appeared to us in the past and declared,
"I have loved you with an everlasting love; I have drawn you with
lovingkindness." **JEREMIAH 31:3**

I am serene because I know thou lovest me.
Because thou lovest me, naught can move me from thy peace.
Because thou lovest me, I am as one to whom all good has come.
    ALISTAIR MACLEAN, *Scottish novelist (1922–1987) [PL, 112]*

I love You, Father, because You first loved me and sent Your Son to atone
for my sins. And I stand amazed that Jesus, who by nature had always
been God, did not cling to His rights as Your equal . . . that He laid aside
all His privileges, to be born as a human being . . . that He totally humbled
Himself, submitting to the death of a common criminal, enduring infinite
humiliation and pain . . . that on the cross You laid on Him the compressed
weight of all my sin and guilt and shame, of all my griefs and sorrows, and
He became sin for me, dying the death I deserved.

    And how much I praise You that it was impossible for death to hold
Him in its power . . . that You raised Him from the dead to be my Savior, to
make me righteous in Your sight . . . that He is able to save me completely,
for He lives forever and prays for me, and for all of us who have come to You
through Him. I glorify You, my Father, with gratefulness and joy.

    And I bow at the feet of Him who was dead, and is now alive forever
and ever. I exalt Him, I yield myself to Him, for He is worthy of the total
response of my entire being.
    RUTH MYERS, *American missionary (1928–2010) [EGA, 46–47]*

A PRAYER FOR TODAY

Lord, I thank You for what You have done in the past. . . .
I thank You for what You have promised for the future. . . .

PRAYERS *of* CONFESSION

O Lord, I know that my life is not my own;
It is not for me to direct my steps.
O Lord, correct me, but do it with gentle justice—
Not in anger, lest You reduce me to nothing.   JEREMIAH 10:23–24

Most merciful God, we confess that we have sinned against thee in thought, word, and deed,
By what we have done, and by what we have left undone.
We have not loved thee with our whole heart;
We have not loved our neighbors as ourselves.
We are truly sorry and we humbly repent.
For the sake of thy Son Jesus Christ, have mercy on us and forgive us;
That we may delight in Thy will, and walk in thy ways,
To the glory of thy Name. Amen.
   "PRAYER OF CONFESSION," *Book of Common Prayer* [*BCP, 331* PD]

I praise You now that there is no condemnation for those who are in Christ Jesus, because the law of the Spirit of life in You has set me free from the law of sin and death.
(Greek for *condemnation* is *katakrima: a judgment against, deserved punishment, guilty verdict*)   ROMANS 8:1–2

Fix the centre of my heart in yourself, O Lord,
   for only thus will I resist temptation and live according to your will.
   MEISTER ECKHART, *German theologian (1260–1327)* [*BTP, 125* PD]

A PRAYER FOR TODAY

Most gracious and good God, I pause today to confess
My personal sins and affronts to You . . .
The sins of my family . . .
The sins of my church . . .
The sins of my country . . .
I am mindful that we have not only sinned in what we have done, but in what we have left undone; so most gracious and good God, I pause today to confess to You:
   The good things I have left undone . . .
   The good things my family has left undone . . .
   The good things my church has left undone . . .
   The good things my country has neglected to do . . .
Thank You for Your restoring grace. Amen.

PRAYERS *of* AFFIRMATION

You, Lord, formed my inward parts;
You knitted me together while I was still in my mother's womb.
I praise You, for I am fearfully and wonderfully made.
Wonderful are Your deeds; my soul knows it well.
Your eyes saw my unformed substance;
in Your book were written every one of them,
the days that were formed for me, when as yet there were none of them.
PSALM 139:13–16

Father, we live in a world that often identifies us by numbers.
Our social security numbers, area codes, zip codes, credit card codes, cell phone numbers, and other personal identification numbers all take precedence over our names.
But that is not how You know me.
It is not how You identify me.
You have known me by name. You care about every detail in my life.
Before the foundation of the earth, You knew all about me.
To You, I am not a faceless number or a mere cog in the wheel.
I am not just another person in the sea of humanity. I am known and loved.
KURT BJORKLUND, *American minister (1968–present day)*

Behold what manner of love the Father has bestowed on me, that I should be called the child of God! 1 JOHN 3:1

Father God, if nothing in us can win Thy love, nothing in the universe can prevent Thee from loving us. Thy love is uncaused and undeserved. Thou are thyself the reason for the love wherewith we are loved. Help us to believe in the intensity, the eternity of the love that has found us. Then love will cast out fear; and our troubled hearts will be at peace.
A. W. TOZER, *American pastor (1897–1963) [SOL, 232]*

A PRAYER FOR TODAY

Father, thank You for caring about me personally in all the details of my life.
I affirm that there is nothing in my life that You do not care about. You care about . . .
I affirm that the basis for Your love of me is in Your character, not my performance.
I affirm that You have been good to me in so many ways, such as . . .
You have called me Your child. You are my heavenly Father;
I affirm that worry is pointless and an expression of doubt. Amen.

PRAYERS *of* PETITION

To You, O Lord, I lift up my soul. *("Soul" connotes what is inside me, my essence, my emotions.)*
In You I trust, O my God.
Do not let me be put to shame,
Nor let my enemies triumph over me.
No one whose hope is in You will ever be put to shame. . . .
Show me Your ways, O Lord,
Teach me Your paths;
Guide me in Your truth and teach me,
For You are God my Savior,
And my hope is in You all day long.   **PSALM 25:1–5**

Help me, Lord, to see You are about me. **You are my hope.**
In my laying down and rising, in my travelling and arriving
    Help me, Lord, to see You are about me. **You are my hope.**
In my sorrow and enjoyment, in my work and unemployment
    Help me, Lord, to see You are about me. **You are my hope.**
In my health and in my sickness, in my strength and in my weakness
    Help me, Lord, to see You are about me. **You are my hope.**
In my peacefulness and strife, in my going from this life
    Help me, Lord, to see You are about me. **You are my hope.**
In my achievement and its waning, in my losing or my gaining
    Help me, Lord, to see You are about me. **You are my hope.**
(Note: *The final word may be changed from hope to peace or life, or this may be prayed three times with the last word read differently each time. Or change me/my to the identity of a loved one.*)
    CELTIC PRAYER, *"Help Me Lord" [PL, 6–7]*

A PRAYER FOR TODAY

Father, there are areas of my life where I face discouragement and
    hopelessness like . . .
But I affirm that You alone are my hope.
I place these areas of hopelessness in Your hands . . .
I sense that I have some friends and family who may be struggling with
    discouragement and who may be in need of hope.
I ask that You would meet them in their discouragement by . . .
I ask that You would bring hope to their lives by . . . Amen.

PRAYERS *for* RENEWAL

❧ Lord God, I will be careful how to keep all Your commandments . . .
and to love You, to walk in obedience to You, to keep Your commands, to
hold fast to You
and to serve You with all my heart and with all my soul.   JOSHUA 22:5

❧ Lord, give me I pray:
A remembering heart for the things that have happened
An attentive heart to what I have heard
A forgiving heart for what has hurt
A grateful heart for what has blessed
A brave heart for what may be required
An open heart to all that may come
A trusting heart to go forth with You
A loving heart for You and all Your creation
A longing heart for the reconciliation of all things.
A willing heart to say "Yes" to what You will.
       LEIGHTON FORD, *American evangelist/spiritual mentor (1926–present day)*
       [PE, n.p.]

❧ Almighty God, by whose mercy my life has continued for another year,
I pray that, as my years increase, my sins may not increase.
As my age advances, let me become more open, more faithful and more
trusting in you.
Let me not be distracted by lesser things from what is truly important.
And if I become infirm as I grow old, may I not be overwhelmed by self-
pity or bitterness.
Continue and increase your loving kindness toward me, so that when you
finally call me to yourself,
I may enter into eternal happiness with you, through Jesus Christ my Lord.
       SAMUEL JOHNSON, *English author and lexicographer (1709–1784)*
       [BTP, 310 PD]

A PRAYER FOR TODAY

Father, replenish my heart today, orient it toward You.
As I pray the lines above, this line strikes me most today . . .
Allow my heart to feel . . .
Allow me to act . . .
Renew my passion for You.
Renew my commitment to You. Amen.

PRAYERS of PRAISE/ADORATION

I know that You alone, whose name is the Lord,
are the Most Highly Exalted One over all the earth.   PSALM 83:18

You are great, Lord, and greatly to be praised.
Great is your power, and of your wisdom there is no end.
Men and women, who *are* part of what you have created, *desire* to praise you.
For you have stirred up *our hearts* so that *we take* pleasure in praising you.
You have created us for yourself, and our hearts are restless until they rest
in you.
> AUGUSTINE, *bishop of Hippo (354–430)* [BHE, 72 PD]

No one is like You, O Lord;
You are great, and Your name is mighty in power.
Who should not revere You, O King of the nations? This is Your due.
Among all the wise people of the nations and in all their kingdoms,
there is no one like You!   JEREMIAH 10:6–7

O Lord my God, when I in awesome wonder consider all the worlds
   Thy hands have made,
I see the stars, I hear the rolling thunder, Thy power throughout the
   universe displayed!
And when I think that God, His Son not sparing, sent Him to die, I scarce
   can take it in—
That on the cross, my burden gladly bearing, He bled and died to take away
   my sin!
When Christ shall come with shout of acclamation and take me home,
   what joy shall fill my heart!
Then I shall bow in humble adoration and there proclaim, my God, how
   great Thou art!

Then sings my soul, my Savior God to Thee: How great Thou art, how great
   Thou art!
> "HOW GREAT THOU ART," STUART K. HINE, *American writer*
> *(1899–1989)* [PD]

A PRAYER FOR TODAY

Father, today I am praising You for all Your greatness. I see it in so many ways. . . .
My heart is restless, as seen in . . .
And it will be restless until it finds its rest in You.
I desire to praise You. I take pleasure in praising You for . . .

PRAYERS *for* CHRISTLIKE CHARACTER

- I want to abound in faith, in speech, in knowledge, in all diligence, in love, and in the grace of giving.   2 CORINTHIANS 8:7

- I want to abound in love and faith toward You, Lord Jesus, and toward all the saints.   PHILEMON 5

- My salvation is closer now than when I first believed. . . .
  Therefore I will cast off the works of darkness and put on the armor of light.
      ROMANS 13:11–12

- Almighty and most merciful Father, whose clemency I now presume to implore, after a long life of carelessness and wickedness, have mercy upon me. I have committed many trespasses; I have neglected many duties, I have done what Thou hast forbidden, and left undone what Thou hast commanded. Forgive, merciful Lord, my sins, negligences, and ignorances, and enable me, by the Holy Spirit, to amend my life according to Thy Holy Word, for Jesus Christ's sake. Amen.
      SAMUEL JOHNSON, *English author/lexicographer (1709–1784) [GMO, 281]*

- Merciful Father, . . . let me now in Thy holy presence inquire into the secrets of my heart.
  Have I today done anything to fulfill the purpose for which Thou didst cause me to be born?
  Have I performed without omission the plain duties of the day?
  Have I kept my imagination pure and healthy?
  Have I been . . . sincere in all I have professed to be, to feel or to do?
  Give me the grace to answer honestly, O God. . . .
  May I more and more be delivered from my besetting sins. Amen.
      JOHN BAILLIE, *Scottish theologian (1886–1960) [DPP, 43]*

A PRAYER FOR TODAY

Father, forgive me for where I have fallen short. . . .
Father, show me where I have sinned ignorantly and willfully. . . .
Show me where I have neglected duties or left undone what should have been done. . . .
Empower me to live in a way that pleases You by . . .
Move me from indifference and inaction to embodying faith in every action, conversation, and moment.
Grant me assurance of Your love for me, both when I fall short and when I abound in faith.
Give me the grace to live in a way that pleases You—
but without the law creeping into my sense of rightness with You. Amen.

PRAYERS *for* WISDOM/GUIDANCE

O Lord, Your word is upright and all Your work is accomplished in faithfulness.
You love righteousness and justice; the earth is full of Your lovingkindness.
PSALM 33:4–5

Our God, whose Son is the light of the world,
in his penetrating light we acknowledge our darkness;
in his constant grace, our careless love;
in his generous giving, our sordid grasping;
in his equal justice, our dire prejudice;
in his fortitude, our fearful failure;
in his inclusive love, our deep divisions;
in his pure sacrifice, our soiling sins.
HORTON DAVIES, *American professor (1915–2005) [COS, 28]*

Many will make war against the Lamb, but the Lamb will overcome them all because He is the Lord of lords and the King of kings.
REVELATION 17:14

Lord, the two-word affirmation Kyrios Jesous (Jesus is Lord) . . . has far-reaching ramifications. Not only does it express *my* conviction that Jesus is God and Saviour, but it also indicates *my* radical commitment to him. . . .
The dimensions of this commitment are
intellectual (bringing our minds under Christ's yoke),
moral (accepting his standards and obeying his commands),
vocational (spending our lives in his liberating service),
social (seeking to penetrate society with his values),
political (refusing to idolize human institutions),
and global (being jealous for the honour and glory of his name).
JOHN W. STOTT, *English minister and author (1921–2011) [AC, 243]*

A PRAYER FOR TODAY

Lord, I commit all my ways to You.
You are my true light; show me where I am prone to wander in darkness by . . .
You are constant grace; show me where I can squander grace by . . .
You are generous giving; show me where I may hold tightly to things by . . .
You are equal justice; show me where I display prejudice by . . .
You are strength; show me where I am driven by fear by . . .
In Jesus there is love; show me where I drive division by . . .
I know that despite my reckless handling of Your grace, You are good and
what You do is right. You have the right to rule my life. Amen.

PRAYERS *of* INTERCESSION

⚜ Lord Jesus Christ, I affirm that no one comes to the Father, except through You. JOHN 14:6

⚜ Lord Jesus Christ, I affirm that salvation is found in no one else, for there is no other name given under heaven by which we must be saved. ACTS 4:12

⚜ I pray that words may be given me, that I may open my mouth boldly to make known the mystery of the gospel. EPHESIANS 6:19

⚜ Father God, Free me:

> From the unbelief in the truth that the only way to You is through Jesus Christ;
> From the distaste of stating Your truth about this one way;
> From the timidity that worries more about what others will think of me;
> From the fear of rejection;
> From the isolation that keeps me far from those who are far from You;
> From the veiled eyes that no longer see the need around me;
> From the uncertainty about my words and my credibility;
> From the selfishness that doesn't want to invest the time or energy in other people's lives;
> From the spiritualization that says it isn't my calling or my season;
> From the grand plan that tries to share with hundreds while ignoring the one before me;
> From the indifference that affirms truth but doesn't act;
> From the busyness that dominates my life with non-essential things;
> From the good and legitimate things that dominate my time; and

Replace these emotions and realities, I pray, with a passionate love of one beggar pointing another to where bread may be found. Amen.

KURT BJORKLUND, *American minister (1968–present day)*

A PRAYER FOR TODAY

Father, I ask that You would open the eyes of my friends, coworkers, and family to see Your salvation *(name people you would like to see come to believe in Jesus as the Savior)*. . . .

I ask that You would give me appropriate boldness seeing opportunities when they arise.

I ask that I would be bold enough to create opportunities by . . . Amen.

PRAYERS *of* SURRENDER

I will love the Lord my God with all my heart,
with all my soul, and with all my strength.   DEUTERONOMY 6:5

My Jesus, I love Thee, I know Thou art mine. For Thee all the follies of sin
I resign.
My gracious Redeemer, my Savior art Thou: If ever I loved Thee, my Jesus
'tis now.

I love Thee because Thou hast first loved me. And purchased my pardon
on Calvary's tree;
I love Thee for wearing the thorns on Thy brow: If ever I loved Thee, my
Jesus 'tis now.

I'll love Thee in life, I will love Thee in death. And praise Thee as long as
Thou lendest me breath;
And say when the death dew lies cold on my brow,
"If ever I loved Thee, my Jesus 'tis now."
   "MY JESUS I LOVE THEE," WILLIAM R. FEATHERSTON *(1848–1875)*
   [*PSH, 386* PD]

I will not love the world, nor the things of this world. For if I love the
world, Your love is not in me. Everything that is in this world,
   the drive to increase possessions, the drive to indulge self,
   and the desire to impress people, is not from You, but originates in
   this world.
And the world is passing away, and also all of its drives;
   but when I do Your will, O God, that will last forever.   1 JOHN 2:15–17

Father, I have only one life that will soon be past.
Only what is done for You will last.
   CLASSIC SAYING *[US]*

A PRAYER FOR TODAY

Father, I love many things—many good things. . . .
Yet, I know that they are not ultimate things.
Help me to see my affections of the things of this world for what they are. . . .
Help me to surrender my affection for these things to You. . . .
I ask that You would replace my earthly affections with affections that are
   centered upon You. . . . Renew my love and affection for You.
Father, to help foster this love and affection for You I purpose to . . . Amen.

PRAYERS *of* THANKSGIVING

Lord, You strengthen the feeble hands, You steady the knees that give way. Therefore, I can say to those with fearful hearts, "Be strong, do not fear; Your God will come. . . ." **ISAIAH 35:3–4A**

Lord God, the strongest and brightest of us are fragile as a floating bubble, unsteady as a newborn kitten on a waxed kitchen floor. If we keep our footing in the shaky space between our arrival and departure from this world, we owe our survival—not to mention our success—to many other people who held us up and helped us crawl or fly or muck our way through.

And to *You*, God, who keeps breathing life into our lungs the way a child keeps puffing air into a leaking balloon. We take our every step in the energy of mercy. . . . We see each flower, taste each drop of water, sense the presence of each person around us, through the gift of consciousness. For all this [may we] be grateful.

LEWIS SMEDES, *American professor/author (1921–2002) [DOG, 172]*

When I suffer loss, Lord, may I in my grief, still fall to the ground in worship, proclaiming:

"Naked I came from my mother's womb, and naked I will depart.

O Lord, You give and take away; may Your name be praised, O Lord."

And in my suffering, may I not sin by charging You with wrongdoing.

JOB 1:20–22

Lord, You sometimes take away what I value most.

It is easy to praise You when You give to me what I want most.

And it is easy to blame You when I suffer.

It is hard for me to imagine that there is a good reason for suffering if I can't think of one. Yet You, my maker, know better about my life than I.

Should I accept good and not bad from Your hand?

So in faith, no matter the circumstance, I *shall* praise Your name.

When laughter and success are my current reality, I shall praise Your name.

When abundance and plenty mark my path, I shall praise Your name.

And when hardship and loss are my current reality, I shall praise Your name.

When scarcity and need mark my path, I shall praise Your name.

When all seems broken, I shall praise Your name.

Lord, whatever I experience, I will choose to praise Your name. Amen.

KURT BJORKLUND, *American minister (1968–present day)*

A PRAYER FOR TODAY

Lord, I thank You for all that You have given me. . . .

And for the people You have sent along to help me on this journey. . . .

And I praise You too in the things You have taken away. . . .

Help me today to say—either way—praise Your name! Amen.

PRAYERS *of* CONFESSION

Search me, O God, and know my heart;
Try me, and know my worries, concerns, and anxieties;
And see if there is any wicked way in me,
And lead me in the way everlasting.   PSALM 139:23–24

My Lord and my God, take me from all that keeps me from thee.
My Lord and my God, grant me all that leads me to thee.
My Lord and my God, take me from myself and give me completely to thee.
NICOLAS OF FLUE, *Swiss hermit (1417–1487)* [PD]

We come to you in penitence, confessing our sins:
the vows we have forgotten, the opportunities we have let slip,
the excuses whereby we have sought to deceive ourselves and you.
Forgive us that we talk so much and are silent so seldom *before you.*
Forgive us that we talk so much and are silent so seldom;
that we are in such constant motion and so rarely still; . . .
Teach us to wait upon you, that we may renew our strength, mount up with
wings as eagles, run and not be weary, walk and not faint.
WILLIAM SLOANE COFFIN JR., *American minister (1924–present day)*
[COS, 93]

Incline my heart to Your testimonies,
And not to covetous thoughts.
Turn away my eyes from looking at worthless things,
And revive me in Your way.   PSALM 119:36–37

A PRAYER FOR TODAY

Pray the words of Nicolas of Flue again. Can you pray them sincerely?
Ask God to reveal any areas of unconfessed sin in your life. . . .
Lord, help me to sincerely want what leads me to You even if it is not pleasing
to me.
Help me to sincerely want nothing that leads me away from You. . . .
Allow me to see where I do not live as You have called me to live. . . .
Grant me the courage to acknowledge my sin to You and to those I have hurt or
offended. . . .
Incline my heart toward You and Your Word. Turn my eyes away from things
that are vain so I can ponder what is most important and worthy. Amen.

PRAYERS *of* AFFIRMATION

- What the law was powerless to do, in that it was weakened through the flesh, You did by sending Your own Son in the likeness of sinful flesh, on account of sin; You condemned sin in the flesh, in order that the requirement of the law might be fully met in us, who do not walk according to the flesh, but according to Your Spirit.   ROMANS 8:3–4

- I confess that Jesus is Lord.

    I confess that Jesus shares the name and nature, the holiness, the authority, power, majesty and eternality of the one and only true God.

    I confess that Jesus died and was raised, opening heaven up to unworthy sinners. I am such a sinner, and I gladly embrace his atonement for me.

    I confess that Jesus rightfully owns me, every part of me, every moment of my time, every dollar in my possession, every opportunity granted me, every responsibility thrust upon me, every hope I cherish, every person whom I love and treasure. I am personal property of the Lord Jesus Christ. He deserves my allegiance, loyalty and trust 24 hours a day, in all places, in all aspects of my life, both public and private. He is worthy of my obedience. He is worthy of my utmost. He is worthy of my very blood.

    RAYMOND ORTLUND JR., *American minister (1946–present day) [PFG, 143–44]*

- Who is like you, Jesus, sweet Jesus?
    You are the light of those who are spiritually lost.
    You are the life of those who are spiritually dead.
    You are the liberation of those who are imprisoned by guilt.
    You are the glory of those who hate themselves.
    You are the guardian of those who are *paralyzed* by fear.
    You are the guide of those who are bewildered by falsehood.
    You are the peace of those who are in turmoil.
    You are the prince of those who yearn to be led.
    You are the priest of those who seek the truth.

    JOHANN FREYLINGHAUSEN, *German pietist (1670–1739) [BHE, 135 PD]*

A PRAYER FOR TODAY

Father, I affirm the reality of Jesus. *(Pause to consider each line of the Freylinghausen prayer. Then identify the line that speaks most to where you are today; take the time to affirm that Jesus is that to you.)* . . .
I affirm that Jesus rightfully owns every part of my life. *(Open your hands as you pray as a tangible sign of living with hands open to God. Reread every line of Ortlund's affirmation, allowing the words to become your reality. If you cannot say the words with integrity, tell that to God.)* . . .
I affirm that Jesus is worthy of my utmost. For me this means . . . Amen.

PRAYERS *of* PETITION

Father God, as You were with *Christians through the ages* . . . so You will be with me; You will never leave me nor forsake me. . . .
May I be strong and courageous and careful to obey Your word; may I not turn from it to the right or to the left, that I may act wisely wherever I go. May I not turn from Your law. Then You will give me success. . . .
May I be strong and courageous. May I not be afraid. May I not be discouraged, for You are the Lord my God, and You will be with me wherever I go. JOSHUA 1:5, 7, 9

This day is Your gift to me; I take it, Lord, from Your hand, and thank You for the wonder of it.
God, *may I see Your presence* in this Your day, every day and every way. . . .
All that I am, Lord, I place into Your hands.
All that I do, Lord, I place into Your hands.

Everything I work for, I place into Your hands.
Everything I hope for, I place into Your hands.

The troubles that weary me, I place into Your hands.
The thoughts that disturb me, I place into Your hands.
I place into Your hands, Lord, the choices that I face.
Guard me from choosing the way perilous of which the end is heart-pain and the secret tear.
Rich in counsel, show us the way that is plain and safe.
May I feel Your presence at the heart of my desire, and so know it for Your desire for me. . . .
Help me to find my happiness in my acceptance of what is Your purpose for me:
> In friendly eyes, in work well done,
> In quietness born of trust,
> And, most of all, in the awareness of Your presence in my spirit.
> **OSWALD OF NORTHUMBRIA**, *Celtic monk (605–642)* [*CDP, 155–57* PD]

A PRAYER FOR TODAY

Father, Here are my fears, my worries and my concerns this week . . .
(go deeper to what is behind them—be blatantly honest.)
Father, here is where I might be scared . . . and here is why . . .
Father, please grant me an eternal perspective about what I'm facing. . . .
Father, please show me insight from Your Word about what I'm facing. . . .

PRAYERS *for* RENEWAL

I will be careful to do all that You have commanded, my Lord. I will not turn to the right or the left.   DEUTERONOMY 5:32

Give us, O Lord,
> A steadfast heart—which no unworthy thought can drag downwards
> An unconquered heart—which no tribulation can wear out
> An upright heart—which no unworthy purpose can tempt aside

Give us, O Lord,
> Understanding to know you,
> Diligence to seek you,
> Wisdom to find you,
> And a faithfulness that may embrace you, through Jesus Christ our Lord.
>> THOMAS AQUINAS, *Italian theologian (1225–1274)* [*PL, 97* PD]

Lord, how much juice you can squeeze from a single grape.
How much water you can draw from a single well.
How great a fire you can kindle from a tiny spark.
How great a tree you can grow from a tiny seed.
My soul is so dry that by itself it cannot pray;
Yet you can squeeze from it the juice of a thousand prayers.
My soul is so parched that by itself it cannot love;
Yet you can draw from it boundless love for you and for my neighbor.
My soul is so cold that by itself it has not joy;
Yet you can light the fire of heavenly joy within me.
My soul is so feeble that by itself it has no faith;
Yet by your power my faith grows to a great height.
> GUIGO THE CARTHUSIAN, *monk and originator of* Lectio Devinia *(twelfth century)* [*BHE, 307–308* PD]

A PRAYER FOR TODAY

Lord, I ask that You would touch my soul in such a way that I would desire what I have prayed today.
Here is the primary area that I resist Your leadership . . . I give it to you.
I ask to be renewed where my soul is empty and dry. . . .
Make my heart steadfast in . . . *(Where is it difficult to persevere in what is right and good?)*
Grant me an "unconquered heart" through . . . *(What trials are you currently facing?)*
Make my heart upright in . . . *(What temptations are you currently facing?)*
Make me prayerful, loving, joyful, and faithful today. Amen.

PRAYERS *of* PRAISE/ADORATION

I would have lost heart unless I had believed that I would see Your goodness, O Lord, in the land of the living.
I will hope in You and be of good courage, and You will strengthen my heart;
Yes, I will hope in You, O Lord.   **PSALM 27:13–14**

You long to be gracious and rise to show compassion.
For You are a God of justice;
Blessed are all those who wait for You.   **ISAIAH 30:18**

May you be blessed forever, Lord, for not abandoning me when I abandoned you.
May you be blessed forever, Lord, for offering your hand of love in my darkest, most lonely moment.
May you be blessed forever, Lord, for putting up with such a stubborn soul as mine.
May you be blessed forever, Lord, for loving me more than I love myself.
May you be blessed forever, Lord, for continuing to pour out your blessing upon me,
even though I respond so poorly. . . .
May you be blessed forever, Lord, for repaying our sin with your love.
May you be blessed forever, Lord, for being constant and unchanging, amidst all the changes of the world.
May you be blessed forever, Lord, for your countless blessings on me and on all your creatures.
TERESA OF ÁVILA, *Spanish nun (1515–1582)* [*BHE, 126* PD]

A PRAYER FOR TODAY

Which line of Teresa of Ávila's prayer most resonates in your own soul? . . .
Take a few moments to ponder every word of that line.
Now turn those words into genuine praise and blessing of God. . . .
Create your own lines of praise:
   May You be blessed forever, Lord, for . . .
   May You be blessed forever, Lord, for . . .
   May You be blessed forever, Lord, for . . .

Father, today I praise Your goodness.
I praise Your grace and compassion.
I praise Your justice.
I praise Your care for those who wait for and fear You.
I place my hope in You. . . . Amen.

PRAYERS *for* CHRISTLIKE CHARACTER

🌸 Lord, we all stumble in a variety of ways. However, those who are never at fault in what they say are perfectly mature, able to keep their whole being in check. **JAMES 3:2**

🌸 O Eternal God, sanctify my body and soul, my thought and my intentions, my words and actions, that whatsoever I shall think or speak or do, may be by me designed for the glorification of Thy Name, and by Thy blessing, it may be effective and successful in the work of God, according as it can be capable. Lord, turn my necessities into virtue; the works of nature into the works of grace; by making them orderly, regular, temperate; and let no pride or self-seeking, no covetousness or revenge, no little ends and low imaginations, pollute my spirit, and unhallow any of my words and actions.
   JEREMY TAYLOR, *English clergyman (1613–1667)* [*MOP, 135–36* PD]

🌸 Whatever is true, whatever is noble, whatever is right,
   whatever is pure, whatever is lovely, whatever is of good report;
   if anything is excellent or praiseworthy, I will think about such things.
   The things I have learned and received and heard and seen in those who
   walk with You, Christ Jesus, I will practice! And You, the God of peace, will
   be with me. **PHILIPPIANS 4:8–9**

🌸 *O Lord, my heart is* weary and troubled. No light in the darkness *I* see.
   But there's light for a look at the Savior, and life more abundant and free.
   So I turn my eyes upon Jesus, *looking* full in His wonderful face, and the
   things of earth will grow strangely dim in the light of His glory and grace.
      "TURN YOUR EYES UPON JESUS," HELEN LEMMEL, *English hymn writer
   (1864–1961)* [*PSH, 284* PD]

A PRAYER FOR TODAY

Father, free me from my attempts to impress You or others. . . .
I realize that my words reveal what is in my heart.
Help me to stop excusing gossiping, slanderous, bitter, and envious words.
Help me instead to deal with the reality of what these words point to. . . .
Free my mind from the cynical and critical. . . .
Let it rest on what is good *(reread Philippians 4:8–9 a line at a time contemplating each word).* . . .
Teach me how to have my mind dwell on the noble, right, pure, and lovely things.
Today I choose to dwell on what is good and excellent and praiseworthy. . . .
I will choose to look full in Your face and speak of what I see. Amen.

You, Holy Spirit, convict the world concerning sin, righteousness, and judgment.   JOHN 16:8

Spirit, we know that we have done wrong by You.
Please forgive us for grieving, resisting and quenching You.
We have resisted You through sin, through our rebellion, and through our hardness of heart.
At times we have been spiritually blind.
At other times, we knew what You wanted us to do, but we chose to ignore Your promptings.
Yet this is not how we want to live now.
We need You to change us. Only through You can we truly worship.
Spirit of the Lord, You are the one who brings us to a place where we can worship. . . .
Come, Holy Spirit come.

> FRANCIS CHAN, *American minister (1967–present day) [TFG, 165–66]*

Heavenly Father, thank you for sacrificing what was most precious to you in order to make it possible for me to know you. Give me eyes to see past the temporal and into the eternal. Remind me to measure every supposed sacrifice by the standard you set at Calvary and by the certainty of eternity. You have shown the way. I pray for wisdom and courage to follow.

> CHARLES STANLEY, *American pastor (1932–present day) [THF, 124]*

A PRAYER FOR TODAY

Spirit of Truth, You have come and guided me in all truth, for You do not speak on Your own authority, but only whatever You have heard.
You will declare to me the things that are to come.
You will glorify Jesus, and take what is His and declare it to me.
Father God—show me where I have been resisting or quenching Your Spirit. . . .
Show me where I have knowingly or unknowingly embraced wrong. . . .
Show me where I have missed the Spirit due to my busyness. . . .
Show me where I have missed the Spirit due to my own fears. . . .
And empower me to live in the fullness of Your Spirit. Amen.

PRAYERS *of* INTERCESSION

O Lord, I know that You will maintain the cause of the afflicted.
And You will maintain justice for the poor.   PSALM 140:12

Lord, may I learn to do good by:
    Seeking justice,
    removing the oppressor,
    defending the orphan,
    and pleading for the widow.   ISAIAH 1:17

Make us worthy, Lord, to serve our fellow men through the world who live
and die in poverty and hunger. Give them through our hands this day their
daily bread, and by our understanding love, give peace and joy.
    MOTHER TERESA, *Albanian nun who served the poor of Calcutta*
    (1910–1997) [CPB, 148]

We beseech Thee, Lord and master, to be our help and succor.
Save those who are in tribulation; have mercy on the lonely; lift up the
    fallen; show Thyself unto the needy; heal the ungodly; convert the
    wanderers of Thy people; feed the hungry; raise up the weak; comfort
    the faint-hearted.
Let all the peoples know that Thou art God alone,
and Jesus Christ is Thy Son,
and we are Thy people and the sheep of Thy pasture;
for the sake of Christ Jesus. Amen.
    CLEMENT OF ROME, *bishop (first century) [MOP, 132* PD]

God give me work till my life shall end.
And life till my work is done.
    WINIFRED HOLTBY, *English activist and author (1898–1935) [PL, 108* PD]

A PRAYER FOR TODAY

Take a few moments to pray for the poor and hungry in the world, . . .
The oppressed and persecuted, . . .
Those who have suffered from a natural disaster. . . .
Offer prayers for peace among the nations regarding current events, . . .
Pray for those on the front lines of work with the marginalized in our world. . . .

Lord, how can I better aid those in need? . . .
Lord, how can I better seek justice? . . .
Lord, is there an oppressor that You are calling me to oppose and remove? . . .

PRAYERS *of* SURRENDER

Long enough, God—you have ignored me long enough.
I've looked at the back of your head long enough.
Long enough I've carried this ton of trouble, lived with a stomach full of pain.
Long enough my arrogant enemies have looked down their noses at me.
Take a good look at me, God, my God;
I want to look life in the eye, so no enemy can get the best of me or laugh when I fall on my face.
I've thrown myself headlong into your arms—I'm celebrating your rescue.
I will sing to you Lord, for you have been good to me.

>   PSALM 13:1–6 [adapted from MSG]

Lord, where shall I find you? High and hidden is your place.
And where shall I not find you? The world is full of your glory.
I have sought your nearness, with all my heart I called you
And in going out to meet you I found you coming in to meet me.

>   JUDAH HALEVI, *Spanish poet (1075–1141)* [CPB, 208 PD]

Grant to me, O Lord, to worship thee in spirit and in truth; to submit all my nature to thee,

> that my conscience may be quickened by thy holiness,
> my mind nourished by thy truth,
> my imagination purified by thy beauty,
> my heart drawn to thy love
> and my will surrendered to thy purpose,

so I may lift up my heart to thee in selfless adoration and love,
through Jesus Christ my Lord.

>   CREDITED TO MANY SOURCES [PD]

A PRAYER FOR TODAY

Father, I have felt at times like You haven't seen my plight.
I have felt at times that You have turned Your back on me.
I have felt at times that I have carried trouble with no aid . . .
that the godless have thrived . . .
that those same people have looked on me with contempt.
So today I throw myself into Your care. Even if I can't see how You care for me today, I trust that You do. When I think back, I *can* see the ways You have been good to me. . . .
So I surrender my life to You today. Keep my whole being fixed on You.
Sensitize my conscience to Your holiness by . . .
Nourish my mind on Your truth by . . .
Purify my imagination by Your beauty. Amen.

PRAYERS *of* THANKSGIVING

❧ My heart of hearts affirms You, O Lord; and all that is within me blesses
Your holy name.
My soul blesses You, O Lord, and I will not forget all Your benefits;
You forgive all my iniquities and heal all my diseases;
You redeem my life from the pit and crown me with love and compassion;
You satisfy my desires with good things, so that my youth is renewed like
the eagle's. **PSALM 103:1–5**

❧ I confess that I deserve nothing good from Thee.
My heart is given too much to worldly things, and too little to Thee.
O Lord! Give me grace to raise my affections above earthly pleasures, and to
fix them in heaven with Thee where alone true joys are to be found.
Make me feel how short and uncertain life is, and enable me to spend this
day, and every day I have to live, in the way I should wish to have done
when I come to die.
     JW, *unknown author of Prayer Book, 1859* [SSP, 11 PD]

❧ O Lord God, from whom we come, in whom we are enfolded, to whom we
shall return:
I thank You for bringing us in our pilgrimage through life;
     with the power of the Father protecting,
     with the love of Jesus indwelling,
     and the light of the Spirit guiding,
until we come to our ending, in life and love eternal.
     PETER NOTT, *English bishop (1933–present day)* [EOP, 136]

A PRAYER FOR TODAY

Father God, today I thank You for the provisions of my life. . . .
I thank You for the people in my life. . . .
I thank You for the opportunities You have given to me in my life. . . .
I thank You for the acceptance and forgiveness You have lavished upon me in
     spite of my sinful actions and choices. . . .
I thank You for the healing You have brought into my life—physical and
     emotional. . . .
I thank You for the way You have brought me back from the darkness that
     lurks in my soul and the choices I could have made that would have landed
     me in a pit—or the choices I have made that did land me in a pit. . . .
I thank You for the desires of my heart that You have satisfied with good
     things . . .
and the desires that I have not yet seen satisfied. Help me to be confident
because of the grace You have given to me in so many other ways, that even my
unmet desires would be something I could be grateful for. Amen.

PRAYERS *of* CONFESSION

We will all stand before Your judgment seat, O Lord.
For one day every knee will bow before You, and every tongue will confess that You are God.
So then, each of us will give a full account of our lives to You.
ROMANS 14:10–12

Behold, Lord, an empty vessel that needs to be filled. My Lord, fill it.
I am weak in faith, strengthen thou me.
I am cold in love; warm me and make me fervent that my love may go out to my neighbor.
I do not have a strong and firm faith; at times I doubt and am unable to trust thee altogether.
O Lord, help me.
MARTIN LUTHER, *German Reformer (1483–1546)* [OBP, 53 PD]

Lord Jesus, we are silly sheep who have dared to stand before you and try to bribe you with our preposterous portfolios. Suddenly we have come to our senses. We are sorry and ask you to forgive us. Give us the grace to admit we are ragamuffins, to embrace our brokenness, to celebrate your mercy when we are at our weakest, to rely on your mercy no matter what we may do. Dear Jesus, gift us to stop grandstanding and trying to get attention, to do the truth quietly without display, to let the dishonesties in our lives fade away, to accept our limitations, to cling to the gospel of grace, and to delight in your love.
BRENNAN MANNING, *American author (twentieth century)* [MRG, 132]

You, my Savior, have swept away my offenses like a thick cloud,
and my sins like the morning mist. You have redeemed me; therefore, I return to You. **ISAIAH 44:22**

A PRAYER FOR TODAY

Father God, I ask You to heal my brokenness and fill my emptiness. . . .
But I also ask You to allow me rest in the fact that my brokenness and emptiness are in Your hands.
Allow me to not resent what is broken but to trust that even my weakness will be turned for Your glory and my good. . . .
I know that even what is hidden from others is not hidden from You. . . .
I know that what others might see and then reject, You have accepted and forgiven. . . .
Thank you for sweeping away my sin—let me live in that reality today.

PRAYERS *of* AFFIRMATION

⚜ Your Day, Lord, will come like a thief. . . .
Since I am looking forward to this, I will make every effort to be found spotless, blameless, and at peace with You, my Lord. **2 PETER 3:10, 14**

⚜ Behold, You, Lord God, will create a new heaven and a new earth. The former struggles and injustices will not be remembered nor will they come to mind. I will be glad and rejoice forever in what You will create.
ISAIAH 65:17–18

⚜ God, *You are* the highest good of the reasonable creature, and the enjoyment of *You* is the only happiness with which our souls can be satisfied.
To go to heaven fully to enjoy *You*, is infinitely better than the most pleasant accommodations here. Fathers and mothers, husbands, wives, children, or the company of earthly friends, are but shadows. But the enjoyment of *You* is the substance.
These are but scattered beams, but *You are* the sun.
These are but streams, but *You are* the fountain.
These are but drops, but *You are* the ocean.
JONATHAN EDWARDS, *American pastor (1703–1758)* [*GST, 1163* PD]

⚜ *Lord,* we dream the dream of justice. We glimpse for a moment, a world at one, a world put to rights, a world where things work out, where societies function fairly and efficiently, where we not only know what we ought to do but actually do it. And then we wake up and come back to reality.
. . . From the very beginning, two thousand years ago, *we* the followers of Jesus have always maintained that *You* took the tears of the world and made them *Your* own, carrying them all the way to *Your* cruel and unjust death to carry out God's rescue operation; and that *You* took the joy of the world and brought it to new birth as *You* rose from the dead and thereby launched God's new creation. That double claim is huge.
N. T. WRIGHT, *English theologian (1948–present day)* [*WSC, 3, 11–12*]

A PRAYER FOR TODAY

Lord, I know that this earth as it is presently constituted is not my future.
My future is in the new heavens and the new earth. There You will put the world to rights.
How glorious and assuring it is to think about putting the world right! . . .
Remind me that the best things here are but mere shadows of what will be there.
Since I can affirm this magnificent future, I will make every effort to be found spotless by . . .
I will endeavor to store up treasures in heaven by . . . Amen.

Day 34

PRAYERS *of* PETITION

🌿 Lord Jesus, You have said, "Come unto me, all you who are weary and burdened, and I will give you rest. Take my yoke upon you and learn from me, for I am gentle and humble in heart, and you will find rest for your souls. For my yoke is easy and my burden is light."
(Greek for "weary" is *kopiao: to be exhausted from sustained effort*)
(Greek for "burdened" is *phortizo: to load or carry a heavy weight*)
(Greek for "rest" is *anapausis: rest, intermission, refreshment, to gain relief*)
MATTHEW 11:28–30

🌿 Lord, You promised to Your people that Your presence would go with them and that You would give rest.   **EXODUS 33:14**

🌿 Often in the past, Lord, I have come to Thee with heavy heart and burdened life.
And Thou hast answered my prayers and graciously lifted the burden from me.
Yet with a strange perversion, I still refuse to leave my burdens with Thee.
Always I gather them up—those heavy bundles of fears and anxieties—and shoulder them again.
PETER MARSHALL, *chaplain of U.S. Senate (1902–1949) [CDP, 533]*

🌿 Almighty God, who knows our necessities before we ask, and our ignorance in asking:
Set free your servants from all anxious thoughts about tomorrow;
    make us content with your good gifts;
    and confirm our faith that as we seek your kingdom,
    you will not allow us to lack any good thing;
through Jesus Christ our Lord.
AUGUSTINE, *bishop of Hippo (354–430) [EOP, 91 PD]*

A PRAYER FOR TODAY

Father, here is where I am weary . . .
Here is where I am heavy burdened . . .
(What would it mean for you to come to Jesus? To take His yoke? . . .)
(Imagine your life being hitched to Jesus—what would be different? . . .)
I affirm that Your burden is not heavy, and that You are gentle and humble.
I give You my concerns, . . . my activities, . . . and my ambitions. . . .
Make me content with the good gifts You have given. . . .
Amen.

PRAYERS *for* RENEWAL

❦ I will be glad and rejoice in Your love, for You saw my affliction and have known the anguish of my soul.   **PSALM 31:7**

❦ Lord, *when* I have nothing;
> Help me to give even what I do not have.
Lord, *when* I feel nothing,
> Help me not to be jealous, that You may use me to touch others' hearts.
Lord, *when* I am weary;
> Help me to remember that You have been weary, too.
Lord, *when* I need refreshing,
> Help me to refresh others and to forget about my own needs.
Lord, *when* I can't see the way ahead,
> Help me not to get in the way of those who can.
Lord, *when* I am disappointed,
> Help me not to bring disappointment to others.
Lord, *when* I have no one to help me,
> Help me to trust in You.
Lord, *when* I can't see You, yet You see me—
> Help me to remember that.
Lord, *though* I am not worthy to receive You,
> [Only] say the word and I shall be healed.
> > **HUGH BARNEY,** *Celtic monk (unknown era)* [*CDP, 714* PD]

A PRAYER FOR TODAY

Father, You know where I need renewal.
> Where I am devoid of emotion . . .
> Where I am weary I need . . .
> Where I need refreshing in . . .
> Where I need guidance through . . .
> Where I am disappointed . . .
> Where I feel alone . . .
> Where I can't sense Your presence . . .
> Where I feel unworthy . . .
Please touch those places in me—and allow me to experience Your renewal.
Amen.

PRAYERS *of* PRAISE/ADORATION

You sit enthroned above the circle of the earth, O God,
    and its people are like grasshoppers.
You stretch out the heavens like a curtain
    and spread them out like a tent to dwell in.
You reduce rulers and power brokers to nothing
    and make the judges of this world meaningless. . . .
You, O Holy One, have asked,
"To whom will you compare Me? Or who is My equal?"
We lift our eyes to the heavens and see You who created them.
You bring out the starry host by number and call them each by name.
Because of Your great might and the strength of Your power,
    not one of them is missing. . . .
Do we not know? Have we not heard?
You are the everlasting God, the Lord, the Creator of the ends of the earth.
You do not grow tired or weary.
No one can fathom Your understanding.
      ISAIAH 40:22–23, 25–26, 28

Father, I praise You for being great beyond my comprehension;
    For being big so I can be small; powerful so I can be weak;
    forgiving so I can be flawed; wise so I can be foolish;
    sovereign so I can be restful; good so I can be comforted;
    tireless so I can be exhausted; eternal so I can be confident.
I praise You for being loving so I can be free from approval seeking;
    For being God so I can be me.
      KURT BJORKLUND, *American minister (1968–present day)*

A PRAYER FOR TODAY

Father, I praise You for what makes You like no other.
I acknowledge that You alone possess greatness like this.
I admit my smallness and inability to meet all the demands in front of me. . . .
(Name the demands you have been holding—and give them to God.)
I praise You that nothing in my life is beyond You.
I praise You that no problem in this world is beyond You.
Remind me often that even those who seem most significant are like
grasshoppers before You.
I praise You that You will not grow tired or weary of my problems. Amen.

PRAYERS *for* CHRISTLIKE CHARACTER

God, I do not want even a hint of immorality, or any impurity or greed in my life—as these are not proper for a child of God. Nor will I give myself over to obscenity, foolish talk, or coarse joking, which are not fitting. Rather, I will give myself to thanksgiving.   EPHESIANS 5:3–4

Grant me, O Lord,
> To know what is worth knowing
> To love what is worth loving
> To praise what delights you most
> To value what is precious in your sight
> To hate what is offensive to you.

[May I] search out and do what pleases you, through Jesus Christ our Lord.
THOMAS Á KEMPIS, *German theologian (1380–1471)* [*OBP, 92* PD]

O my Saviour, let me not fall by little and little. Or think myself able to bear the indulgence of any known sin because it seems so insignificant.
CHARLES HADDON SPURGEON, *English pastor (1834–1892)* [*CBP, 271* PD]

Your divine power, O God, has given me all things that pertain to life and godliness, through the knowledge of You who called me by Your own glory and virtue. Through these You have given me Your very great and precious promises, so that I may be a partaker of the divine nature, having escaped the corruption that is in the world by lust. Now for this very reason also, applying all diligence in my faith, please supply to me:
Moral excellence—and in moral excellence, knowledge;
And in knowledge, self-control;
And in self-control, perseverance;
And in perseverance, godliness;
And in godliness, brotherly kindness;
And in brotherly kindness, love.   2 PETER 1:3–7

A PRAYER FOR TODAY

Father, here is where immorality, impurity, and greed lurk in my life . . .
Here is where obscenity, foolish talk, and coarse joking appear . . .
I really don't want a hint of these things in my life.
Remind me that there is no sinful indulgence that is insignificant.
But instead, fill me with the things spoken of in 2 Peter 1:5–7.
(Take a few moments to reflect on the list, asking God to build one or two of these areas into your life in a new and powerful way.) . . .
Father, I want to search out what pleases You today by . . . Amen.

> If You call me, then I will say, "Speak, Lord, for Your servant is listening."
> **1 SAMUEL 3:9**

> Lord, teach me to listen. The times are noisy and my ears are weary with the thousand raucous sounds which continuously assault them. Give me the spirit of the boy Samuel when he said to Thee, "Speak, for thy servant heareth." Let me hear Thee speaking in my heart. Let me get used to the sound of Thy voice, that its tones may be familiar. . . . Amen.
> **A. W. TOZER**, *American pastor (1897–1963) [BHE, 320]*

> You will instruct me and teach me in the way I should go;
> You will counsel me and watch over me. **PSALM 32:8**

> Oh Lord, I know not what to ask of thee.
> Thou alone knowest what are my true needs.
> Thou lovest me more than I know how to love myself.
> Help me to see my real needs which are concealed from me.
> I dare not ask either a cross or consolation,
> I can only wait on thee.
> My heart is open to thee;
> visit and help me for thy great mercy's sake;
> strike me and heal me,
> cast me down and raise me up.
> **ANONYMOUS** [*CBP,* 47 PD]

A PRAYER FOR TODAY

God, You are the God who knows and loves me. I acknowledge that often I don't even seek to hear Your voice or to understand Your leadings. Sometimes I do know what You want, but I want something else—so I ignore Your leadings. Sometimes I do not know what to ask, so I need You to even reveal to me how to pray.

But I know that You know my deepest needs, and You love me more than I love myself.

Today, I will allow the voices of friends, of culture, and even other Christians to take a place behind Your voice.

Today, I quiet my heart to hear what You might say to me. . . .

(Do not rush past the last line; sit quietly until You sense the leading of God.)

What I have heard, I will evaluate to see that it is in line with Scripture. . . .

And if it is, I will act today upon what You have shown me by . . .

Teach me to hear Your counsel. Amen.

PRAYERS *of* INTERCESSION

Almighty God, I subject myself to the governing authorities, for You have established the authorities over me. The authorities that are, You have established. Consequently, if I rebel I rebel against what You have instituted and will bring judgment on myself. . . . Therefore, it is necessary for me to submit to the authorities, not only because of possible punishment but also as a matter of conscience. **ROMANS 13:1–2, 5**

Almighty God our heavenly Father, send down upon those who hold office in this place *(Nation, Province, Commonwealth, State, City or Town)* the spirit of wisdom, charity and justice; that with steadfast purpose they may faithfully serve in their offices to promote the well-being of all people.
"PRAYER FOR GOVERNMENT," BOOK OF COMMON PRAYER [*BCP, 822* PD]

Almighty God, who sittest in the throne judging right: We humbly beseech thee to bless the courts of justice and the magistrates in all this land; and give unto them the spirit of wisdom and understanding, that they may discern the truth, and impartially administer the law in the fear of thee alone. Amen.
"PRAYER FOR COURTS," BOOK OF COMMON PRAYER [*BCP, 821* PD]

Almighty God, we commend to your gracious care and keeping all the men and women of our armed forces at home and abroad. Defend them day by day with your heavenly grace; strengthen them in their trials and temptations; give them courage to face the perils which beset them; and grant them a sense of your abiding presence wherever they may be.
"PRAYER FOR THE MILITARY," BOOK OF COMMON PRAYER [*BCP, 823* PD]

A PRAYER FOR TODAY

Take a few moments to pray specifically for your governmental leaders by name—even those from a party you do not support. . . .
Pray that decisions would be made with wisdom. . . .
Pray that their agendas would be driven by what is good for the people and not governed by special interest. . . .
Pray that corruption would be uncovered and brought to light. . . .
Pray for justice to be administered by those in power. . . .
Pray for peace in the world, lifting up particular hot spots. . . .
Pray that any military conflicts your nation is involved in would be carried out without self-serving agendas, but rather for a higher cause of justice. . . .
Pray for a spiritual renewal in your nation. . . .
Lord, show me where I have not been subject to my nation's authorities. . . .
I affirm that it is right for them to have authority, even if misused. Amen.

PRAYERS of SURRENDER

As I walk in You, O Spirit, I will not fulfill the desires of my flesh. . . . If I am led by the Spirit, I am not under the law.

The works of the flesh are evident: *(Pray slowly, articulating areas of each)*

Immorality . . . Gk.=*porneia*: any illicit sexual activity

Impurity . . . Gk.=*akatharsi*: uncleanness

Sensuality . . . Gk.=*aselgeia*: unrestrained actions, shocking

Idolatry . . . Gk.=*eidololatria*: worship of something other than God

Sorcery . . . Gk.=*thapmakei*: consulting the supernatural

Hatred . . . Gk.=*exthra*: hostility

Discord . . . Gk.=*eris*: strife, failure to get along, arguing

Jealousy . . . Gk.=*zelos*: the desire to be as well off as another

Fits of rage . . . Gk.=*thumos*: anger, flare-up, or rage

Selfish ambition . . . Gk.=*eritheia*: selfishness, self-seeking, runaway ambition

Dissension . . . Gk.=*dixostasia*: causing divisions, purposely bring strife

Factions . . . Gk.=*airesis*: factions organized into cliques

Envy . . . Gk.=*phthonos*: the desire for another's possessions or prestige

Drunkenness . . . Gk.=*methe*: using substances to change states of consciousness

Revelry and the like . . . Gk.=*komos*: carousing, a drinking party, intoxication

I know that those who practice such things will not inherit Your kingdom.

But the fruit of Your Spirit is:

Love . . . Gk.=*agape*: unconditional, undeserved love, happily meeting needs

Joy . . . Gk.=*chara*: delight grounded in the reality and beauty of God

Peace . . . Gk.=*eirene*: confidence in God regardless of circumstance

Patience . . . Gk.=*makrothumia*: long-suffering, enduring hurts and hardships

Kindness . . . Gk.=*chrestotes*: a kindly disposition toward others

Goodness . . . Gk.=*agathosune*: living with honesty and transparency

Faithfulness . . . Gk.=*pistis*: faithfulness, reliability, loyalty

Gentleness . . . Gk.=*prautes*: meekness, self-forgetfulness, not self-absorbed

And self-control . . . Gk.=*egkrateia*: controlling passions and appetites

Against such things there is no law.   **GALATIANS 5:16, 19–23**

With me there is an abundance of sin;
In thee is the fullness of righteousness.
Therefore, I will remain with thee.
   MARTIN LUTHER, *German Reformer (1483–1546)* [OBP, 53 PD]

A PRAYER FOR TODAY

Lord, today as I pray through Galatians 5, I invite You to reveal to me where I am driven by my flesh. . . .

I ask that You would produce Your Spirit's fruit in my life. Amen.

PRAYERS *of* THANKSGIVING

Many are the sorrows of the wicked, but the one who trusts in You, O Lord, will be surrounded by Your lovingkindness. **PSALM 32:10**

Father, I thank You for the people in my life who seem to bring more pain than joy, for I believe You have let our paths cross for important reasons. Thank You for the good things You want to do in my life through the things that bother me (their irritating habits? their moodiness? their unloving ways? their demands? their insensitivity? their unrealistic expectations?). I'm grateful that You are with me, to meet my needs when others—even those close to me—fail to do so. I'm so glad that You are also within me, working to make me more like Jesus, more patient, more gentle, more loving, through the very things I dislike.

Thank You too that You love these people, and that Your love is adequate to meet their needs and to transform their lives, however willful or unwise they may sometimes be. Thank You that You care for them deeply, and that each of them has the potential of being a vast reservoir from which You could receive eternal pleasure. And so, though I may not feel grateful, I give thanks for them by faith, trusting Your goodness, Your wisdom, Your power, and Your love for them as well as for me.

And I praise You that I need not fret about these people, or be envious, or mull over angry thoughts to prove I'm right. Thank You that by Your power I can receive them as You receive me: just as I am, warts and wrinkles and hang-ups and all . . . that I can choose not to judge them, but to forgive them . . . to cancel any debts I feel they owe me—any apologies, any obligations . . . that through Your grace, I can choose to wipe clean any slate of grievances I have within me, and to view these people with a heart that says, "You no longer owe me a thing." Thank You for Your Spirit who empowers me, so that I can do them good.

RUTH MYERS, *American missionary (1928–2010) [EGA, 88–89]*

A PRAYER FOR TODAY

Lord, I thank You for the people who have been so hard for me. . . .
I can see what You have developed in my life through these people. . . .
I thank You that You are working in their lives and I pray Your grace upon them. . . .
I surrender my sinful attitudes toward them. . . .
Thank You for accepting me as I am. Because You have accepted me,
I can accept those who are difficult for me.
Thank You for surrounding me with Your lovingkindness when I have not found love from those around me on earth. . . . Amen.

PRAYERS *of* CONFESSION

O God, the Lord,
Deal with me for Your name's sake;
Because Your mercy is good, deliver me.   PSALM 109:21

Father, if anyone sins, *(and I have),*
we have an Advocate with you *(and I do).*
It is Jesus Christ, the righteous One.
And He Himself is the propitiation for our sins,
And not only for ours, but also for the whole world.   1 JOHN 2:1–2

For our insensitivity to your creation, for vandalism and violence, for crass-
ness and carelessness,
> **Forgive us, O Lord.**
For hardness and hatred, for cruelty and callousness,
> **Forgive us, O Lord.**
For greed and gracelessness, for indifference and ignorance,
> **Forgive us, O Lord.**
For disrespect and drabness, for lack of sense and laziness,
> **Forgive us, O Lord.**
Grace and goodness,
Love and liveliness,
> **Give us, O Lord.**
Calm and carefulness,
Generosity and goodness,
> **Give us, O Lord.**
Peace and prosperity,
Hope and healthiness,
> **Give us, O Lord.**
Strength and security,
Employment and enjoyment,
> **Give us, O Lord.**
> "O LORD, FORGIVE AND GIVE"; A CELTIC PRAYER *[PL, 86–87]*

A PRAYER FOR TODAY

Father, reveal to me any areas of unconfessed sin. . . .
Reveal to me any areas of unknown sin. . . .
Draw me through Your kindness and grace—replace my waywardness with the
gifts of Your Spirit.
Thank You for providing Jesus Christ as my Advocate with You. Amen.

PRAYERS *of* AFFIRMATION

🍃 Because of Your great love, O Lord, we are not consumed, for Your
compassions never fail.
They are new every morning; great is Your faithfulness.
I say to myself, "You, Lord, are my portion; therefore I will wait for You."
You are good to those who hope in You and to those who seek You.
      LAMENTATIONS 3:22–25

🍃 Great is Thy faithfulness, O God my Father. There is no shadow of
turning with Thee;
Thou changest not, Thy compassions, they fail not; as Thou hast been
Thou forever wilt be.
Pardon for sin and a peace that endureth, Thy own dear presence to cheer
and to guide;
Strength for today and bright hope for tomorrow, blessings all mine, with
ten thousand beside!

Great is Thy faithfulness! Great is Thy faithfulness! Morning by morning
new mercies I see;
All I have needed Thy hand hath provided; great is Thy faithfulness, Lord,
unto me!
      "GREAT IS THY FAITHFULNESS," THOMAS CHISHOLM, *American hymn
writer (1866–1960)* [PSH, 54 PD]

🍃 You have heard the crying out of Your people, and You are concerned about
our suffering. EXODUS 3:7

A PRAYER FOR TODAY

Ponder the lines in Lamentations 3:22–25:
"Your compassions never fail"—*meaning His mercy will never let you down.*
"They are new every morning"—*meaning His mercy won't be delayed.*
"You are good to those who hope"—*meaning His mercy won't disappoint.*
Here is where I have stopped believing that Your compassions will not fail . . .
I affirm that Your compassions will never fail.
Here is where I have doubted You know when I need Your compassion . . .
I affirm that You know exactly when I need Your hand—and You may not come
when I expect You to come, but You will always come on time.
Here is where I can begin to think that Your ways will not fully satisfy me . . .
I affirm that what You have done and are doing is what I need most, and it will
be good.
You are good all the time; all the time You are good. Amen.

PRAYERS *of* PETITION

⚜ Lord, direct me in the path of Your commands, for there I find delight.
Turn my heart toward Your statutes and not toward selfish gain.
Turn my eyes away from worthless things; preserve my life according to
Your word. PSALM 119:35–37

⚜ Take me often from the tumult of things into Thy presence.
There show me what I am, and what Thou hast purposed me to be.
Then hide me from Thy tears. . . .

The will of God be done by us
The law of God be kept by us
Our evil will controlled by us
Our sharp tongue checked by us
Quick forgiveness offered by us
Speedy repentance made by us
Temptation sternly shunned by us
Blessed death welcomed by us . . .
God's highest praise sung by us.

Christ, You are the truth; You are the light.
You are the Keeper of the treasure we seek so blindly.
My soul's desire is to see the face of God and to rest in His house.
My soul's desire is to study the Scriptures and to learn the ways of God.
My soul's desire is to be freed from all fear and sadness, and to share
Christ's risen life.
My soul's desire is to imitate my King, and to sing His purpose always. . . .

Dear Lord, You alone know what my soul truly desires,
And You alone can satisfy those desires. . . .
My times are in Thy hand, my times are in Thy hand.
        HILD OF WHITBY, *English monk (614–680)* [*CDP, 168–70* PD]

A PRAYER FOR TODAY

Lord, as I consider the words above, I sense You directing my thoughts to
    this phrase or idea . . .
I ask that You would work the thought behind this phrase or idea into my
    activities today by . . .
I ask for Your divine enablement for all I am facing this week. . . .
I ask for insight into my true identity in Christ. . . .
Pray for any other special concerns that you have right now. . . . Amen.

PRAYERS *for* RENEWAL

You are my shepherd, Lord. My Shepherd. One who is always looking out for me. Leading me. Guiding me. Protecting me. What more could I ask?

I ask that You make me to lie down in some green pastures. You know how much I need the rest.

Lead me beside some place of quiet waters. A place where the rippling sounds can float my cares away. You know how much my soul needs restoring.

You know how weary I am now, Lord, how hungry, how thirsty.

Don't let me stray from the path You are leading me down. You know how prone to wander I am.

I try not to look too far ahead on that path, but You know how anxious I am. I know that somewhere down the path is a dark valley through which I someday must travel.

If I had to go through it alone, I'd be terrified. But I don't have to go through it alone. You will be there. With me. Leading me through it.

Thank you that I don't have to go through life—with all its uncertain shadows—alone. I don't even have to go through today alone.

PSALM 23, ANONYMOUS *[BHE, 222]*

Savior, like a Shepherd lead us, much we need thy tender care; in thy pleasant pastures feed us, for our use thy folds prepare: Blessed Jesus, blessed Jesus, thou has bought us, thine we are. . . .

We are thine, do thou befriend us, be the guardian of our way; keep thy flock, from sin defend us, seek us when we go astray: Blessed Jesus, blessed Jesus, hear, O hear us when we pray. . . .

"SAVIOR LIKE A SHEPHERD LEAD US," DOROTHY A. THRUPP, *hymn writer (1779–1847)* [PD]

A PRAYER FOR TODAY

Think about the image of a shepherd—the care, the protection, the nurture. Perhaps the closest modern equivalent is having a parent caring for a young child. Now think about that kind of care, protection, and nurture from God Himself toward you. . . . Then pray the following:

Lord God, I know that there is nothing beyond or above You. Yet I affirm that You care for me as a shepherd cares for his or her sheep.

Lord, here is where I need rest . . .

Lord, here is where my soul needs restoring . . .

Here is where I am prone to wander . . . Allow me to see what wandering will really do to me. Lord, here is the dark valley I'm facing . . .

Thank You for being here to lead me, to shepherd me through these things.

Thank You for renewing me today. Amen.

O Son of Man, You will come with the clouds of heaven. In the presence of the Ancient of Days, You will be given dominion and glory and a kingdom, so that people of every nation and language will worship You. Your dominion is an everlasting dominion that will not pass away, and Your kingdom is one that will never be destroyed. **DANIEL 7:13–14**

You took always the lowest place
And did it so completely that no one ever since has been able to wrest it
 from You.
  ABBE HUVELIN, *desert monk (unknown era)* [*CDP, 654* PD]

You are the great, the mighty, and the awesome God, who keeps Your promises of lovingkindness. . . . In all that has happened to us, You have been just, You have acted faithfully, even while we did wrong.
  NEHEMIAH 9:32–33

Praise to the Lord, the Almighty, the King of creation!
O my soul, praise Him, for He is thy health and salvation.
All ye who hear, now to His temple draw near,
Join me in glad adoration!

Praise to the Lord, O let all that is in me adore Him!
All that hath life and breath, come now with praises before Him!
Let the Amen sound from His people again;
Gladly for aye we adore Him!
  "PRAISE TO THE LORD THE ALMIGHTY," JOACHIM NEANDER,
  German hymn writer (1650–1680) [PD]

As the ripples of the river glance up to the light, *let my heart glance up to You in little looks of love very often through the day.*
  AMY CARMICHAEL, *American missionary (1867–1951)* [*CDP, 572*]

A PRAYER FOR TODAY

I praise You Lord for the way You took on human form to accomplish light,
 life, and liberation.
All people will worship You someday, even if today is not that day.
Today I choose to worship You, for You are my health and salvation.
Today I choose to worship You, and I know You keep Your promises of
 lovingkindness.
Today I choose to worship You for . . . Amen.

PRAYERS *for* CHRISTLIKE CHARACTER

I will not be arrogant, proud, haughty, or full of myself, or wise in my own estimation—but I will associate with the humble and lowly.
> **ROMANS 12:16**

O Father, give us the humility which
> Realizes its ignorance, admits its mistakes,
> Recognizes its need, welcomes advice,
> Accepts rebuke.

Help us always
To praise rather than to criticize,
> To sympathize rather than to condemn,
> To encourage rather than discourage,
> To build rather than to destroy,
> And to think of people at their best rather than at their worst.
> **WILLIAM BARCLAY**, *Scottish Bible professor (1907–1978) [CPB, 215]*

When I am blessed with abundance, I will be on my guard lest my heart become proud, and I forget to honor You, O Lord my God, who is the one who provides all good things . . . lest I think that it was my power and the strength of my hand that brought this abundance.
> **DEUTERONOMY 8:12–14, 17**

Lord Jesus Christ, my almighty yet humble God.
Your word teaches that You bring down the proud and lift up the humble.
I am tempted even in this prayer to be humble so I can be made much of.
> Forgive me. Help me be free from the desire to be exalted.
> Help me to admit when I am wrong or mistaken.
> Help me to rejoice in another's success even if it comes at my expense.
> Help me to be content when I am not on top.
> Help me to weep when those who have been against me weep, not
> taking secret joy in their misfortune.
> Help me not to be miffed when I am not recognized or appreciated.
> Help me not to feel insulted when I am not chosen or consulted.
> Help me not to be disheartened when I am passed over.
> Help me to recognize that all I have that is good is a gift from Your
> hand. Amen.
> **KURT BJORKLUND**, *American minister (1968–present day)*

A PRAYER FOR TODAY

Add your own prayers around what it would mean to be humble. . . .
Ask to be rescued from pride—and to see pride for what it is. . . .

PRAYERS *for* WISDOM/GUIDANCE

O God, wisdom has declared. . . .
Out of my window I can see it—the simple, those without sense, going out looking for a sexual liaison.
Those looking for a sexual liaison are found by loose people with crafty intent who don't value their own homes. Such people linger in the streets, in the trendy hangouts, and around corners, waiting to take hold of me and kiss me.
> "Come, let's make love all night long. Let's enjoy being lovers.
> My spouse is away and will never know."
> At once I am tempted to follow. If I do, I will be like
>> an ox going to slaughter, a deer stepping into a noose,
>> a bird darting into a snare, little knowing it will cost me my life.
But I will listen and pay attention to what You say:
I will not let my heart turn to his or her ways or stray into his or her paths.
Many are the victims who have gone down that path.
Seductive urges have slain a mighty throng.
The lodging of sexual indiscretion is a highway to hell—leading to the death of all that is good.   **PROVERBS 7:1, 6–27**

Merciful Father, how often have we failed to fight lust!
We have embraced the enemy that makes war on our souls.
Forgive us according to Your promise to be slow to anger and abounding in mercy.
Come now and give us new resolve,
> and new power,
> and a new view of Your promises and Your supreme value.
Satisfy us in the evening with Your steadfast love, and sever the root of lust with a superior pleasure. Amen.
> **JOHN PIPER,** *American pastor (1946–present day) [PBW, 111]*

A PRAYER FOR TODAY

Father, let me see the places that I could be sexually seduced. . . .
Allow me to see the places that I could fall to sexual temptations. . . .
Save me from the false hope that romance and sexuality are the ultimate in satisfaction.
Lead me from the inordinate lure of human love.
May I see the trap of sexual expression outside Your prescribed boundaries.
I ask for the insight to see sexuality through Your eyes.
Let me be satisfied in Your love first, so I can enter human love as a giver and not a taker. Amen.

PRAYERS *of* INTERCESSION

Father, whatever I do for one of the least of these, I do for You.
MATTHEW 25:40

I pray for all who are in despair.
All who have been betrayed
All who are dismayed
All who are distressed
All who feel depressed . . .
All whose hope has flown
All who are alone . . .
Lord, who came down to share our plight,
Lift them into your love and light.
CELTIC PRAYER [*PL, 32* PD]

I pray you would give me a heart for those . . . who, for whatever
reason, are not in the mainstream of life.
    For those who lie crumpled and cast aside.
    For those who are forgotten and ignored.
    For those who are in some way blinded to the fullness of life.
Help me not to turn a deaf ear when they call out.
Help me to stop, regardless of what the crowd may say.
Help me to give them my undivided attention.
Help me to give myself to them as you did—to show mercy, to do what I
can.
Although I may not be able to loose them from their chains or free them
from their separate prisons,
Help me to visit faithfully so they may know that someone cares;
Help me to bring a meal so they may be nourished;
Help me to say a kind word so they may be encouraged;
Help me to give a gentle touch so they may be comforted; . . .
Help me to lend a listening ear so their stories may be heard.
Help me whenever, wherever, and however I can to bring light to someone
who sits in darkness.
KEN GIRE, *American writer (1950–present day)* [*MWS, 272–73*]

A PRAYER FOR TODAY

Pray specifically for those who are the "least" whom you have contact with. . . .
Ask God to open your eyes to see an opportunity to "do for" them. . . .
Father, help me not to be smug in the good fortune that I have experienced but
to be aware of the grace that I have received. . . .
Keep me from lame excuses and a hardened heart. . . . Amen.

You are close to the brokenhearted, Lord,
and save those who are crushed in spirit.
Many are the afflictions of the righteous,
but You deliver the righteous from all of them.   **PSALM 34:18–19**

You are my refuge and You are my strength, O God,
my ever-present help in trouble.
Therefore I will not fear, though the earth changes
and the mountains slip into the heart of the sea.   **PSALM 46:1–2**

I pray, O God, that I may know you,
that I may love you,
so that I may rejoice in you.
And if I cannot do this to the full in this life, at least let me go forward from
day to day until that joy comes to fullness.
Let the knowledge of you go forward in me here, and there let it be made
full.
Let love for you increase, and there let it be full, so that here my joy may be
great in hope and there it may be full in reality.
O Lord, through your Son, you command us—rather, you counsel us—to
ask, and you promise that we shall receive, that our joy may be full.
O Lord, I ask what you counsel through our wonderful Counselor.
Let me receive what you promise through your truth, that my joy may be
full.
Meanwhile, let my mind meditate upon it, let my tongue speak of it.
Let my heart love it, let my tongue discourse upon it.
Let my soul hunger for it, let my flesh thirst for it, let my whole being
desire it, until I enter into the joy of my Lord,
who is the triune and one God, blessed forever. Amen.
       ANSELM, *Italian monk (1033–1109)* [*PFG, 118* PD]

A PRAYER FOR TODAY

Open your hands as a posture of reception and submission to God.
Father, I ask for a heart that longs for You like the psalmist and those who have
gone before me.
Today my heart is broken in the following ways . . .
My spirit is crushed in the following ways . . .
I am afflicted in the following ways . . .
Yet I acknowledge that You are close to me, that You save me,
that You deliver me from all my afflictions,
that You are my refuge—my strength—my ever-present help.
I thank You and I will live today without being dominated by fear. Amen.

PRAYERS *of* THANKSGIVING

What a God you are! And how fortunate I am to have you as my Infinite Father, the same Father as the Lord Jesus. Because Jesus was raised from the dead, I have been given a brand-new life and have everything to live for, including a future in heaven—and that future starts now! *You are* keeping careful watch over me and the future. The Day is coming when I'll have it all—life healed and whole.
> 1 PETER 1:3–5 [MSG; plural changed to singular]

Almighty God, Father of all mercies, we your unworthy servants give you humble thanks for all your goodness and loving-kindness to us and to all whom you have made.
We bless you for your creation, preservation, and all the blessings of this life; but above all for your immeasurable love in the redemption of the world by our Lord Jesus Christ;
for the means of grace, and for the hope of glory.
And, we pray, give us such an awareness for your mercies,
> that with truly thankful hearts we may show forth your praise,
> not only with our lips, but in our lives,
> by giving up our selves to your service,
> and by walking before you in holiness and righteousness all our days;
> through Jesus Christ our Lord, Amen.
> "GENERAL THANKSGIVING" [*BCP, 101* PD]

For Your provisions to me in the past,
for Your abundance to me in the present,
and for Your hope that leads me into the future,
I thank You, my savior, my sustainer, my God. Amen.
> KURT BJORKLUND, *American minister (1968–present day)*

A PRAYER FOR TODAY

Father, I express to You thanks for the material things in my life. . . .
I express to You thanks for the people in my life. . . .
I express to You thanks for the opportunities I have been given. . . .
I express to You thanks for the spiritual realities You have brought into my life. . . .
I express to You thanks for Your goodness to me that supersedes what I deserve. . . .
I express to You thanks for the assurance of future blessings. . . . Amen.

Day 52

PRAYERS *of* CONFESSION

You are not a God who takes pleasure in wickedness;
Evil cannot abide with You.   **PSALM 5:4**

Be gracious to me, O God, according to Your patient and enduring love;
according to the greatness of Your compassion blot out my transgressions.
Wash me thoroughly from my iniquity
and cleanse me from my sin.
For I know my transgressions, and my sin is ever before me.
Against You, You alone, have I sinned
and done what is evil in Your sight.   **PSALM 51:1–4**

O Father in heaven, I acknowledge . . . the faults and failures of this day . . .
My failure to be true even to my own accepted standards:
My deception in the face of temptation:
My choosing of the worse when I know better: **O Lord, forgive.**
My failure to apply to myself the standards of conduct I demand of others:
My blindness to the suffering of others and my slowness to be taught by my own:
My complacence towards wrongs that do not touch my own case and my over-sensitiveness to those that do: **O Lord, forgive.**
        JOHN BAILLIE, *Scottish theologian (1886–1960) [DPP, 15]*

Our Father, teach us not only Thy will, but how to do it.
Teach us the best way of doing the best thing,
lest we spoil the end by unworthy means;
for the sake of Christ Jesus our Lord. Amen.
        JOHN HENRY JOWETT, *English minister (1864–1923) [EPP, 114]*

A PRAYER FOR TODAY

Contemplate the statement that evil cannot abide with God. . . .
Pure God, You take no pleasure in wickedness.
I confess that sin is not just something I do,
but it is something I think, and it is something I am.
Here is where I can see evil in myself . . .
Often even when I have a worthy end I spoil it with unworthy means.
I am not powerful in my own strength to change my patterns.
I can only turn to You for cleansing and deliverance.
I pray with the psalmist in Psalm 51. . . . *(Pray Psalm 51 above.)*

PRAYERS *of* AFFIRMATION

Here is a true saying that deserves full acceptance:
Christ Jesus came into the world to save sinners—of whom I am the worst.
But for that very reason I was shown mercy, so that Christ Jesus might display His unlimited patience as an example for those who would believe on Him and receive eternal life.   1 TIMOTHY 1:15–16

I believe in You, the one God and Father Almighty;
maker of heaven and earth, and of all things visible and invisible.

And I believe in You, the one Lord Jesus Christ, the only-begotten Son of God, very God of very God,
begotten, not made, being of one substance with the Father; by whom all things were made;
who, for us men and for our salvation, came down from heaven,
and was incarnate by the Holy Spirit of the Virgin Mary,
and was made man,
and was crucified also for us under Pontius Pilate;
You suffered and were buried; and on the third day You rose again,
according to the Scriptures; and ascended into heaven,
and sitteth on the right hand of the Father;
and You shall come again, with glory, to judge both the quick and the dead;
whose kingdom shall have no end.

And I believe in You, the Holy Spirit, the Lord and Giver of Life;
who proceedeth from the Father and the Son;
who with the Father and Son together is worshiped and glorified;
who spake by the Prophets.

And I believe in the one Universal Church.
I acknowledge one *confession* for the remission of sins; and I look for the resurrection of the dead, and the life of the world to come. Amen.
    THE NICENE CREED, *(AD 325) [adapted from GST, 1163]*

A PRAYER FOR TODAY

Father, I affirm the greatness of Your self-revelation and mercy. . . .
I ponder where I would be without Your initiating grace. . . .
Father, today I affirm that You have worked in this world to win my salvation and my heart.
The greatness of what You have done is beyond my ability to comprehend.
Let my heart be moved afresh with the reality of Your goodness. Amen.

PRAYERS *of* PETITION

We who are strong ought to bear with the shortcomings of those who are weak and not seek to please ourselves.
Lord, let me please my neighbors and friends for their good,
in order to build them up.
For even You, Jesus, did not please Yourself.   ROMANS 15:1–3

God, why do *I* call impossible what *You* call possible?
Why do *I* call unforgivable what *You* have forgiven?
Why do *I* compromise with what *You* call sin?
How *I* need to know *Your* heart, and reach out in *Your* love and wisdom to others.
It's easy to love the people who are standing hard and fast, pressing on to meet that higher calling.
But the ones who might be struggling, we tend to judge too harshly and refuse to try to catch them when they're falling.
We put people into boxes and we draw our hard conclusions when they do the things we know they should not do.
We sometimes write them off as hopeless and we throw them to the dogs.
Our compassion and forgiveness sometimes seem in short supply.
We can love them and forgive them when their sin does not exceed our own, for we too have been down bumpy roads before.
But when they commit offences outside the boundaries we have set, we judge them in a word and we turn them out, and we close the door.
   CHUCK GIRARD, *Celtic author (unknown era)* [*CDP, 307–308* PD]

A PRAYER FOR TODAY

Lord, I ask that You would give me the grace to see the shortcomings in my life. . . .
(Silently allow God to highlight your own shortcomings and faults.)
I ask for forgiveness where I have made much of the shortcomings and faults of others. . . .
I ask for forgiveness where I have drawn hard conclusions to satisfy my own desire to feel like I am somehow in a favorable place with You. . . .
Grant me grace in dealing with everyone You bring into my life. . . .
Grant me the perspective that sees myself as part of the community of sinners.
Keep me from vilifying those who fall or let me down. . . .
How I need Your heart and wisdom! Amen.

PRAYERS *for* RENEWAL

🌿 Father, may I, like Paul, not be disobedient to the heavenly vision that You give me. First, I will proclaim Your Word to those close to me, then to those in my extended network, then to whomever and wherever I may go. I will do this so that they should repent and turn to You and prove their repentance by their deeds. **ACTS 26:19–20**

🌿 For a clearer vision of the work you have set before us and for a better understanding of your gospel,
Lord, direct us.
For a deeper commitment in your service and a greater love for all your children,
Lord, direct us.
For a fresh understanding of the task before us and for a sense of urgency in our proclamation,
Lord, direct us.
For a great respect and acceptance among Christians of different traditions and for a common goal in evangelism,
Lord, direct us.
   PRAYER FROM THE ANGLICAN PROVINCE of the Indian Ocean
   [*CBP, 433* PD]

🌿 Here, Lord, I abandon myself to thee. I have tried in every way I could think of to manage myself, and to make myself what I know I ought to be, but have always failed. Now I give it up to thee. Do thou take entire possession of me. Work in me all the good pleasure of thy will. Mold and fashion me into such a vessel as seemeth good to thee. I leave myself in thy hands, and I believe thou wilt according to thy promise, make me into a vessel unto thy own honor. . . . *I* lay off every other burden, *my* health, *my* reputation, *my* Christian work, *my* houses, *my* children, *my* business, *my* servants, everything, in short, *all* that concerns *me*, whether inward or outward.
   HANNAH WHITALL SMITH, *American author (1832–1911)* [*GMO, 359* PD]

A PRAYER FOR TODAY

Lord, what vision do You have for me in this season of my life? . . .
I can be tempted to project my vision of my life onto You.
Help me to truly discern Your leading.
I know that Your vision usually involves a sacrificial mission of sorts. . . .
Grant me the courage to pursue Your vision for my life. . . .
Let Your vision renew in me a joyful self-denial, a sacrificing of comforts. . . .
Renew in me Your vision and purpose, a passion, vigor, joy, and love. Amen.

Day 56
PRAYERS *of* PRAISE/ADORATION

God, You made the earth by Your power; You founded the world by Your wisdom and You stretched out the heavens by Your understanding.
When You thunder, the waters in the heavens roar; You make the clouds rise from the ends of the earth. You send lightning with the rain and bring out the wind from Your storehouses. JEREMIAH 10:12–13

I bless you, O Lord, though I am powerless, you strengthen my weakness. You stretch forth from above your helping hand and bring me back unto yourself.
What shall I render to you, O all-good Master, for all the good things you have done and continue to do for me, the sinner?
I will cease not to bless you all the days of my life, my creator, my benefactor, my guardian.
> BASIL, *bishop of Caesarea (330–379)* [PD]

Praise is an expression of wonder, approval, and appreciation.
At times, my heart is filled with spontaneous praise for You.
But more often, my heart is indifferent or preoccupied.
But today as an act of the will, I offer my praise to You.
> I praise You because You are more powerful than any other.
> I praise You by offering my wonder.
> I praise You because You are worthy.
> I praise You by offering my approval.
> I praise You because You are gracious.
> I praise You by offering my appreciation.
> KURT BJORKLUND, *American minister (1968–present day)*

Praise the Lord!
Praise God in His sanctuary.
Praise Him in His mighty expanse.
Praise Him for his mighty deeds;
Praise Him according to His excellent greatness.
Let everything that has breath praise the Lord.
Praise the Lord! PSALM 150:1–2, 6 [NASB]

A PRAYER FOR TODAY

Lord, I want to contemplate Your great power in creating the universe. . . .
I know that You have power over all the natural forces that You created.
I know that I could not take a breath or be sustained upon this earth but by Your grace.
So I join the psalmist in exclaiming Your praise. . . .

PRAYERS *for* CHRISTLIKE CHARACTER

To fear (Heb.=*yira*: from *yare, to reverence or fear, hold with awe*)
You, O Lord, is the beginning of wisdom,
And to know (Heb.=*data: knowledge, understanding, learning*) You,
O Holy One, is understanding.   **PROVERBS 9:10**

The greatest commandment is this: Hear, O Israel; the Lord our God, the
Lord is one; and you shall love the Lord your God
with all your heart and with all your soul and with all your mind and
with all your strength.
The second is this: You shall love your neighbor as yourself.
There is no commandment greater than these, O God.   **MARK 12:29–31**

O God, who hast taught us to keep all thy commandments by loving thee
and our neighbor: Grant us the grace of thy Holy Spirit, that we may be
devoted to thee with our whole heart, and united to one another with pure
affection; through Jesus Christ our Lord, who liveth and reigneth with thee
and the same Spirit, one God, for ever and ever. Amen.
FROM THE BOOK OF COMMON PRAYER [*BCP, 179* PD]

Thanks be to thee, my Lord Jesus Christ,
for all the benefits thou hast won for me,
for all the pains and insults thou hast borne for me.
O most merciful Redeemer, Friend and Brother,
may I know thee more clearly,
love thee more dearly,
and follow thee more nearly, day by day.
RICHARD OF CHICHESTER, *English minister (1197–1253)* [*BTP, 58* PD]

A PRAYER FOR TODAY

God, You are a God of love.
I recognize that my character is the result of thousands of little choices.
I ask You to help me this day, to make choices that reflect the values of Jesus
Christ. I know that I'm commanded to love You and others above anything else,
but sometimes I love these things or people more . . .
I invite the work of the Holy Spirit to reign in my heart and life by . . .
Father, where Your values are not my values . . .
please change my heart.
Where I share Your values, but lack courage, strength, or perseverance . . .
grant those in abundance.
To love You with my whole heart, soul, mind, and strength means . . . Amen.

PRAYERS for WISDOM/GUIDANCE

I will not let Your word depart from my mouth, O Lord,
    but I will meditate on it day and night,
    so that I may be careful to do all that is written in it;
for then I will be prosperous and I will act with wisdom. **JOSHUA 1:8**

Grant, O Lord, to all teachers and students,
    to know what is worth knowing,
    to love what is worth loving,
    to praise what pleases you most,
    and to dislike whatsoever is evil in your sight.
Grant us with true judgment to distinguish things that differ,
and above all to search out and do what is well-pleasing to you,
through Jesus Christ our Lord.
      THOMAS Á KEMPIS, *German monk (1379–1471)* [COS, 119 PD]

O Lord, I do not know what to ask of You.
You alone know what are my true needs.
You love me more than I myself know how to love.
Help me to see my real needs which are concealed from me. . . .
I can only wait on You. My heart is open to You.
Visit and help me, for the sake of Your great mercy.
Strike me and heal me; cast me down and raise me up.
I worship in silence Your holy will and Your unsearchable ways.
Teach me to pray. . . . Amen
      PHILARET, *Russian theologian (1782–1867)* [EOP, 17 PD]

A PRAYER FOR TODAY

Lord, today I sense the need to love what You love . . .
    and to praise what You praise . . .
    and to dislike what You dislike. . . .
I know that this perception will come to me only as I meditate on Your Word.
Show me today Your ways. . . .
Often I don't know what I really need.
But You know. And I trust You.
As I become increasingly aware of You and Your ways, draw me to be fully committed to You. For me, being fully committed to You would involve . . . Amen.

PRAYERS *of* INTERCESSION

⚜ I will declare Your glory among the nations, Your marvelous deeds among all people. **PSALM 96:3**

⚜ John saw an angel flying in midair, holding the eternal gospel to proclaim to those who live on the earth . . . declaring in a loud voice, "Fear God and give Him glory, because the hour of His judgment has come. Worship Him who made the heavens, the earth, the sea. . . ." **REVELATION 14:6–7**

⚜ Great God of overflowing grace, move our hearts to pray for Your
    saving power among the nations.
Burden us with the plight of people who have no access to the gospel.
Grant us to pray big, global, God-sized, Bible saturated prayers.
Don't let us lose sight of the one lost sheep nearby.
But, O Father, give us a passion for Your worldwide purpose to call Your
    sheep from every people on the earth.
For the glory of Christ, and in His name we pray. Amen.
      JOHN PIPER, *American pastor (1946–present day) [PBW, 14]*

A PRAYER FOR TODAY

God's mission is to the whole earth. Traditional missions send people cross-culturally to proclaim the Word of God. Consider also praying for those who labor locally and are within their own culture doing things to proclaim the Word of God.
Lord, I ask that Your glory be declared in . . . *(name country or community)*
I ask that You would empower Your workers there. . . .
I pray specifically for . . . *(Name missionary. If you don't know any, learn one's name today and pray for him, her, or them.)*
I ask that You, God, would provide for them financially.
I ask that You would protect them from all that is bent on their harm.
I ask that You would show them Your agenda and that their efforts would be
    directed toward it.
I ask that You would allow them to see enough fruit of their work to not
    become weary.
I ask that You would resolve their greatest challenges. . . . *(name them if you are aware)*
I ask that You would grant them favor with the local community.
I ask that You would allow them to experience favor with the local
    government.
I ask that You would renew their spiritual passion and walk with You . . .
that it would be the source of their strength and joy.

PRAYERS *of* SURRENDER

I lift up my eyes to the hills. Where does my help come from?
It comes from You, O Lord, the One who made heaven and earth.
You will not allow my foot to slip; You, the One who watches over me,
    will not slumber.
You are my keeper; You are my shade at my right hand. The sun will not
    harm me by day, nor the moon by night.   PSALM 121:1–3, 5–6

O God, our Father, we thank you for waking us to see the light of this new
day.
Grant that we may waste none of its hours; soil none of its moments;
neglect none of its opportunities; fail none of its duties.
And bring us to the evening time undefeated by any temptation, at peace
with ourselves, and with you. This we ask for your love's sake.
    WILLIAM BARCLAY, *Scottish Bible professor (1907–1978) [CPB, 142]*

I hand over to your care, Lord,
My soul and body,
My mind and thoughts, my prayers and my hopes,
My health and my work, my life and my death,
My parents and my family, my friends and my *neighbors,*
My country and all men. Today and always.
    LANCELOT ANDREWES, *English minister (1555–1626) [CPB, 150–51* PD]

A PRAYER FOR TODAY

Father, my hours today will be filled with . . .
    Help me not to waste any of them.
The opportunities that I have today are . . .
    Help me to neglect none of these.
I have these duties . . .
    Help me to fulfill them with gladness.
I will likely face these temptations . . .
    Help me to be undefeated.
I give You my moments,
    my physical well-being,
    my intellect,
    and my hopes and dreams.
I acknowledge that You do not sleep or slumber;
You are up all night—so I don't need to be. Allow me to rest in You. Amen.

PRAYERS *of* THANKSGIVING

🌿 It was You, Lord,
Who created the heavens and stretched them out,
Who spread out the earth and all that grows on it;
You give breath to its people and spirit to those who walk on it.
      ISAIAH 42:5

🌿 I will praise You, Lord!
I will give thanks to You with my whole heart, along with others who are
    upright within the congregation.
Great are Your works, Lord; they are studied by all who delight in them.
Full of splendor and majesty is Your work, and Your righteousness endures
    forever.
You have caused Your wonderful works to be remembered; You are
    gracious and merciful. PSALM 111:1–4

🌿 *Father, You* giveth more grace when the burdens grow greater,
You sendeth more strength when the labors increase;
to added affliction *You* addeth *Your* mercy,
to multiplied trials *Your* multiplied peace.
When we have exhausted our store of endurance,
when our strength has failed ere the day is half done,
when we reach the end of our hoarded resources, *Father Your* full giving is
only begun.
Your love has no limit, *Your* grace has no measure;
Your power no boundary known unto men;
for out of *Your* infinite riches in Jesus, *You* giveth and giveth and giveth again.
    "HE GIVETH MORE GRACE," ANNIE JOHNSON FLINT, *American poet*
    (1866–1932) [PD]

🌿 *Thank You, God, that You* are for us—*which* is a . . . summary of redemptive
history. Amen.
    MARTIN H. FRANZMANN, *American professor (twentieth century)*
    [FRC, 157]

A PRAYER FOR TODAY

Lord, thank You for who You are . . . and Your mighty works. . . .
Thank You that Your love has no limit and Your grace no measure. . . .
Thank You that nothing is beyond Your power. . . .
Thank You for being my. . . .
Thank You for never forsaking me in my weaknesses. . . . Amen.

PRAYERS *of* CONFESSION

You, O Lord, are my Redeemer, the Holy One of Israel. You have said:
"I am the Lord your God, who teaches you what is best for you,
and who leads you in the way you should go." ISAIAH 48:17

O Lord our God, we have looked for riches, which would corrupt us.
We have wanted human approval more than yours.
And we have expected you to guard our worldly goods.
Forgive us, we pray, and take us back to Christ and to the least of his
brothers and sisters. Amen.
> CORNELIUS PLANTINGA JR., *American seminary president (1946–present day)*
> *[BDD, 203]*

If I claim to be without sin, I am deceived and the truth is not in me.
If I confess my sins, You are faithful and just and will forgive me of my sins
and purify me from all unrighteousness.
If I claim I have not sinned, I make You out to be a liar and Your word is not
in me. 1 JOHN 1:8–10

From the cowardice that dare not face new truth,
From the laziness that is contented with half truth,
From the arrogance that thinks it knows all truth,
Good Lord, deliver me.
> UNKNOWN SOURCE

God grant me the serenity
To accept the things I cannot change,
The courage to change the things I can,
And the wisdom to know the difference.
> REINHOLD NIEBUHR, *American minister (1892–1971) [PL, 102]*

A PRAYER FOR TODAY

Father—I pause to ask You to reveal to me anything I am doing that is not
pleasing to You. . . .
Please reveal to me anything that I am neglecting to do that would be pleasing
to You. . . .
Please reveal to me any areas of unconfessed sin. . . .
Please reveal to me the ways I have adopted cultural values. . . .
Please reveal to me where I have been hardened to the needs of others. . . .
I confess these things to You, and ask You to grant me the courage to change and
the will to surrender.

PRAYERS *of* AFFIRMATION

Jesus, I affirm that I will see You, the Son of Man, sitting at the right hand of the Mighty One and coming on the clouds of heaven.   **MARK 14:62**

Lord Jesus, I affirm that You have all authority in heaven and on earth and that You have commanded Your followers to go and make disciples of all people, baptizing them in the name of the Father, the Son, and the Holy Spirit, and teaching them to obey all that You have commanded. And in doing this, You will be with us to the very end of the age.
MATTHEW 28:18–20

We believe that Jesus Christ will return personally and visibly, in power and glory, to consummate his salvation and his judgment.

This promise of his coming is a further spur to our evangelism, for we remember his words that the gospel must first be preached to all nations. We believe that the interim period between Christ's ascension and return is to be filled with the mission of the people of God, who have no liberty to stop before the end.

We also remember his warning that false Christs and false prophets will arise as precursors of the final Antichrist. We therefore reject as a proud, self-confident dream the notion that people can ever build a utopia on earth. Our Christian confidence is that God will perfect his kingdom, and we look forward with eager anticipation to that day, and to the new heaven and earth in which righteousness will dwell and God will reign forever.

Meanwhile, we rededicate ourselves to the service of Christ and of people in joyful submission to his authority over the whole of our lives.
THE LAUSANNE COVENANT, *1973* [PD]

Lord, You bore our sins in Your body on the tree, so that we might die to sin and live for righteousness; for by Your wounds we have been healed.
1 PETER 2:24

A PRAYER FOR TODAY

God, I believe that Jesus is the provision of redemption.
I believe that faith in Jesus Christ alone brings about salvation.
I affirm that my life is to be about the declaration and spreading of this message.
I will make it my aim to spread this message today by . . .
I will seek to declare this message to . . . *(name person)*

PRAYERS *of* PETITION

Father God, since I am surrounded by such a great cloud of witnesses, let me throw off everything that hinders and the sin that so easily entangles, and let me run with endurance the race marked out for me.
Let me fix my eyes on Jesus, the author and perfecter of my faith, who for the joy set before Him endured the cross, scorning its shame, and sat down at the right hand of the throne of God.
I will consider Him who endured such opposition from sinful men, so that I will not grow weary and lose heart. **HEBREWS 12:1–3**

Give us grace, almighty Father, to address thee with all our hearts as well as with our lips. . . .
Teach us to fix our thoughts on thee, reverently and with love,
so that our prayers are not in vain,
but are acceptable to thee, now and always;
through Jesus Christ our Lord.
JANE AUSTEN, *English novelist (1775–1817)* [CBP, 11 PD]

Dear Jesus,
Help us to spread your fragrance everywhere we go.
Flood our souls with your spirit and life.
Penetrate and possess our whole being so utterly that our lives may only be a radiance of yours.
Shine through us and be so in us that every soul we come in contact with may feel your presence in our soul.
Let them look up and see no longer us but only Jesus.
Stay with us and then we shall begin to shine as you shine, so to shine as to be light to others.
The light, O Jesus, will be all from you.
None of it will be ours.
It will be you shining on others through us.
Let us thus praise you in the way you love best by shining on those around us.
MOTHER TERESA, *Albanian nun (1910–1997)* [GSG, 49]

A PRAYER FOR TODAY

Lord, I give up the sin that so easily entangles me. . . .
I give up what is not sinful, but has become an encumbrance to my spiritual passion. . . .
I will move with steady perseverance toward the life You have called me to live. . . .
I will fix my eyes on You today by . . . Amen.

PRAYERS *for* RENEWAL

I will trust in You, Lord, with all my heart
And lean not on my own understanding;
In all my ways I will acknowledge You,
And You will make my paths straight.
I will not be wise in my own eyes,
But I will fear You, Lord, and depart from evil.   PROVERBS 3:5–7

Dear Lord, help me to see the "nowness" of my Christian faith. The past is
the past, and put aside; the future is in Your hands, Lord, but the "now" is
up to me. This is where I either reflect You or not, in how I live today. . . .
Fill me with Your Spirit; enable me to be more than I am, that I may seize
this precious time that will not come again, and live today to Your glory.
      D. L. HAMMOND, *devotional writer (unknown era) [EOP, 1034]*

Lord, High and Holy, Meek and Lowly,
Thou hast brought me to the valley of vision,
Where I live in the depths, but see Thee in the heights;
Hemmed in by mountains of sin I behold Thy glory.
Let me learn by paradox
    That the way down is up,
    That to be low is to be high,
    That the broken heart is the healed heart,
    That the contrite spirit is the rejoicing spirit,
    That the repenting soul is the victorious soul,
    That to have nothing is to possess all,
    That to bear the cross is to wear the crown,
    That to give is to receive,
    That the valley is the place of vision.
Lord, in the daytime stars can be seen from the deepest wells,
And the deeper the wells the brighter Thy stars shine;
Let me find Thy light in my darkness,
Thy life in my death,
Thy joy in my sorrow,
Thy grace in my sin,
Thy glory in my valley.
      "THE VALLEY OF VISION," ARTHUR BENNETT, *English author (1915–1994)*
      [as quoted in BHE, 255–56]

A PRAYER FOR TODAY

Lord, when I lean on my own understanding it leads me toward this . . .
But when I acknowledge You and I am directed this way . . .
Amen.

Day 66
PRAYERS of PRAISE/ADORATION

❦ Who is like You, O Lord? Who is like You—
majestic in holiness, awesome in praises, working wonders?
EXODUS 15:11

❦ It is . . . right, and fitting, and due, in all things, and for all things,
at all times, in all places, by all means, in every season, every spot,
ever, everywhere, every way, to make mention of Thee, to Worship Thee,
to confess to Thee, to praise Thee, to bless Thee,
to sing to Thee, to give thanks to Thee.
For You are the Maker, Nourisher, Preserver, Governor, Protector, Author,
Finisher of all, the Lord and Father, the King and God,
the Fountain of life and immortality,
the Treasure of eternal good things.
LANCELOT ANDREWES, *English pastor (1555–1626)* [*PDL, 43–44* PD]

❦ Lord, I have heard of Your fame; I stand in awe of Your deeds, O Lord.
Renew them in our day, in our time make them known; in wrath remember
mercy. **HABAKKUK 3:2**

❦ O my God, give me thy grace so that the things of this earth and things
more naturally pleasing to me, may not be as close as thou art to me.
Keep thou my eyes, my ears, my heart from clinging to the things of this
world.
Break my bonds, raise my heart.
Keep my whole being fixed on thee.
Let me never lose sight of thee; and while I gaze on thee,
let my love of thee grow more and more every day.
JOHN HENRY NEWMAN, *English clergy (1801–1890)* [*CBP, 65* PD]

A PRAYER FOR TODAY

Lord, I praise You today!
I acknowledge Your fame among all people.
I praise You for working wonders. There is no one like You.
You are the Maker . . .
My Nourisher . . .
My Preserver . . . My Protector . . .
My King . . .
Let me not lose sight of You in the rush of my life. Amen.

PRAYERS *for* CHRISTLIKE CHARACTER

I will not lay up for myself treasures on earth,
    where moth and rust destroy and where thieves break in and steal.
But I will lay up for myself treasures in heaven,
    where moth and rust do not destroy and where thieves do not break in
    and steal. MATTHEW 6:19–20

God, I will keep my life free from the love of money, and I will be content
with what I have, for You have said, "I will never leave you nor forsake you."
    HEBREWS 13:5

Dig out of us, O Lord, the venomous roots of covetousness,
    or else so repress them with your grace, that we may be contented with
your provision of necessaries, and not labor, as we do, with all toil, skill,
    guile *(defined as shrewdness, crafty, using tricks to deceive)*,
    wrong and oppression,
    to pamper ourselves with vain superfluities.
    EDMUND GRINDAL, *English bishop (1519–1583)* [COS, 78 PD]

O Merciful God, let me fully and entirely resign myself to thy disposal,
    to have no desires of my own,
    but a perfect satisfaction in thy choice for me;
    that so, in whatsoever state I am, I may be therein content;
Lord, grant I may never look with murmuring on my own condition, nor
with envy on other men's.
And, to that end, I beseech thee purge my heart of all covetous affections.
    SAMUEL VON PUFENDORF, *German philosopher (1632–1694)* [HBP, 392 PD]

A PRAYER FOR TODAY

Make a list of the things you would like to have right now.
Which things on your list are real needs and which things are mere wants?
Lord, I can see how this list can turn into a great desire for earthly things.
I can see that when others have something, it can spur a desire to have more.
I confess to You my covetous affections. . . .
I confess to You my murmuring of my own condition. . . .
I confess to You how I seek to pamper myself with vain superfluities. . . .
I ask that You would grant me contentedness in You. . . .
I ask that You would grant me contentedness in what You have given me. . . .
Show me how covetous affections breed dissatisfaction of soul. . . .
May I not love money but rest in the promise of Your constancy. . . . Amen.

If I listen to a life-giving rebuke, (Heb.=*tokahat: correction, reproof, punishment*)
    I will be at home among the wise.
If I refuse instruction, (Heb.=*musar: correction, discipline, instruction*)
    I despise myself,
but if I heed correction, (Heb.=*tokahat: correction, reproof, punishment*)
    I will gain understanding.
When I fear You, Lord,
I learn wisdom. **PROVERBS 15:31–33**

Grant us, Lord, to know in weakness the strength of your incarnation:
    in pain the triumph of your passion:
    in poverty the riches of your Godhead:
    in reproach the satisfaction of your sympathy:
    in loneliness the comfort of your continual presence:
    in difficulty the efficacy of your intercession:
    in perplexity the guidance of your wisdom:
and by your glorious death and resurrection bring us at last to the joy of
seeing you face to face.
    ANONYMOUS *[EOP, 126]*

Grant us a vision, Lord,
    To see what we can achieve
    To reach out beyond ourselves
    To share our lives with others
    To stretch our capabilities
    To increase our sense of purpose
    To be aware of where we can help
    To be sensitive to your Presence
    To give heed to your constant call.
    "BEYOND OURSELVES," CELTIC PRAYER *[PL, 45]*

A PRAYER FOR TODAY

Lord, show me where I am currently experiencing life-giving rebuke. . . .
What are You teaching me in pain? . . . in poverty? . . . in reproach? . . . in
loneliness? . . .
I sense the wisdom and understanding I am to gain through this is . . .
Help me to heed this correction by taking the following steps . . .
(Articulate a few clear action steps in this area of your life.)
I ask for vision in the midst of this to see this as about more than me. Amen.

PRAYERS *of* INTERCESSION

🌸 Father, when I come before you, I won't turn it into a theatrical produc-
tion. A lot of people make a regular show out of their prayers, hoping for
stardom! But I know that you don't sit in a box seat.

Here is what I will do—find a quiet, secluded place so I won't be
tempted to role-play before you. I will just be there as simply and honestly
as I can be and my focus will shift from myself to you, I will begin to sense
your grace.

The world is full of so-called prayer warriors who are prayer-ignorant.
They're full of formulas and programs and advice, peddling techniques for
getting what you want from God. I won't fall for that nonsense. You are my
father that I'm dealing with, and you know better than I do what I need.
With a God like you loving me, this is how I pray:

Our Father in heaven, *(Our Father in heaven)*
Reveal who you are. *(Hallowed be your name)*
Set the world right; *(Your kingdom come)*
Do what is best—as above, so below.
(Your will be done on earth as it is in heaven)
Keep us alive with three square meals. *(Give us today our daily bread)*
Keep us forgiven with you and forgiving others.
(Forgive us our debts, as we also have forgiven our debtors)
Keep us safe from ourselves and the Devil.
(And lead us not into temptation, but deliver us from the evil one)
You're in charge!
You can do anything you want!
MATTHEW 6:5–13 (Adapted from MSG—*words of NIV in parentheses*)

🌸 *Lord, I will* not have as *my* motive the desire to be known as a praying *person.*
I will seek an inner chamber in which to pray where no one knows that *I* am
praying, *and I will* shut the door and talk to *You*, God, in secret. *I will* have
no other motive than to know *You, my* Father in heaven. It is impossible to
conduct *my* life as a disciple without definite times of secret prayer.
OSWALD CHAMBERS, *English chaplain, teacher (1874–1917) [MUH, 191]*

A PRAYER FOR TODAY

Consider what it would be like for God to "set the world right." . . .
Lord, reveal who You are in this world and to this world.
Set this world right. You are in charge. You are beautiful.
Letting Your kingdom become foremost in my life today would mean . . .
Bring a taste of Your kingdom to the following people and situations in our
world. . . . Amen.

Day 70
PRAYERS *of* SURRENDER

- For I joyfully concur with Your law, O God, even in the deepest parts of my being. **ROMANS 7:22**

- Your word is a lamp to my feet and a light for my path.
  I pledge to confirm and to follow Your righteous laws. . . .
  Accept, O Lord, the willing praise of my mouth, and teach me Your laws.
  PSALM 119:105–106, 108

- Eternal God, who *is* the light of the minds that know you,
      the joy of the hearts that love you,
      and the strength of the hands that serve you.
  Grant us so to know you, that we may truly love you, and so to love you
      that we may fully serve you, whom to serve is perfect freedom,
  in Jesus Christ our Lord.
  AUGUSTINE, *bishop of Hippo (354–430)* [CPB, 141 PD]

- Heavenly Father, thank you for loving me enough to set limits on what I may and may not do. Grant me the wisdom to stay within the confines you have so wisely established. By sending Christ to die you have assured me that you have my best interest in mind. I willingly surrender every area of my life with the assurance that in doing so I am guaranteed freedom. Amen.
  CHARLES STANLEY, *American pastor (1932–present day)* [THF, 20]

- O Lord, I really want to be in control. No, I need to be in control. That's it isn't it? I'm afraid to give up control, afraid of what might happen. Heal my fear, Lord. How good of You to reveal my blind spots even in the midst of my stumbling attempts to pray. Thank You! But now what do I do? How do I give up control? Jesus, please, teach me Your way of relinquishment.
  RICHARD FOSTER, *American author (1942–present day)* [PHH, 56]

A PRAYER FOR TODAY

What is God directing in your life right now? . . .
What has God been showing you in His Word in recent days? . . .
What would total submission to these things look like? . . .
What don't you want to relinquish control of? . . .
What scares you about following God's leading? . . .
Father, here is what I have been holding on to . . .
I surrender it to You. . . .
I trust that all things are better when they are in Your control. . . . Amen.

PRAYERS *of* THANKSGIVING

🍃 Jesus, You are before all things and in You all things are held together. You have made Him the head of the body—the church; and You are the beginning, the firstborn from the dead; so that You might come to have first place in everything. COLOSSIANS 1:17–18

🍃 Eternal God, the heaven of heavens cannot contain you, much less the walls of this *building* made with hands. Graciously receive our thanks for this place, and accept the work of our hands, offered to your honor and glory. For the church universal, of which these visible buildings are the symbol,
> **we thank you, Lord.**

For your presence whenever two or three have gathered together in your Name,
> **we thank you, Lord.**

For making us your children by adoption and grace, and refreshing us day by day with the bread of life,
> **we thank you, Lord.**

For the knowledge of your will and the grace to perform it,
> **we thank you, Lord.**

For the fulfilling of our desires and petitions as you see best for us,
> **we thank you, Lord.**

For the pardon of our sins, which restores us to the company of your faithful people,
> **we thank you, Lord.** . . .

For the faith of those who have gone before us and for our encouragement by their perseverance
> **we thank you, Lord.** . . .

Yours, O Lord, is the greatness, the power, the glory, the victory, and the majesty;
And you are exalted as head over all. Amen.
> **"A LITANY OF THANKSGIVING FOR THE CHURCH"** [*BCP, 578-79* PD]

A PRAYER FOR TODAY

I thank You for the foundation of the church in Jesus Christ.
I acknowledge that You are the head of this church.
I thank You for the imperfect people who make up my church. . . .
I thank You for the leadership of my church. . . .
I thank You for those who irritate me within the church. . . .
I thank You for those who serve consistently within the church. . . .
I thank You for the teaching of Your Word in my church. . . . And for
how You have used this church in my own spiritual journey. . . . Amen.

PRAYERS *of* CONFESSION

You, O Lord, search me and know me.
You know when I sit down and when I rise up.
You understand my thoughts from afar.
You scrutinize my path and my lying down,
And are intimately acquainted with all my ways.
Even before there is a word on my tongue,
You, O Lord, know it all.
You have enclosed me, behind and before,
And laid Your hand on me.   **PSALM 139:1–5**

Father God, You know all of me, and
Oh the comfort, the inexpressible comfort of feeling safe with *You*;
having neither to weigh thoughts nor measure words, but to pour them
out, just as they are, chaff and grain together, knowing that a faithful hand
will take and sift them,
keep what is worth keeping, and then, with the breath of kindness, blow
the rest away.
   GEORGE ELIOT, *English writer (1819–1880)* [*CDP, 523* PD]

O God, whose Spirit searcheth all things, and whose love beareth all things,
encourage us to draw near to Thee in sincerity and in truth. Save us from
a worship of the lips while our hearts are far away. Save us from the useless labor of attempting to conceal ourselves from Thee who searchest the
heart.
Enable us to lay aside all those cloaks and disguises which we wear in the
light of day and here to bare ourselves, with all our weakness, disease and
sin, naked to Thy Spirit.
   W. E. ORCHARD, *author (nineteenth century)* [*MOP, 128* PD]

A PRAYER FOR TODAY

Father, I consider what is deep inside me that few or no one knows. . . .
I acknowledge that I have tried to manage my image before others.
I acknowledge that I have tried to even manage my image before You.
Please bring to mind what is not aligned with Your purposes for my life. . . .
I confess what is not aligned to You and turn away from it. . . .
Now I see that part of me as accepted in the grace of God through Jesus Christ.
Now I celebrate the acceptance that I have received in Jesus. . . .
Now I rejoice that You love me when I find it hard to believe anyone else could
love me if they were to see what You have seen. . . . Amen.

PRAYERS *of* AFFIRMATION

Lord Jesus Christ, I acknowledge that You suffered for me,
leaving for me an example that I should follow in Your footsteps.
For You committed no sin, and no deceit was found in Your mouth.
When You were reviled, You did not retaliate;
when You suffered You made no threats,
but entrusted Yourself to the One who judges fairly.   1 PETER 2:21–23

Jesus, *You* suffered not that we might not suffer,
but that when we suffer we might become like *You.*
> AMY CARMICHAEL, *American missionary (1868–1951) [US]*

God, like a father, *You* don't just give advice. *You* give *yourself.*
You become the husband to the grieving widow (Isaiah 54:5).
You become the comforter to the barren woman (Isaiah 54:1).
You become the father to the orphaned (Psalm 10:14).
You become the bridegroom to the single person (Isaiah 62:5).
You are the healer to the sick (Exodus 15:26).
You are the wonderful counselor to the confused and depressed (Isaiah 9:6).
> JONI EARECKSON TADA AND STEVEN ESTES, *American authors (twentieth century) [WGW, 125] At seventeen Joni was paralyzed in a diving accident.*

O my sweet Saviour Christ, which in thine undeserved love towards *humanity* so kindly wouldst suffer the painful death of the cross, suffer me not to be cold nor lukewarm in love again towards thee.
> THOMAS MORE, *English philosopher/author (1478–1535) [CBP, 65 PD]*

A PRAYER FOR TODAY

Lord, I acknowledge that You suffered unjustly.
Yet You did not retaliate.
Rather You entrusted Yourself to the One who judges fairly.
I know that when I suffer You become what I need and change me to be who You want me to be.
Help me to see my suffering as a means to experience Your presence.
Help me to see my suffering as a means to be transformed into Your likeness.
Help me to desire to be like You more than I desire a pain-free life.
Help me to entrust my life to You, the One who judges fairly. Amen.

PRAYERS *of* PETITION

I call on You, God, for I know You will answer me;
   Incline Your ear to me and hear my prayer.
   Show the wonders of Your great love.
   You are the Savior of those who take refuge in You from their adversaries.
   Keep me as the apple of Your eye;
   hide me in the shadow of Your wings. **PSALM 17:6–8**

O Lord, hear our prayers,
   not according to the poverty of our asking but according to the richness of
      your grace,
   so that our lives may conform to those desires which accord with your will;
   through Jesus Christ our Lord.
      REINHOLD NIEBUHR, *American minister (1892–1971) [CBP, 13]*

Lord, teach me to seek you,
      and reveal yourself to me as I look for you.
   For I cannot seek you unless first you teach me,
      nor find you unless first you reveal yourself to me.
      AMBROSE, *bishop of Milan (340–397) [BTP, 21]*

For You Lord will rescue (Gk.=*rhyomai: rescue, deliver, save, preserve*)
   me from every evil attack
   and will bring me safely (Gk.=*sozo: to keep safe from harm, rescue;* related
   word *soteria* used for salvation) to Your heavenly kingdom.
   To You be glory for ever and ever. Amen. **2 TIMOTHY 4:18**

A PRAYER FOR TODAY

Lord, this is what I am most concerned about today . . .
Please work in this situation by . . .
Please adjust my mind to see this as You see it *(what is God's reality?)*. . . .
This is my dominant feeling or emotion today . . .
Please work in my emotions today by . . .
Please adjust my feelings to Your reality. . . .
Please show me the wonder of Your love and grace in the midst of these things.
Please remind me of how You see me. *(What images besides "apple of Your eye"
come to mind?)*. . . .
Please remind me that You care deeply for me even when things seem to be
moving against me. Amen.

PRAYERS *for* RENEWAL

🖋 We have received Your power in the coming of the Holy Spirit, and we will be Your witnesses. **ACTS 1:8**

🖋 But I ask that You would make me
   clear minded in all situations,
   enduring in hardship,
   passionate in working for others to hear Your good news,
   and one who fulfills the ministry You have given me.
For I am willing to be poured out as a drink offering. . . . **2 TIMOTHY 4:5–6**

🖋 O Lord, how trivial are my aspirations and desires. I pursue the amusements and toys and *culture* of the modern world, while the higher longings of my soul weaken from neglect. What do I need to remove from my life, in order to throw myself without reserve or impediment into the great cause of the gospel? This is my brief moment in history. I do not have forever. Now is my time to speak to my generation. Purify my heart, Lord. Energize my desires. Open my eyes. Compel me with my personal responsibility to serve the interests of the gospel in the world today. O Lord, let me spend my life for you, disregarding all risks, accepting all consequences. Let the power of the gospel so grip me that I act upon it, come what may. Let me recover the power to live and to die for my faith. In the holy name of Christ. Amen.
   RAYMOND ORTLUND JR., *American minister (1946–present day) [PFG, 31]*

🖋 Dearest Lord, teach me to be generous;
   and to serve Thee as Thou deservest;
   To give and not to count the cost,
   To fight and not to heed the wounds,
   To toil and not to seek for rest,
   To *labor* and not to ask for any reward
   Save that of knowing that I do Thy will.
   IGNATIUS OF LOYOLA, *Spanish hermit (1491–1556) [PL, 105 PD]*

A PRAYER FOR TODAY

Lord, grant me sustained passion to give my life to a greater cause than my own comfort. . . .
Help me to see things with a clear mind, one that is not clouded by my cultural viewpoint. . . .
When hardships enter my life, help me to endure joyfully and disregard the risks in serving You. . . . Amen.

PRAYERS of PRAISE/ADORATION

I lift you high in praise, my God, O my King! And I'll bless your name into eternity.

I'll bless you every day, and keep it up from now to eternity.

You are magnificent and can never be praised enough.

Generation after generation stands in awe of your work; each one tells stories of your mighty acts.

Your beauty and splendor have everyone talking; I compose songs on your wonders. . . .

You are all mercy and grace—not quick to anger, *and* rich in love.

You are good to one and all; everything *you* do is suffused with grace.

Creation and creatures applaud you, God; your holy people bless you.

They talk about the glories of your rule, they exclaim over your splendor, letting the world know of your power for good, the lavish splendor of your kingdom.

Your kingdom is a kingdom eternal; you never get voted out of office.

You always do what you say, and you are gracious *in everything you do*. . . .

Generous to a fault, you lavish your favor on all creatures.

Everything *you do* is right—the trademark on all *your works* is love. . . .

My mouth is filled with *your* praise. Let everything living bless *you*.

Bless *your* holy name from now to eternity.

      PSALM 145:1–5, 8–13, 16–17, 21 [MSG]

To God be the glory, great things He hath done,
So loved He the world that He gave us His Son,
Who yielded His life an atonement for sin,
And opened the life gate that all may go in.
Praise the Lord, praise the Lord, let the earth hear His voice!
Praise the Lord, praise the Lord, let the people rejoice!
O come to the Father thru Jesus the Son, and give Him the glory,
Great things He hath done!

      "TO GOD BE THE GLORY," FANNY CROSBY, *American hymn writer (1820–1915) [PSH, 8]*

A PRAYER FOR TODAY

Lord, if I were to praise You for all eternity it would not be enough.

Help me to not be so focused on my problems that I miss the splendor of Your glory.

I add my own words of praise to the voices of others . . .

I add my own posture of praise *(symbolically move to a position that expresses praise)* . . .

I praise You! Amen.

PRAYERS *for* CHRISTLIKE CHARACTER

You are the Lord my God, . . . I will have no other gods before You.
I will not make for myself an idol in the form of anything in heaven above or on the earth beneath or in the waters below.
I will not bow down to them or worship them, for You are a jealous God. . . .
I will not misuse Your name, Lord God, . . .
I will remember Your Sabbath by keeping it holy. Six days I will labor and do my work, but I will devote one day to worship You and to rest. . . .
I will honor my father and mother. . . .
I will not murder.
I will not commit adultery.
I will not steal.
I will not give false testimony against my neighbor.
I will not covet my neighbor's house or my neighbor's spouse, or my neighbor's empire, or my neighbor's possessions. EXODUS 20:2–17

To my God a heart of flame,
To my fellow man a heart of love,
To myself a heart of steel.
AUGUSTINE, *bishop of Hippo in North Africa (354–430)* [PL, 101 PD]

A PRAYER FOR TODAY

Lord, show me what gods I am prone to have before You. . . .
Show me the idols of my heart that capture my affection. . . .
Show me the ways I misuse Your name—how I use it too casually, as a curse, and when I invoke it to gain an advantage, rather than in humble submission. . . .
Give me the courage to keep one day reserved for worship and rest. . . .
Help me to know what it looks like to really honor my parents, and then to choose to do it. . . .
Show me where I have hate. . . . (Matthew 5:21–22)
Show me where I have lust. . . . (Matthew 5:27–28)
Show me where I take what isn't mine—including another's reputation, purity, or intellectual property, and when I squander another's possessions through misuse. . . .
Keep me from speaking falsely or from my silence giving false impressions. . . .
Grant me contentment so I will not covet what is not mine. . . .
Lord, You know and want what is best for me. Amen.

PRAYERS for WISDOM/GUIDANCE

Teach me to do Your will, for You are my God;
may Your good Spirit lead me on level ground.   **PSALM 143:10**

O God, who am I now? Once I was secure in familiar territory in my sense of belonging, unquestioning of the norms of my culture, the assumptions built into my language, the values shared by my society. But now you have called me out and away from home, and I do not know where you are leading. I am empty, unsure, *and* uncomfortable. I have only a beckoning star to follow.

Journeying God, *guide me*
so that I may not become deterred by hardship, strangeness, doubt.
Show me the movement I must make
    toward a wealth not dependent on possessions
    toward a wisdom not based on books
    toward a strength not bolstered by might
    toward a God not confined to heaven
but scandalously earthed, poor, unrecognized . . .
Help me to find myself as I walk in other's shoes.
    KATE COMPSTON, *Jesuit poet, unknown era [BTP, 112–13]*

Whether I turn to the right or to the left, my ears will hear Your voice behind me, saying, "This is the way; walk in it."   **ISAIAH 30:21**

Help me today to realize that you speak primarily through your Word.
Help me today to realize that you *also* will be speaking to me through the events of the day, through people, through things, and through creation.
Give me ears, eyes and heart to perceive you, however veiled your presence may be.
Give me insight to see through the exterior of things to the interior truth.
Give me your Spirit of discernment.
    JACOB ASTLEY, *English royalty (1579–1652)* [CPB, 146 PD]

A PRAYER FOR TODAY

Lord, show me Your will. . . .
Show me what level ground is in my situation. . . .
Help me to hear Your voice leading me. . . .
How are You speaking through Your Word? . . .
How are You speaking through events? . . .
How are You speaking through people? . . .
How are You speaking through things / creation? . . .
I return to You! Amen.

PRAYERS *of* INTERCESSION

⚜ Heavenly Father, You have called us into fellowship with Your Son Jesus; therefore, help us to agree with one another, so that there are no divisions among us, and that we may be perfectly joined together in the same mind and in the same judgments. **1 CORINTHIANS 1:9–10**

⚜ Jesus, You prayed to the Father that all Your followers would be one, just as the Father is in You and You are in the Father. **JOHN 17:21**

⚜ If my soul has turned perversely to the dark;
If I have left some brother wounded by the way;
If I have preferred my aims to thine;
If I have been impatient and would not wait;
If I have marred the pattern drawn out of my life;
If I have cost tears to those I loved;
If my heart has murmured against thy will,
O Lord, forgive.
　　F. B. MEYER, *English evangelist/minister (1847–1929) [CBP, 259]*

⚜ O God, give us patience when those who are wicked hurt us. O how impatient and angry we are when we think ourselves unjustly slandered, reviled and hurt! Christ suffers blows upon his cheek, the innocent for the guilty; yet we may not abide one rough word for his sake. O Lord, grant us virtue and patience, power and strength, that we may take all adversity with goodwill, and with a gentle mind overcome it. And if necessity and thy honour require us to speak, grant that we may do so with meekness and patience, that thy truth and thy glory may be defended, and our patience and steadfast continuance perceived.
　　MILES COVERDALE, *English Bible translator (1488–1569)* [CBP, 221 PD]

A PRAYER FOR TODAY

Lord, often those who claim to follow You are characterized by strife and conflict rather than unity and like-mindedness.
I pray for unity in *(insert name)* church and/or *(insert name)* organization. . . .
Show those involved:
　　if they have left another wounded by the way and cost others tears;
　　where they have elevated their own ambitions and goals above others;
　　where they have been impatient and murmured against You or others;
　　how to overlook offenses . . .
　　how to speak with meekness, patience, and the goal that Your truth and glory be defended, not that another be put in his or her place. Amen.

PRAYERS *of* SURRENDER

Christ Jesus, may I prepare my mind for action and be self-controlled, setting my hope fully on the grace to be given to me at Your coming.
1 PETER 1:13

O God, our Father, help us all through this day so to live that we may bring help to others, credit to ourselves and to the name we bear, and joy to those that love us and to you.
Help us to be:
Cheerful when things go wrong;
Persevering when things are difficult;
Serene when things are irritating.
Enable us to be:
Helpful to those in difficulties;
Kind to those in need;
Sympathetic to those whose hearts are sore and sad.
Grant that:
Nothing may make us lose our tempers;
Nothing may take away our joy;
Nothing may ruffle our peace;
Nothing may make us bitter towards anyone. . . .
This we ask for your love's sake.
WILLIAM BARCLAY, *Scottish Bible professor (1907–1978) [CPB, 143]*

Lord, I commit today to:
Do all the good *I* can
By all the means *I* can
In all the ways *I* can
In all the places *I* can
At all the times *I* can
To all the people *I* can
As long as *I* ever can.
JOHN WESLEY, *English minister/founder of Methodism (1703–1791)* [PD]

A PRAYER FOR TODAY

Lord, where do You want me to help others today? . . .
Where can I be an encouragement to others? . . .
Where can I be sympathetic? . . .
Where can I show Your joy? . . .
Where can I reflect You more fully? . . .
Renew me in my commitment to reflect You in all that I do. Amen.

PRAYERS *of* THANKSGIVING

I give thanks to You Lord, for You are good, **Your love endures forever.**
I give thanks to You God of all gods, **Your love endures forever.**
I give thanks to the Lord of lords, **Your love endures forever.**
You alone do great wonders, **Your love endures forever.**
You have made the heavens by Your understanding, **Your love endures forever.**
You spread out the earth upon the waters, **Your love endures forever.**
You made the great lights, **Your love endures forever.**
You set the sun to govern the day, **Your love endures forever.**
You set the moon and the stars to govern the night, **Your love endures forever.** . . .
You are the One who remembered us in our low estate, **Your love endures forever.**
You freed us from our enemies, **Your love endures forever.**
You give food to every creature, **Your love endures forever.**
I will give thanks to You, the God of heaven, **Your love endures forever.**
PSALM 136:1–9, 23–26

I arise today through God's strength to pilot me,
God's might to uphold me,
God's wisdom to guide me,
God's eye to look before me,
God's ear to hear me,
God's word to speak for me,
God's hand to guard me, . . .
God's shield to protect me,
God's hosts to save me
from snares of the devil, from temptations of vices,
from every one who desires me ill, . . .
Christ with me, Christ before me, Christ behind me,
Christ in me, Christ beneath me, Christ above me,
Christ on my right, Christ on my left,
Christ when I lie down, Christ when I sit down, . . .
PATRICK, *Irish missionary (387–493)* [BJD, 199 PD]

A PRAYER FOR TODAY

Lord, I thank You for how Your goodness impacts me. . . .
If it weren't for Your goodness I would be lost in . . .
I thank You that Your love endures forever.
Let me never lose sight of Your great love for me. Amen.

Day 82

PRAYERS *of* CONFESSION

Jesus, You have said, "Blessed are the poor in spirit for theirs is the
kingdom of heaven"—I acknowledge that I have often been proud in
my spirit and full of arrogance.

Jesus, You have said, "Blessed are those who mourn, for they shall be
comforted"—I acknowledge that I have often glossed over things that
should make me sad and chosen petty amusements.

You have said, "Blessed are the gentle for they shall inherit the earth"—
I acknowledge that I have often been anything but gentle; I have been
pushy and domineering to get my way.

You have said, "Blessed are those who hunger and thirst for righteousness,
for they shall be satisfied"—I acknowledge that I often hunger and
thirst after things that are not righteous.

You have said, "Blessed are the merciful, for they shall receive mercy"—
I acknowledge that I am often too consumed with my own life to show
genuine mercy to those around me.

You have said, "Blessed are the pure in heart, for they shall see God"—
I acknowledge that often my heart is not pure. Rather it is filled with
mixed motives and impure desires.

Jesus, You have said, "Blessed are the peacemakers, for they shall be called
the sons of God"—I acknowledge that I often stir up strife and am part
of discord rather than peace.

MATTHEW 5:2–9, with additional confession by Kurt Bjorklund

Dear Lord, forgive me in that so much of my religion is concerned with
myself.
I want harmony with thee. I want peace of mind.
I want health of body—and so I pray.
Forgive me, for I have made thee the means and myself the end.
I know it will take long to wean me from this terrible self-concern,
but O God, help me, for hell can be nothing else but a life on which self is
the center.

LESLIE WEATHERHEAD, *English minister (1893–1976) [BHE, 315]*

A PRAYER FOR TODAY

Allow me to see the ways my sin impacts me, . . . Forgive me.
Allow me to see the ways my sin impacts those I love, . . . Forgive me.
Allow me to see the ways my sin impacts You, . . . Forgive me.
I know that much of my seeking You is really about me, . . . Forgive me.
Free me from the bondage of being preoccupied with myself.
Grant me the vision of life as a kingdom participant. . . . Amen.

PRAYERS *of* AFFIRMATION

You, O Lord, are my rock and my fortress and my deliverer;
You are my rock; I will take refuge in You.
You are my shield and the horn of my salvation,
My stronghold (Heb.=*mesuda: fortress, a place difficult to access by foes*)
and my refuge (Heb.=*manos: a place of escape, a place of strength and safety*)
My Savior, You save me from violence.
I call on You, Lord; You are worthy of praise,
And I am saved from my enemies.   2 SAMUEL 22:2–4

I believe, O God of all gods, that you are present,
that this day begins in you and in your Presence there is Peace.
I believe, O God of all gods, that you are present,
that this journey is in you and in your Presence there is Peace.
I believe, O God of all gods, that you are present,
that this work place is in you and in your Presence there is Peace.
I believe, O God of all gods, that you are present,
that we dwell in you and in your Presence there is Peace.
"THE PEACE OF THE PRESENCE," CELTIC PRAYER [*PL, 12–13* PD]

You, eternal Godhead, are life and I am death.
You are wisdom and I am ignorance.
You are light and I am darkness.
You are infinite and I am finite.
You are absolute directness and I am terrible twistedness.
You are the doctor and I am the sick.
CATHERINE OF SIENA, *Italian author (1347–1380)* [*US* PD]

A PRAYER FOR TODAY

Father—there are places where I do not sense Your presence, . . .
Where I do not sense Your peace, . . .
Where I do not sense Your security, . . .
I affirm today, that in You is peace.
I affirm today, that You are security.
I affirm that You are my rock, my fortress, and my deliverer.
I affirm that You are eternal, wise, light, and infinite.
I give You my places of doubt and darkness. . . .
I give You my twistedness and neediness. . . .
I run into an awareness of Your presence. Amen.

PRAYERS *of* PETITION

Lord, I will give You my burdens (Heb.=*yehab: cares, anxieties*)
and You will sustain (Heb.=*kul: contain, endure, hold, provide, supply*) me.
You will never permit the righteous to fall.   PSALM 55:22

Lord Christ, help us to have the courage and humility to name our burdens
and lay them down so that we are light to walk across the water to where
you beckon us. Our pride, armoring us, hardening us, making us defend
our dignity by belittling others
We name it and we lay it down.
The memory of hurts and insults, driving us to lash out, to strike back
We name it and we lay it down.
Our antagonism against those whose actions, differences, presence,
threaten our comfort or security
We name it and we lay it down.
Our fear, or unsolved questions, of the unknown, of fear itself
We name it and we lay it down.
We do not need these burdens, but we have grown used to carrying them,
have forgotten what it is like to be light. Beckon us to lightness of being,
for you show us it is not unbearable. . . . Blessed are you, Lord Christ, who
makes the heavy burdens light.
    KATHY GALLOWAY, *Scottish Iona Community (twentieth century) [CBP, 253]*

Give me, Lord,
    a stout heart to bear my own burdens,
    a tender heart to bear the burdens of others,
    and a believing heart to lay all my burdens on you, for you care for us.
    LESSLIE NEWBIGIN, *Scottish missionary/author (1901–1998) [CBP, 189]*

A PRAYER FOR TODAY

Lord, here are the burdens of my heart today . . . I give them to You knowing
that You care for me, knowing that You will not let me fall.
Some of my burdens are external. . . .
Some of my burdens are internal. . . . *(like those noted by Kathy Galloway)*
Now that I have named these burdens, I lay them down. I ask that You would
show me the burdens of others that You want me to carry. . . .
Show me how to carry their burdens. . . .
Show me the burdens that I am not called to carry. . . .
Let me be a comforting and encouraging presence by . . .
Let me be a challenging presence by . . . Amen.

PRAYERS *for* RENEWAL

One thing I ask of You, Lord; this is what I seek:
That I may dwell in Your house all the days of my life,
That I may gaze upon Your beauty and to seek You in Your temple.
   PSALM 27:4

[Like the psalmist, I desire not only to gaze on *Your* beauty in heaven but to catch transforming glimpses here and now.]
Lord, I desire to become all that *You* created me to be.
I desire to live each moment as a human fully alive and redeemed.
I desire that Christ may be seen in the features of my face. . . .
I desire to know fully and to be known fully even as now I am fully known
by God.   **1 CORINTHIANS 13:12**

I desire that the pattern of the glory will emerge. . . .
I desire to have my imagination quickened with a preview of heaven.
I desire the clarity and the centeredness that are marks of heaven where
"the Lamb is at the center of the throne" (Rev. 5:6) to mark my life now.
I desire to be part of what will bring joy and glory to the Creator—the restoration of all things that is surely coming.
I desire to have a home for God in my heart and to come home each day,
each hour, from now to eternity.
I desire to look with more and more attention until that longing for home
becomes a reality.
   LEIGHTON FORD, *American evangelist (1931–present day)* [TAL, 196–97]

I praise You for the honor of being made in Your image, personally formed
by You for Your glory, and gifted spiritually just as it has pleased You.
Thank You for each strength and ability and desirable trait You have given
me.
   RUTH MYERS, *American missionary (1928–2010)* [EGA, 58]

A PRAYER FOR TODAY

Reread Leighton Ford's prayer aloud slowly—thinking about each line.
Lord, I want to live every day, every moment, with an awareness of Your
presence.
When I experience You it sparks desire in me. Yet at times my desire is languid.
Fill me with a longing to be filled with You.
Show me the experiences and disciplines that spark this longing. . . .
Renew my desire for all that is related to You.

PRAYERS *of* PRAISE/ADORATION

I will praise You, O Lord, with all my heart; I will tell of all Your wonders. I will be glad and rejoice in You; I will sing praise to Your name, O Most High. PSALM 9:1–2

Father, we come to You in worship *which* is the submission of all our nature to *You.*
It is the quickening of conscience by *Your* holiness;
the nourishment of mind with *Your* truth;
the purifying of the imagination by *Your* beauty;
the opening of the heart to *Your* love;
the surrender of will to *Your* purpose—
and all of this gather up in adoration,
the most selfless emotion of which our nature is capable
and therefore the chief remedy of that self-centeredness
which is our original sin and the source of all actual sin.
   WILLIAM TEMPLE, *English bishop (1881–1944) [OBP, 3]*

Let all who fear You, O Lord, come and listen,
   and I will tell them what You have done for my soul.
   I cried out to You with my mouth; Your praise was on my tongue.
   If I had esteemed sin in my heart, You would not have heard.
   But You have heard, even the very words of my prayers.
   Praise be to You, O God. Neither my prayer nor Your love have been turned
   away. PSALM 66:16–20

A PRAYER FOR TODAY

Lord, as an act of worship I submit all of who I am to You. . . .
I consider Your holiness—and I experience greater sensitivity in my conscience. . . .
I consider Your truth—and I am nourished in my mind. . . .
I consider Your beauty—and I am purified in my imagination. . . .
I consider Your love—and I am opened in my heart. . . .
I consider Your purposes—and I surrender my will to Yours. . . .
I consider Your selflessness—and I begin to move beyond my selfishness. . . .
I consider Your hearing of my prayers—and I am encouraged to bring all to You. . . .
I consider Your wonders—and I am moved to adoration and love. . . .
I consider Your rule—and I am moved to lay my life before You. . . .
When I speak of Your wonders, they become even sweeter to me. Amen.

PRAYERS *for* CHRISTLIKE CHARACTER

I will not love the world or anything in the world.
For if I love the world, it proves that I do not love You, Father God.
For everything in the world:
> the cravings of sinful people
> the lust of the eyes
> and the boasting of what we have and do

does not come from You, but from the world.
The world and its desires pass away, but the person who does the will of
God will live forever.   1 JOHN 2:15–17

Increase our faith, O merciful Father, that we do not swerve at any time
from thy heavenly words,
but augment in us hope and love,
with a careful keeping of all thy commandments,
that no hardness of heart,
no hypocrisy,
no concupiscence of thy eye,
no enticement of the world,
draw us away from thy obedience. Amen
> **JOHN KNOX,** *Scottish Reformer (1513–1572)* [*EOP, 88* PD]

Lord, make me a crisis man. Let me not be a mile-post on a single road, but
make me a fork that men must turn one way or another in facing Christ in
me.
> **JIM ELLIOT,** *American missionary/martyr (1927–1956)* [*US*]

A PRAYER FOR TODAY

Lord, the world has a strong allure.
Please let me see the stuff of this world for what it is. . . .
Help me to understand that all this world offers is passing away. . . .
Let me see that the end of increasing possessions is . . .
Let me see that the end of indulging self is . . .
Let me see that the end of impressing people is . . .
And give me a greater love for You.
Let this love be so evident that my life makes those who love the world
uncomfortable.

Day 88

PRAYERS *for* WISDOM/GUIDANCE

- Lord, Your law is perfect, reviving my soul.
  Your statutes are trustworthy, making me wise where I am simple.
  Your precepts are right, giving joy to my heart.
  Your commands are radiant, giving light to my eyes.
  The fear of You is pure, enduring forever.
  Your ordinances are sure, and altogether righteous.
  They are more precious than gold—than much pure gold.
  They are sweeter than honey, than the honey from the comb.
  By them I am warned, and in keeping them there is great reward.
  Can I discern my own errors? Forgive my faults that are hidden from me.
  May the words of my mouth and the meditation of my heart be pleasing in
  Your sight, O Lord, my Rock and my Redeemer. PSALM 19:7–12, 14

- My Lord God, I have no idea where I am going.
  I do not see the road ahead of me.
  I cannot know for certain where it will end.
  Nor do I really know myself, and the fact that I think that I am following
  your will does not mean that I am actually doing so.
  But I believe that the desire to please you does in fact please you. . . .
  I hope that I will never do anything apart from that desire.
  And I know that if I do this, you will lead me by the right road though I may
  know nothing about it.
       THOMAS MERTON, *American priest (1915–1968) [CPB, 147–48]*

- Lord, I know not what I ought to ask of Thee; Thou only knowest what I
  need;
  Thou lovest me better than I know how to love myself.
  O Father! Give to Thy child that which he himself knows not how to ask. . . .
  I open my heart to Thee.
       FRANÇOIS FÉNELON, *French theologian (1651–1715) [MOP, 55 PD]*

A PRAYER FOR TODAY

Father, here is where I need guidance in my life . . .
In this area of my life . . . I don't even know what to ask.
But I trust that You know and love me better than I know and love myself.
As I reflect on and search Your law, statutes, precepts, and commands I see . . .
So may my external words and actions and my internal thoughts be pleasing to
You.
I simply present all that is before me to You. . . .
Wherever You lead me I will go. Whatever You ask of me I will do. Amen.

PRAYERS *of* INTERCESSION

❧ May we always thank You, O God, for other believers and pray that their faith would grow consistently, demonstrating more and more evidence of that faith, and that their love for each other would increase.
> 2 THESSALONIANS 1:3

❧ O Lord, the help of the helpless,
> the hope of the hopeless,
> the saviour of the storm-tossed,
> the harbour of voyagers,
> the physician of the sick;
we pray to you.
O Lord, you know each of us and our petitions;
You know each house and its needs.
> BASIL, *Greek bishop (330–379)* [BTP, 60 PD]

❧ All this day, O Lord,
let me touch as many lives as possible for thee;
and every life I touch, do thou by thy Spirit quicken,
> whether through the word I speak,
> the prayer I breathe,
> or the life I live.
> MARY SUMNER, *English founder of Mother's Union (1828–1921)* [CBP, 317 PD]

❧ Oh, that we would always have such a mind to fear You and keep all Your commandments, so that it might go well with us and with our children forever. DEUTERONOMY 5:29

A PRAYER FOR TODAY

Lord, I lift up the needs of my family and friends to You. . . .
I ask that You would meet their physical and obvious needs.
I ask that You would meet their emotional and less obvious needs.
Meet also their spiritual and ultimate needs.
Cause their faith to grow so that they would fear You.
Create in them a desire to love others.
I ask that You would help me to point them to You today in my words by . . .
I ask that You would help me to point them to You today in my life by . . .
Amen.

PRAYERS *of* SURRENDER

I want to serve You, God, being commendable in all I do:
   with great endurance,
   in afflictions, in needs, in distresses, in beatings,
   in imprisonments, in tumults, in hard labor,
   in sleepless nights, in hunger,
   in purity, in knowledge,
   in patience, in kindness,
   in Your Holy Spirit,
   in sincere love,
   in the word of truth, in Your power, O God—
through the weapons of righteousness in the right hand and in the left,
through glory and dishonor,
through bad report and good report—
as deceivers, and yet true;
as unknown, yet as well-known;
as dying, and yet living;
as beaten, and yet not killed;
as sorrowful, yet always rejoicing;
as poor, yet making many rich;
as having nothing and yet possessing everything.   2 CORINTHIANS 6:4–10

May the love of the Lord Jesus draw us to himself;
May the power of the Lord Jesus strengthen us in his service;
May the joy of the Lord Jesus fill our souls.
May the blessing of God almighty, the Father, the Son, and the Holy Spirit,
be amongst you and remain with you always.
   WILLIAM TEMPLE, *English bishop (1881–1944) [OBP, 172]*

A PRAYER FOR TODAY

Pick the phrase above that most represents your current experience....
Lord, whatever You bring my way I want to surrender myself to You. . . .
May Your love draw me, . . .
Your power strengthen me, . . .
and Your joy fill me. . . .
So I may be commendable in all that I do and all that I am.

PRAYERS *of* THANKSGIVING

For unto us a child is born and unto us a son is given,
and the government shall be upon his shoulders, and he shall be called
Wonderful Counselor, Mighty God,
Everlasting Father, the Prince of Peace.
Of the increase of his government and peace there will be no end.
He will reign on David's throne and over his kingdom, establishing and
upholding it with justice and righteousness from that time on and forever.
Your zeal, Lord Almighty, will accomplish this.   ISAIAH 9:6–7

To God the Father, who first loved us, and made us accepted in the beloved:
To God the Son, who loved us, and washed us from our sins in his own
blood:
To God the Holy Spirit, who sheds the love of God abroad in our hearts:
Be all love and all glory, for all time and for eternity.
THOMAS KEN, *English clergy/hymn writer (1637–1711)* [*CBP, 463* PD]

Your grace, God, the grace that brings salvation, has appeared to all people.
It teaches us to say "no" to ungodliness and worldly passions, and to live
self-controlled, upright, and godly lives in this present age, while we wait
for the blessed hope—the glorious appearing of our great God and Savior,
Jesus Christ, who gave Himself for us to redeem us from all wickedness and
to purify for Himself a people that are His very own, eager to do what is good.
TITUS 2:11–14

Gracious God, I don't think, feel, or express thanks to You for Your
incredible grace often.
I get caught up in the details of my life. I get consumed with current
concerns.
Today, I thank You for all the grace You have given to me.
Thank You for the hope for the future that this grace inspires. Amen.
KURT BJORKLUND, *American minister (1968–present day)*

A PRAYER FOR TODAY

Lord, I thank You for the things You have done in the past. . . .
I thank You for being my . . . *(Meditate upon one of the titles found in Isaiah 9.)*
I thank You for the blessed hope and the desires that will one day be fulfilled. . . .
Remind me that the best things of this earth are only meant to arouse and
suggest ultimate satisfaction.
Thank You for giving us something beyond this world for which to hope.

PRAYERS *of* CONFESSION

○ O God, You know my foolishness,
And my guilt is not hidden from You.
May those who hope in You not be ashamed because of me, O Lord God of hosts;
May those who seek You not be dishonored because of me, O God of Israel.
PSALM 69:5–6

○ O God, forgive the poverty and pettiness of our prayers.
Listen not to our words, but to the yearning of our hearts.
Hear beneath our petitions the crying of our need.
PETER MARSHALL, *chaplain of U.S. Senate (1902–1949) [CDP, 522]*

○ You, Lord God, are compassionate and gracious, slow to anger, and abounding in lovingkindness and truth, maintaining love to thousands, and forgiving iniquity, transgression, and sin. **EXODUS 34:6–7**

○ *Father, when You forgive sins, You separate* them as far from us as the east is from the west, *bury* them in the bottom of the deepest sea, and *put* up a sign for the devil that says, NO FISHING.
CORRIE TEN BOOM, *Holocaust survivor (1892–1983) [CDP, 540]*

A PRAYER FOR TODAY

Lord, thank You for the assurance that You remove the stain of my sins.
You know my foolishness. . . .
You know where I am actually guilty. . . .
You know where I try to justify myself and rationalize my behavior. . . .
You know how I have brought shame to other believers. . . .
You know how my actions have discredited the faith of others. . . .
Yet I know that You are compassionate, meaning You still love me. . . .
I know that You are gracious, meaning You want to bring good into my life. . . .
I know that You are slow to anger, meaning You are patient with my faults. . . .
I know that You are abounding in lovingkindness and truth, meaning You have
    more than enough. . . .
I know that You are forgiving, meaning You will not hold me responsible once
    I repent. . . .
I know that You do not fish up my past misdeeds.
So I confess my sins to You. . . .
Lord, thank You for the assurance that You remove the stain of my sins. Amen.

PRAYERS *of* AFFIRMATION

Lord God, I know that it was not with perishable things such as silver or gold that I have been redeemed from the empty way of life that was handed down from my ancestors, but I have been redeemed with the precious blood of Christ, a lamb without blemish or defect.   1 PETER 1:18–19

I proclaim with a loud voice—worthy are You, Lamb who was slain,
to receive power and wealth and wisdom
and strength and honor and glory
and praise!   REVELATION 5:12

Born as a son,
led forth as a lamb, sacrificed as a sheep,
buried as a man, he rose from the dead as a God,
for he was by nature God and man.
He is all things:
he judges, and so he is Law;
he teaches, and so he is Wisdom;
he saves, and so he is Grace;
be begets, and so he is Father;
he is begotten, and so he is Son;
he suffers, and so he is Sacrifice;
he is buried, and so he is man;
he rises again, and so he is God.
This is Jesus Christ, to whom belongs glory for all ages.
     MELITO, *bishop of Sardis (d. 180)* [*EOP, 39* PD]

A PRAYER FOR TODAY

Lord Jesus, Your journey to earth is astounding. . . .
Your journey to earth is effectual. . . .
You are God.
You are Man.
You are the sacrificial Lamb.
You have the right to judge me and all humanity.
You have the perspective to teach me and all humanity.
You have saved me and offer salvation to all humanity.
You have suffered, so You have the ability to lead me through darkness.
You were buried, so You can lead me through the valley of death.
You rose again, so You have defeated death. *(That affirmation is most needed in your life today—take a few moments to ponder it.)*
You are worthy of my worship.

PRAYERS *of* PETITION

Lord, I will put to death whatever belongs to my earthly nature:
Sexual immorality, (Gk.=*porneia: illicit sexual activity*)
impurity, (Gk.=*akatharsia: uncleanness, filthiness*)
lust, (Gk.=*pathos: passion, insatiable desires*)
controlling desires, (Gk.=*epithumia: desires for good and evil things*)
and greed, (Gk.=*pleonexia: selfish desire for more things for self; avarice*)
which is idolatry. (Gk.=*eidololatria: having allegiance to or affection for
    something or someone beyond God*)
Because of these things, the wrath of God is coming. I used to live this way. . . .
But as Your holy, loved, and chosen child, I will clothe myself with:
Compassion, (Gk.=*oiktirmos: mercy, feeling sympathy for others' misfortunes*)
kindness, (Gk.=*chrestotes: extending goodwill, kindness, and helpfulness*)
humility, (Gk.=*tapeinophrosyne: lowliness of mind and attitude, modesty*)
gentleness, (Gk.=*proutes: meekness, obedient submissiveness to God*)
and patience. (Gk.=*makrothumia: long-suffering, handling injustice or difficulty
    well*)
I will bear with others (Gk.=*anechomai: to endure or put up with someone*)
and forgive whatever grievances I have against another.
I will forgive as You have forgiven me.
And over all of these virtues, I will put on love, which binds them together
perfectly. **COLOSSIANS 3:5–7, 12–14**

Lord, why do I keep relating to you as one of my many relationships instead of my only relationship, in which all other ones are grounded? Why do I keep looking for popularity, respect from others, success, acclaim, and sensual pleasures? Why, Lord, is it so hard for me to make you the only one? Why do I keep hesitating to surrender myself totally to you?

Help me, O Lord, to let my old self die, to let die the thousand big and small ways in which I am still building up my false self and trying to cling to my false desires.

I need your loving grace to travel on this hard road that leads to the death of my old self and to a new life in and for you. I know and trust that this is the road of freedom.

HENRI NOUWEN, *American priest (1932–1996) [GSG, 149]*

A PRAYER FOR TODAY

Lord, grant me the grace to put to death these vices . . .
Grant me the grace to be clothed in these virtues . . .
Amen.

PRAYERS *for* RENEWAL

God, I pray that You, according to the riches of Your glory,
would strengthen me with power through Your Spirit in my inner being,
so that Christ may dwell in my heart through faith.
And may I, being rooted and grounded in love, be able to comprehend with all the saints
what is the width and length and height and depth of Your love in Christ,
and to know this love that surpasses knowledge that I may be filled up with Your fullness. EPHESIANS 3:16–19

Lord, *when* I am disturbed
When I am distressed
When I am divided
When I am disgusted.
I come to you for healing
I come to you for peace
I come to you for *restoration*
I come to you for dignity.
Help me, Lord,
To do what you would have me do, to become the person you want me to be.
"ONE IN HIM," CELTIC PRAYER *[PL, 58]*

I will trust in You God at all times.
I will pour out my heart to You, for You are my refuge. PSALM 62:8

Have *Your* own way, Lord, have *Your* own way.
You are the potter, I am the clay
Mold me and make me after *Your* will,
While I am waiting, yielded and still.
"HAVE THINE OWN WAY, LORD," ADELAIDE A. POLLARD, *hymn writer*
(1862–1934) [CDP, 522 PD]

A PRAYER FOR TODAY

Father,
Please bring healing to me in . . .
Please bring peace to me in . . .
Please bring restoration to me in . . .
Please bring strength and power to me in . . .
Please bring awareness of Your love to me in . . .
So that I may be an instrument in Your hands.
Have Your own way in me.
Help me to wait and be yielded to You. Amen.

PRAYERS of PRAISE/ADORATION

I waited patiently for You, Lord,
and You turned to me and heard my cry.
You lifted me out of the slimy pit—out of the muck and mire;
You set my feet on a rock and gave me a firm place to stand.
You put a new song in my mouth, a hymn of praise to You, my God.
Many will see and fear and put their trust in You.   PSALM 40:1–3

Dear Lord Jesus, how do You love me? Let me count the ways—
enough to bless me,
to always be with me,
to heal my wounds,
to strengthen me,
to give Your life for me!
How do I love You?
Enough to praise You in all things?
Enough to be obedient to You?
Enough to commit my life to You? . . .
Oh Lord, help me to love You enough to never count the cost. . . . You didn't.
DONNA L. HAMMOND, *devotional writer (unknown era) [EOP, 975]*

But whatever was to my profit I now consider loss for the sake of You,
Christ.
What is more, I consider everything a loss compared to the surpassing
greatness of knowing You,
Christ Jesus, my Lord, for whose sake I have lost all things.
I consider them rubbish, (Gk.=*skublan: refuse, table scraps*)
that I may gain You, Christ and be found in You,
not having a righteousness of my own that comes from rule keeping,
but that which is through faith in You and is by faith.
PHILIPPIANS 3:7–9

A PRAYER FOR TODAY

Lord, nothing compares to the greatness of knowing You:
Not my career success . . .
Not my family . . .
Not my religious experiences or knowledge . . .
Not my service rendered unto You . . .
Not my money or acquisitions . . .
Not my reputation . . . Not my recreation . . .
Not my friendships . . .
All my aspirations are rubbish compared to the possibility of knowing You.

PRAYERS *for* CHRISTLIKE CHARACTER

Father, let love and faithfulness never leave me, for I will bind them around my neck and write them on the tablet of my heart.
PROVERBS 3:3

O God of love, we ask you to give us love;
Love in our thinking, love in our speaking, love in our doing,
and love in the hidden places of our souls;
Love of those with whom we find it hard to bear,
and love of those who find it hard to bear with us;
Love of those with whom we work,
and love of those with whom we take our ease.
WILLIAM TEMPLE, *English bishop (1881–1944) [BTP, 52]*

Almighty God, I know so little of what love in its fullness can be.
My love is marred by jealousy, scarred by envy, limited by selfishness.
I withhold love at the slightest provocation,
and withdraw myself from involvement with others for fear of being hurt.
Still, I know something of what love can be like.
I can remember being forgiven . . . freely by someone I had wronged.
I can remember being comforted and cared for when, bruised and battered,
I crept home.
I can remember being made strong by the realization that someone cared.
I am grateful for such experiences, for they tell me what love is about.
And if the Lord Jesus be right, to know what love is like is to know what you are like. . . .
Out of the heart of the Lord Jesus came the evidences of his love for all kinds of people and his refusal to give up on any of us.
I am grateful for that love and for that refusal, for in him I have hope. . . .
Will you help me to be more outgoing, less sensitive to slights, and more alert to the feelings of others?
Will you help me to be less quick to judge? . . .
Give me steadiness and firmness and true commitment to the life of faith.
ANONYMOUS *[US]*

A PRAYER FOR TODAY

Father, I ask You to bring to mind situations where I have not shown love. . . .
I ask You to grant me the desire to show love in these situations.
I ask You to empower me to love others as You have loved me.
Under the direction of Your Spirit I will endeavor to demonstrate love to . . .
Amen.

PRAYERS *for* WISDOM/GUIDANCE

🌸 I will receive the words of wisdom and treasure her instruction within my
heart. I will turn my ear to wisdom and apply my heart to understanding.
If I cry out for discernment and lift up my voice to get understanding,
if I seek her as I might seek wealth and search for her hidden treasures,
then I will understand what it is to fear You, Lord,
and I will know what it is to know You, O God. **PROVERBS 2:2–5**

🌸 Should I seek great things for myself? I will not seek them.
      JEREMIAH 45:5

🌸 O Lord,
Open our eyes to your Presence
Open our minds to your grace
Open our lips to your praises
Open our hearts to your love
Open our lives to your healing
And be found among us.
        DAVID ADAM, *English author (unknown era) [BTP, 23]*

🌸 O Gracious and Holy Father,
        give us wisdom to perceive you,
        diligence to seek you,
        patience to wait for you,
        eyes to behold you,
        a heart to meditate upon you,
        and a life to proclaim you,
        through the power of the Spirit of Jesus Christ our Lord.
        BENEDICT, *Italian monk (480–543) [EOP, 14 PD]*

A PRAYER FOR TODAY

Lord, I want to sense Your presence.
I want to know Your grace.
I want my lips to proclaim Your praises.
I need the wisdom to perceive You. I sense You moving in this way . . .
I need the diligence to seek You. I will seek You this week by . . .
Where am I missing opportunities to seek You? . . .
What is keeping me from seeking You? . . .
I need the patience to wait for You. I will wait in this area . . .
I need a life that proclaims You—I will proclaim You this week to . . .
And all of this is only through the power of Your Spirit. Amen.

PRAYERS *of* INTERCESSION

❧ You, God, are not human that You should lie, nor a son of man, that You should change Your mind.
  Do You speak and then not act? Do You promise and then not fulfill? Never!
    NUMBERS 23:19

❧ Lord, lying lips are an abomination to You,
  but those who act faithfully are Your delight. **PROVERBS 12:22**

❧ Almighty God, who sent the Spirit of truth to us to guide us into all truth:
  so rule our lives by your power that we may be truthful in thought and word and deed.
  May no fear or hope ever make us false in act or speech;
  cast out from us whatsoever loves or makes a lie,
  and bring us all into the perfect freedom of your truth,
  through Jesus Christ our Lord.
    B. F. WESTCOTT, *English bishop (1825–1901)* [*COS, 59* PD]

A PRAYER FOR TODAY

Select a person or people close to you and a public figure or figures and pray for them by name:
God, You are a God of truth,
    completely veracious and completely dependable in Your character, words, and actions.
I ask that You would make *(insert name)* a person of truth.
Make *him/her* truthful in big and little things.
Don't let *him/her* tolerate deception in *himself/herself* or in others.
Make *him/her* truthful when it is inconvenient and costly.
Make *him/her* bold to speak for the truth when silence would be easier.
Make *him/her* truthful to *himself/herself* when they do not like the truth.
Don't let *him/her* settle for half truths—but prompt *him/her* to see the good, bad, and ugly about themselves.
Make *him/her* truthful when those around *him/her* are engaging in self-destructive behavior.
Make *him/her* truthful when those around *him/her* are unaware of Your truth.
Make *him/her* bold to speak the truth when those around *him/her* need to be encouraged, exhorted, or comforted.
Make *him/her* a lover of truth.
Make *him/her* one who is guided by truth. Amen.

PRAYERS *of* SURRENDER

Lord, let me do nothing out of
selfish ambition (Gk.=*epitheia: selfishness, jockeying for position or acclaim*)
or vain conceit, (Gk.=*kenodoxia: empty praise, personal vanity, jealousy*)
but in humility help me to consider others as better than myself.
Help me to not look out only for my own interest, but also for the interest
of others.
My attitude should be the same as that of Christ Jesus.   PHILIPPIANS 2:3–5

O Jesus, meek and humble of heart, hear me.
From the desire of being esteemed, **deliver me, Jesus.**
From the desire of being loved, **deliver me, Jesus.**
From the desire of being praised, **deliver me, Jesus.**
From the desire of being preferred to others, **deliver me, Jesus.**
From the desire of being consulted, **deliver me, Jesus.**
From the desire of being approved, **deliver me, Jesus.**
From the fear of being humiliated, **deliver me, Jesus.**
From the fear of being despised, **deliver me, Jesus.**
From the fear of being rebuked, **deliver me, Jesus.**
From the fear of being criticized, **deliver me, Jesus.**
From the fear of being forgotten, **deliver me, Jesus.**
From the fear of being ridiculed, **deliver me, Jesus.**
From the fear of being wronged, **deliver me, Jesus.**
From the fear of being suspected, **deliver me, Jesus.**
That others may be loved more than I, **Jesus grant me the grace to desire it.**
That others may be esteemed more than I, **Jesus grant me the grace to
desire it.**
That in the opinion of the world others may increase and I may decrease,
Jesus grant me the grace to desire it.
That others may be chosen and I set aside, **Jesus grant me the grace to
desire it.**
FRANCIS OF ASSISI, *Italian monk (1181–1226), also credited to Rafael Merry
del Val (1865–1930)* [PD]

A PRAYER FOR TODAY

Which fear listed above is the most intense for you?...
Which desire listed above is the most intense for you?...
Lord, please deliver me from my fear of being belittled. . . .
Lord, please deliver me from my desire to be made much of. . . .
Lord, grant me the desire for things that run contrary to the common values of
this age so I can have the same attitude as my Savior, Christ Jesus. Amen.

PRAYERS *of* THANKSGIVING

God, I will do all things without complaining
(Gk.=*gongysmos*: *murmuring in dissatisfaction, expressing secret discontent*)
or arguing, (Gk.=*dialogismos*: *skeptical questioning or criticism*)
so that I may be blameless and pure as Your child, without fault in a
crooked and perverse generation, among whom I shine as a light in the
world, holding out the word of life. **PHILIPPIANS 2:14–16**

Give us, O Lord, thankful hearts
    which never forget Your goodness to us.
Give *us*, O Lord, grateful hearts,
    which do not waste time complaining.
    THOMAS AQUINAS, *Italian theologian (1225–1274)* [BHE, 122 PD]

Thank you for the privilege of scrubbing this floor.
Thank you for the health and the strength to do it.
That my back is straight and my hands are whole.
I can push the mop. I can feel the hard surface under my knees when I kneel.
I can grasp the brush and let my energy flow down into it as I erase the dirt
    and make this floor bright and clean.
Lord, thank you for everything that has to do with scrubbing this floor.
Bless the soap and the bucket and the brush and the hands that do it.
Bless the feet that are running in right now to track it.
Those feet are the reason I do it. They are the living reasons for my
    kneeling here—half to do a job, half in prayer.
A floor is a foundation. A family is a foundation. You are our foundation.
Bless us all, and our newly scrubbed floor.
    "PRAYING WHILE SCRUBBING A FLOOR," MARJORIE HOLMES, *American
author (1910–2002) [BHE, 167–68]*

A PRAYER FOR TODAY

Lord, sometimes I complain about . . .
Sometimes I criticize and question . . .
But today, I want to choose thankfulness.
I will be thankful for what seems mundane. . . .
I will be thankful for what seems like a chore. . . .
I will be thankful for the work that I must do today. . . .
I will be thankful for the people I must look after. . . .
I know that these things have come from Your hand.
Help my demeanor in the daily routines to shine like a bright light in the world.
Amen.

PRAYERS *of* CONFESSION

⚜ I have been unfaithful to You my God . . . but in spite of this there is still hope. EZRA 10:2

⚜ Father *Almighty*,
Forgive all that in each of us is unprepared for Christ's coming:
Our insensitivity to others;
Our ignoring of the stranger;
Our lack of attention to Your Word.
   DAVID ADAM, *English author (unknown era) [CDP, 772]*

⚜ O God, we have been recipients of the choicest blessings of heaven. We have been preserved, these many years, in peace and prosperity. We have grown in numbers, wealth and power . . . but we have forgotten God. We have forgotten the gracious hand which preserved us in peace, and multiplied and enriched and strengthened us; and we have vainly imagined, in the deceitfulness of our hearts, that all these blessings were produced by some superior wisdom and virtue of our own. Intoxicated with unbroken success, we have become too self-sufficient to feel the necessity of redeeming and preserving grace, too proud to pray to the God that made us.
   It behooves us, then, to humble ourselves before the offended Power, to confess our national sins, and to pray for clemency and forgiveness.
   ABRAHAM LINCOLN, *American president (1809–1865)* [BHE, 74 PD]

A PRAYER FOR TODAY

Lord, I confess my personal unfaithfulness to You:
Concerning my consumption coupled with ignoring needs of other individuals . . .
In my lack of acknowledgement of Your good hand in my blessings . . .
In my neglect to seek You and pay attention to Your Word . . .
In my self-sufficiency and pride . . .
In my *(add your own categories)* . . .
I confess our national unfaithfulness to You:
In our consumption coupled with ignoring the needs of other nations and those within our nation without sufficient resources . . .
In our lack of acknowledgement of Your good hand in our blessings . . .
In our neglect to seek You and pay attention to Your Word . . .
Concerning our self-sufficiency and pride . . .
Concerning our *(add your own categories)* . . .
Amen.

PRAYERS *of* AFFIRMATION

⚜ You, O Lord, are our judge, You are our lawgiver, You are our King;
It is You who will save us. **ISAIAH 33:22**

⚜ Let us proclaim the mystery of faith:
Christ has died, Christ has risen,
Christ will come again.
> Dying you destroyed our death,
> Rising you restored our life.
Lord Jesus, come in glory. . . .
Lord, by your cross and resurrection
You have set us free.
You are the Saviour of the world.
> **"MEMORIAL ACCLAIM OF THE PEOPLE"** [*CBP, 78* PD]

⚜ We believe in one God, the Father, the Almighty, maker of heaven and earth, of all that is seen and unseen.

We believe in one Lord, Jesus Christ, the only Son of God, eternally begotten of the Father, God from God, Light from Light, true God from true God, begotten, not made, one in Being with the Father. Through him all things were made. For us . . . and for our salvation he came down from heaven: by the power of the Holy Spirit he was born of the Virgin Mary, and became man. For our sake he was crucified under Pontius Pilate; he suffered, died, and was buried. On the third day he rose again in fulfillment of the Scriptures; he ascended into heaven and is seated at the right hand of the Father. He will come again in glory to judge the living and the dead, and his kingdom will have no end.

We believe in the Holy Spirit, the Lord, the giver of life, who proceeds from the Father and the Son. With the Father and the Son he is worshipped and glorified. He has spoken through the prophets. . . . Amen.
> **"TRADITIONAL PROFESSION OF FAITH"** [*CPB, 72–74* PD]

A PRAYER FOR TODAY

Lord, as my creator and maker, You have the right to be my lawgiver and judge.
As my King, You have the right to demand my allegiance.
Yet You choose to come as my Savior and win my affection.
Let me realize that I am helpless to earn Your favor. . . .
You have loved all of humanity enough to not write us off for our rebellion.
Let me be moved by this incredible act of love once again. . . .
Let me believe this truth in my core being, not only in words. . . . Amen.

PRAYERS of PETITION

❧ Lord, let my love be sincere.
Let me hate what is evil and cling to what is good.
Help me to be devoted to others with affectionate love, honoring others above myself.
Never let me be lacking in zeal, but keep my spiritual fervor hot to serve You.
Help me to be joyful in hope, patient in affliction, and faithful in prayer.
Lead me to share with Your people who are in need and to practice hospitality.
Help me to bless those who persecute me, to bless and not curse.
Let me rejoice with those who rejoice and mourn with those who mourn.
Help me to live in harmony with others, not being proud.
Make me willing to associate with those that seem of a lower social position; rid me of conceit.
Help me not to repay evil for evil, being careful to do what is right.
Help me not to take revenge but to leave room for Your wrath.
Help me not to be overcome by evil but to overcome evil with good.

>   ROMANS 12:9–19, 21

❧ *Father*, people *can* often *be* unreasonable, irrational and self-centered.
Help me to forgive them anyway.
Father, if *I am* successful, *I* will win some unfaithful friends and some genuine enemies.
Help me to succeed anyway.
Father, if *I am* honest and sincere, people may deceive *me*.
Help me to be honest and sincere anyway.
Father, what *I* spend years creating, others could destroy overnight.
Help me to create anyway. . . .
Father, the good *I* do today, will be forgotten tomorrow.
Help me to do good anyway.
Father, if *I* give the best *I* have, it will never be enough.
Help me to give my best anyway.
Father, in the final analysis
Help me to remember it is only between *you* and *me*.

>   MOTHER TERESA, *Albanian nun (1910–1997)* [US PD]

A PRAYER FOR TODAY

Lord, show me where I have allowed myself to justify or rationalize not choosing what reflects You. . . . *(Reflect on Romans 12:9–21.)*
Grant me the courage to do it "anyway"—despite the possible negative reactions of some. . . . Amen.

PRAYERS *for* RENEWAL

Morning by morning You waken me—
waken my ear to listen as those who are taught.   ISAIAH 50:4B

Teach me Your way, O Lord; I will walk in Your truth;
Give me an undivided heart that I may fear Your name.
I will praise You, O Lord, and I will glorify Your name forever.
For great is Your love toward me; You have delivered me from the depths of
the grave.   PSALM 86:11–13

May your Spirit guide my mind, which is so often dull and empty.
Let my thoughts always be on you,
And let me see you in all things.
May your Spirit quicken my soul, which is so often listless and lethargic.
Let my soul be awake to your presence,
And let me know you in all things.
May your Spirit melt my heart, which is so often cold and indifferent.
Let my heart be warmed by your love,
And let me feel you in all things.
JOHN FREYLINGHAUSEN, *German pietist (1670–1739)* [CBP, 6 PD]

Father in Heaven, great and powerful and full of love, I lift my heart in
praise. . . . Search my heart, Lord, and show me if any sin is hindering Your
work in my life. May I respond without delay whenever You make me conscious of sin. . . . Day by day may Your Spirit work in me, motivating me to
abide in Christ and pray in faith, moving Your mighty hand to fulfill Your
purposes. Keep reminding me that You are able to do infinitely more than
I would ever dare to ask or imagine, by Your mighty power at work within
me.
WARREN AND RUTH MYERS, *American missionaries (twentieth century)*
[MGH, 46–47]

A PRAYER FOR TODAY

Lord, I do want an undivided heart. The natural tendency of my heart is away
from You.
My heart is divided by the desire to . . .
My heart is divided by the fear of . . .
Please renew the singular focus of my heart with affection toward You. . . .
I ask You to guide my mind away from what makes me double-minded. . . .
I ask You to grant me strength to choose the good when my affections are
divided. . . . Amen.

From the rising to the setting of the sun, Your name, O Lord, is to be
praised.
You are high above all nations, Your glory is above all nations.
Who is like You, O Lord our God, the One who is enthroned on high,
You who humble Yourself to behold the things that are in the heavens
and in the earth? **PSALM 113:3–6**

Worthy of praise from every mouth,
Of confession from every tongue,
Of worship from every creature,
Is thy glorious name, O Father, Son and Holy Ghost:
Who didst create the world in thy grace and by thy compassion didst save
the world.
To thy majesty, O God, ten thousand times ten thousand bow down and
adore, singing and praising without ceasing and saying,
Holy, holy, holy, Lord God of hosts;
Heaven and earth are full of thy praises; Hosanna in the highest.
NESTORIAN LITURGY *(fifth century)* [*CBP, 23* PD]

Glory to God in the highest, and peace to his people on earth.
Lord God, heavenly King, almighty God and Father,
we worship you, we give you thanks, we praise you for your glory.
Lord Jesus Christ, only Son of the Father, Lord God, Lamb of God,
you take away the sin of the world: have mercy on us;
you are seated at the right hand of the Father: receive our prayer.
For you alone are the Holy One,
You alone are the Lord,
You alone are the Most High,
Jesus Christ, with the Holy Spirit,
in the glory of God the Father. Amen.
"THE GLORIA," *traditional prayer* [*CPB, 71* PD]

A PRAYER FOR TODAY

Lord, I imagine the great scene of throngs of living creatures worshiping You.
As I do, I add my own words of praise. . . .
My single voice will join the chorus of the ages and the nations in proclaiming
Your excellence.
As I will then, I proclaim Your excellence now. . . . Amen.

PRAYERS *for* CHRISTLIKE CHARACTER

- God, I want to be above reproach, (Gk.=*anepilemptos*: *deservedly beyond criticism, unimpeachable*)

  faithful to my spouse, (Gk.=*gunaikos andra*: *literally a one-woman man, husband of one wife*)

  temperate, (Gk.=*nephalios*: *sober with alcohol; not given to excessive indulgence*)

  self-controlled, (Gk.=*sophro*: *sensible, prudent, able to control emotionally driven urges*)

  respectable, (Gk.=*kosmios*: *orderly in demeanor and fulfillment of duties, ordering inner life*)

  hospitable, (Gk.=*philoxeno*: *warmly receives others not only as a duty; opens life and home to others*)

  able to teach, (Gk.=*didaktikos*: *skillful in understanding, applying, and presenting the content of the Bible*)

  not given to wine, (Gk.=*paroivos*: *one who sits long with his wine; a slave to strong drink*)

  not violent (Gk.=*plektes*: *not a giver of blows, not pugnacious*)

  but gentle, (Gk.=*epieikes*: *kindly, lenient, forbearing*)

  not quarrelsome, (Gk.=*amaxos*: *without fighting, not contentious, not disagreeable*)

  not a lover of money. (Gk.=*aphilargyros*: *love of money*)

  I want to manage my family well and keep my children under control with proper respect. And I want a good reputation with outsiders, so that I will not fall into disgrace and the snare of the devil. 1 TIMOTHY 3:2–4

- I believe, Lord, but let me believe more firmly.

  I hope, Lord, but let me hope more surely.

  I love, Lord, but let me love more ardently.

  I repent, Lord, but let me repent more deeply. . . .

  Teach me to fulfill your will, for you are my God.

  Give me an understanding heart to distinguish right from wrong.

  Father, give me humility, meekness, chastity, patience, and charity.

  Father, teach me goodness, knowledge and discipline.

  Father, give me your love, together with your grace, and I will be rich enough.

  ANTHONY MARY CLARET, *Spanish bishop (1807–1870)* [EOP, 87 PD]

A PRAYER FOR TODAY

Which qualities stand out to you as the ones that you need to foster in your life? . . .
Take some time to ask God to grow you in that area of your life.
What step of action could you take to facilitate growth in these areas? . . .

When I am tempted, God, I will not say that You are tempting me.
For You cannot be tempted by evil, nor do You tempt anyone;
but I am tempted when, by my own evil desire, I am dragged away and enticed.
Then after my desire has conceived, it gives birth to sin;
and sin when it is full-grown gives birth to death.   **JAMES 1:13–15**

Defend me from all temptation, that I may ever accept the right and refuse the wrong.
Defend me from myself, that in your care my weakness may not bring me to shame.
May my lower nature never seize the upper hand.
Defend me from all that would seduce me, that in your power no tempting voice may cause me to listen, no tempting sight fascinate my eyes.
Defend me from discouragement in difficulty and from despair in failure, from pride in success and from forgetting you in the day of prosperity.
Help me to remember that there is no time when you will fail me and no moment when I do not need you.
Grant me this desire: that guided by your light and defended by your grace, I may come in safety and bring honor to my journey's end by the defending work of Jesus Christ my Lord.
   NORMAN SHAWCHUCK, *American author (twentieth century)* *[GSG, 104–105]*

Father, it is confidence in *Your* invariably overriding intention for our good, with respect to all the evil and suffering that may befall us on life's journey, that secures us in peace and joy. *I* must be sure of that intention if *I am* to be free and able . . . to simply do what *I* know to be right.
   DALLAS WILLARD, *American author (1935–present day)* *[GSG, 104]*

A PRAYER FOR TODAY

Begin by affirming to God that He is not the author of temptation—therefore it is from within your heart. . . .
Reread the prayer from Shawchuck carefully, considering each place where it reflects the reality of your current life. Ask God to defend you in those areas. . . .
Look at the places of your life where you see evil and suffering—affirm that God is bringing good even where it doesn't feel like it. . . .

Lord, I choose to do the right and best things even where it doesn't make sense to me. . . .
Lord, I ask for guidance in the circumstances of my life. . . .
Lord, I ask that I would see things as You see them. . . . Amen.

PRAYERS *of* INTERCESSION

Father, if anyone confesses with his or her mouth that "Jesus is Lord,"
   and believes in his or her heart that You raised Jesus from the dead,
   that person will be saved.
For it is with our hearts that we believe and are justified,
   and it is with our mouths that we confess and are saved. . . .
How, then, can they call on the one they have not believed in?
And how can they believe in the one of whom they have not heard?
And how can they hear without someone preaching or proclaiming to them?
And how can they preach or proclaim unless they are sent?
As it is written, "How beautiful are the feet of those who bring good news!"
   ROMANS 10:9-10, 14-15

O Lord God, we modern Christians can be so self-absorbed. We look
with condescension and boredom on the missionary enterprise—when
we think of it at all. God, forgive us. We worship your Son in church on
Sunday morning, we sing our choruses with a euphoric joy, and we think
we have honored him. But what do we know of honoring Christ, when we
remain content to let whole nations of peoples and tribes around the world
live and die without ever bowing to the One whose name is above every
other name? We have privatized our faith. We have trivialized it as a merely
personal benefit, like a favorite television show or a hobby. We do not hear
the gospel as a war cry, as a summons to risk-taking, as a command to see
the Lord Jesus Christ honored in our own hearts as we exert ourselves
toward his being honored in others' hearts. O Lord, give fresh power to the
gospel among us. Revive in us the passion for Christian missions for the
honor and glory of the Son of God. Deliver us from our convenience Christianity and lift us up to the infinite joy of kingdom-advancing missionary
Christianity. In Christ's holy name. Amen.
   RAYMOND ORTLUND JR., *American minister (1946–present day) [PFG, 192–93]*

A PRAYER FOR TODAY

Father, I ask You to empower those I know who are serving in foreign lands. . . .
I pray specifically for this country: the needs that exist there . . .
and the spread of Your gospel there. . . .
I ask You to direct me to any ways I could more fully participate in Your mis-
sionary agenda. . . .
I ask You to grant vision to churches and sending agencies to send many new
people.
I ask You to call many new young people to Your work internationally.
Amen.

PRAYERS *of* SURRENDER

God, You want those of us who trust in You to be careful to devote ourselves to doing what is good. This is what is excellent and profitable for everyone.   **TITUS 3:8**

O God our Father, throned on high, enrobed in ageless splendor,
To thee, in awe and love and joy, ourselves we would surrender—
To live obedient to thy will as servants to each other,
And show our faithfulness to thee by love to one another.
        GEORGE THOMAS COSTER, *English pastor (1835–1912)* [CH, 492 PD]

Thou who art the Lord . . . I submit my will to Thine:
From the stirrings of self-will within my heart:
From cowardly avoidance of necessary duty:
From rebellious shrinking from necessary suffering:
From discontentment with my lot:
From jealousy of those whose lot is easier: . . .
From uncreaturely pride . . . from unwillingness to learn and unreadiness to serve:
O God, set me free . . . Through Jesus Christ our Lord. Amen
        JOHN BAILLIE, *Scottish theologian (1886–1960)* [DPP, 131]

Lord, I am willing
to receive what You give
to lack what You withhold
to relinquish what You take
to suffer what You inflict
to be what You require.
And, Lord, if others are to be Your messengers to me,
I am willing to hear and heed what they have to say. Amen.
        NELSON MINK, *(unknown era)* [TTO, 552–53]

Whom have I in heaven but You? And this earth has nothing that I desire more than You. **PSALM 73:25**

A PRAYER FOR TODAY

Lord, today I devote myself to doing what is good.
I submit my will to Yours by choosing . . .
Lord I am willing to . . . in this area of my life. . . .
Lord, this is what is profitable and excellent for me, and for everyone.
Help me to really be able to say with the psalmist that there is nothing I desire more than You.
To You be all my honor and allegiance. Amen.

PRAYERS *of* THANKSGIVING

Christ, sometimes to keep Your people from becoming conceited . . . You give a thorn in the flesh, a messenger of Satan to torment. Sometimes we repeatedly plead with You to take it away from us. But You assure us that Your grace is sufficient for us, Your power is made perfect in our weakness. Therefore we can boast all the more gladly about our weaknesses so that Your power may rest on us. That is why for Your sake, we delight in weaknesses. For when we are weak, then we are strong.
> **2 CORINTHIANS 12:7–10**

Lord, day after day I've thanked You for saying yes.
But when have I genuinely thanked You for saying no? . . .
So thank You for saying no when my want list for things far exceeded my longing for You. . . .
To my petulant "Just this time, Lord?" thank You for saying no to the senseless excuses, selfish motives, *and* dangerous diversions. . . .
Thank You for saying no when I asked You to leave me alone.
Above all, thank You for saying no when in anguish I asked "If I give You all else may I keep this?"
Lord, my awe increases when I see the wisdom of Your divine no.
> **RUTH HARMS CALKIN**, *American author (unknown era)* [*TTO, 451–52*]

I asked God for strength that I might achieve;
I was made weak, that I might learn to serve.
I asked for health that I might do great things;
I was given infirmity, that I might do better things.
I asked for wealth, that I might be happy;
I was given poverty, that I might be wise.
I asked for power, that I might earn the praise of *people*;
I was given weakness, that I might feel the need of God. . . .
I got nothing I asked for, but all I hoped for.
Despite myself, my unspoken prayers were answered.
And I am, among all *people*, most richly blessed.
> **"PRAYER OF AN ANONYMOUS CONFEDERATE SOLDIER"** [*BHE, 244–45* PD]

A PRAYER FOR TODAY

Lord, I have felt a "no" concerning a desire of my heart. . . .
I thank You for Your wisdom in directing me to the richer blessings.
Lord, here I have experienced a "thorn in my flesh" . . .
I thank You that through this Your grace is sufficient.
I thank You that in my weakness Your strength is revealed. Amen.

Day 112

PRAYERS *of* CONFESSION

🍃 The heart is deceitful above all things and incurably sick.
Who can understand it? You, Lord, search the hearts of people and test
their minds to reward them according to their ways, according to the fruit
of their deeds. JEREMIAH 17:9–10

🍃 Our God and God of our fathers, let our prayer reach You—do not turn
away from our pleading. For we are not so arrogant and obstinate to claim
that we are indeed righteous people and have never sinned. But we know
that both we and our fathers have sinned.
We have abused and betrayed. We are cruel.
We have destroyed and embittered other people's lives.
   We were false to ourselves.
   We have gossiped about others and hated them.
   We have insulted and jeered. We have killed. We have lied.
   We have misled others and neglected them.
   We were obstinate. We have perverted and quarreled.
   We have robbed and stolen.
   We have transgressed through unkindness. . . .
   We have yielded to wrong desires, our zeal was misplaced.
We turn away from Your commandments and good judgment but it does
not help us. Your justice exists whatever happens to us, for You work for
truth, but we bring about evil.
   TRADITIONAL JEWISH CONFESSION *on Day of Atonement* [OBP, 281 PD]

A PRAYER FOR TODAY

*Slowly reread the Jewish Confession, considering any ways that you have knowingly or
unknowingly engaged in actions or attitudes that are counter to the heart of God. . . .*
Lord, I confess to You specifically the ways I have acted or thought that have not
reflected You. . . .
I confess to You the ways I failed to act or think that would reflect You. . . .
I confess that at times this has been willful.
At times I have also been unaware of these patterns in my life.
Please show me where I have been unaware. . . . Amen.

PRAYERS *of* AFFIRMATION

One thing You have spoken; two things I have heard:
that You, O God
    are strong (Heb.=*oz*: *strength, power, might*)
and that You, O Lord,
    are loving. (Heb.=*hesed*: *unfailing love, devotion, kindness, loyalty*)
For You reward us according to what we have done. **PSALM 62:11–12**

Jesus, You have the very nature of God, but You did not consider equality with God something to be grasped, but You made Yourself nothing, taking the very nature of a servant, begin made in human likeness. And being found in appearance as a human being You humbled Yourself and became obedient to death—even death on a cross. **PHILIPPIANS 2:6–8**

O Jesus, poor and abject, unknown and despised, have mercy upon me, and let me not be ashamed to follow thee.
O Jesus, hated, *mistreated*, and persecuted, have mercy upon me, and make me content to be as my master.
O Jesus, blasphemed, accused, and wrongfully condemned, have mercy upon me, and teach me to endure the contradiction of sinners. . . .
O Jesus, insulted, mocked, and spit upon, have mercy upon me, and let me not faint in the fiery trial.
O Jesus, crowned with thorns and hailed in derision;
O Jesus, burdened with our sins and the curses of the people;
O Jesus, affronted, outraged, buffeted, overwhelmed with injuries, griefs, and humiliations;
O Jesus, hanging on the accursed tree, bowing the head, giving up the ghost, have mercy upon me, and conform my whole soul to thy holy, humble, suffering Spirit.
      JOHN WESLEY, *English minister (1703–1791)* [*CBP, 398* PD]

A PRAYER FOR TODAY

Lord, I affirm that You are strong and mighty as seen in . . .
And You are loving, loyal, and tender as seen in . . .
It took both strength and love to be obedient on the cross.
I affirm that You really suffered on the cross *(consider what strikes you most from the prayer of Wesley)*. . . .
I affirm that You call me to not be ashamed—yet sometimes I am fearful of ridicule as seen in . . .
I easily get indignant when I am mistreated . . .
But I want to testify (tell others) all about You by . . . Amen.

PRAYERS *of* PETITION

The waywardness of the simple will destroy them,
and the complacency of the foolish will be their destruction;
But if I listen to wisdom, I will live securely
and be free from the fear of evil.   PROVERBS 1:32–33

When I trust in my own gut instincts, I am foolish,
but when I walk in wisdom, I am delivered.   PROVERBS 28:26

Dearest Lord, may I see you today and every day in the person of your sick,
and whilst nursing them minister unto you.

Though you hide yourself behind the unattractive disguise of the
irritable, the exacting, the unreasonable, may I still recognize you and say:
"Jesus, my patient, how sweet it is to serve you."

Lord, give me this seeing faith, then my work will never be
monotonous. I will ever find joy in humouring the fancies and gratifying
the wishes of all poor sufferers.

O beloved sick, how doubly dear you are to me, when you personify
Christ; and what a privilege is mine to be allowed to tend you.

Sweetest Lord, make me appreciative of the dignity of my high
vocation, and its many responsibilities. Never permit me to disgrace it
by giving way to coldness, unkindness, or impatience. . . .

Lord, increase my faith, bless my efforts and work, now and for evermore.
MOTHER TERESA, *Albanian nun (1910–1997) [OBP, 133]*

A PRAYER FOR TODAY

Father, show me what is wise and right in the things I am facing today. . . .
Show me where I am deceived and where I have followed my gut instincts into
foolishness. . . .
Remind me that the waywardness of the simple will destroy them, but the wise
are delivered.
Grant me the courage to pursue what is right and wise. . . .
Keep me from forgetting to do good, which I can be prone to do when I . . .
Remind me that You are pleased when I sacrifice something of myself for the
good of others.
Help me to see You in the people I am called to serve.
Never permit me to disgrace an attempt to serve others by serving with
coldness, unkindness, or impatience seen in my life through . . .
But grant me the strength to persevere in what is right and true and good. . . .
Amen.

PRAYERS *for* RENEWAL

❧ My soul waits in hope for You, O Lord; You are my help and my shield.
My heart rejoices in You, because I trust in Your holy name.
Let Your unfailing love be upon me, O Lord, even as I put my hope in You.
PSALM 33:20–22

❧ Grant me, O most sweet and loving Jesus, to rest in Thee
    Above every creature
    Above all health and beauty
    Above all glory and honor
    Above all power and dignity
    Above all knowledge and *refinement*
    Above all riches and arts
    Above all joy and exultation
    Above all fame and praise
    Above all sweetness and consolation
    Above all hope and promise . . .
    Above all gifts and presents which Thou art able to bestow or infuse
    Above all joy and gladness which the mind *receives and feels*;
Finally, . . . above all that falls short of Thyself, O Thou, My God.
THOMAS Á KEMPIS, *German theologian (1380–1471)* [*OBP, 54* PD]

❧ O God, You are my God; earnestly I seek You;
my soul thirsts for You, my body longs for You,
in a dry and weary land, where there is no water.   **PSALM 63:1**

A PRAYER FOR TODAY

When was the last time you really longed for God like a person thirsty without the abundance of water? . . .

Lord, I wait in hope for You today above all. . . . *(Be specific in naming things—try to move past the general categories of the á Kempis prayer.)*
Lord, I know that only You can inspire such confidence. Please move in me in such a way.
Lord, raise me from the weary depths I often experience. . . . *(Be specific in naming the places that you are weary.)*
Lord, I know that only You can inspire such enthusiasm. Please move in me in such a way.
Lord, I will earnestly seek You today by . . . *(Be specific in naming what you will do today to earnestly seek God.)*
Lord, I know that only You can inspire such a quest. Amen.

PRAYERS of PRAISE/ADORATION

O Lord, the God of our ancestors, are You not the God who rules in heaven?
Are You not the ruler over all those who rule the nations of the earth?
Power and might are in Your hand,
and not one is able to withstand You.   **2 CHRONICLES 20:6**

You are able to keep me from falling
and to present me before His glorious presence
without fault and with great joy—
to You, the only God my Savior, be
glory, (Gk.=*doxa: to give weight to something, to give supreme place*)
majesty, (Gk.=*megalosyne: greatness, royalty, to consider beautiful*)
power, (Gk.=*kratos: sovereign right or dominion in strength and action*)
and authority (Gk.=*exousia: the right to set direction and make
determinations*)
through Jesus Christ our Lord, before all ages, now and forever more! Amen.
JUDE 24–25

Knowing *You* God without knowing our own wretchedness makes for
pride.
And knowing our own wretchedness without knowing *You* God makes for
despair.
Knowing Jesus Christ strikes the perfect balance because He shows us
both *You*, God, and our own wretchedness. Jesus is a God whom we can
approach without pride and before whom we can humble ourselves
without despair.
BLAISE PASCAL, *French philosopher (1623–1662)* [*CDP, 687* PD]

A PRAYER FOR TODAY

Lord, I praise You because You are able to present me without fault. . . .
You have more power than anyone or anything in the universe. You are mighty
to secure me against any present or future threat to my security in You.
Lord, I praise You because You are willing to present me without fault. . . .
You put my wretchedness on Christ Jesus.
You see me through the reality of Christ Jesus.
I ascribe to You glory. . . .
I ascribe to You majesty. . . .
I ascribe to You power. . . .
I ascribe to You authority. . . . Amen.

PRAYERS *for* CHRISTLIKE CHARACTER

Lord, I will remember the ones who lead me—who I take my cues from—who have taught me the ways of God through the Word of God.
I will consider the outcome of their way of life and imitate their faith.
HEBREWS 13:7

Suffer me never to think that I have knowledge enough to need no teaching,
   wisdom enough to need no correction,
   talents enough to need no grace,
   goodness enough to need no progress,
   humility enough to need no repentance,
   devotion enough to need no quickening,
   strength sufficient without thy Spirit;
lest, standing still, I fall back evermore.
   ERIC MILNER-WHITE, *Dean of York (1884–1963) [MG, n.p.]*

A PRAYER FOR TODAY

Lord, I want to receive verbal instruction and challenges from others well.
I also want to see in those around me what is worth emulating and what does not reflect Your heart.
Help me as I consider the ways of others, not to judge, but rather to see what to, and not to, emulate.

(Now for each person or group of people listed below, consider what is worth emulating, and what is an example of what you don't believe reflects God well.) . . .
My parents: what is worth emulating . . . what doesn't reflect God's heart . . .
My siblings and extended family: what is worth emulating . . . what doesn't reflect God's heart . . .
My spouse (if you have one): what is worth emulating . . . what doesn't reflect God's heart . . .
My children (if you have them): what is worth emulating . . . what doesn't reflect God's heart . . .
My good friends: what is worth emulating . . . what doesn't reflect God's heart . . .
My heroes: what is worth emulating . . . what doesn't reflect God's heart . . .
My Christian leaders: what is worth emulating . . .
what doesn't reflect God's heart . . .
My coworkers: what is worth emulating . . .
what doesn't reflect God's heart . . . Amen.

God, do You really dwell on earth?
The heavens, even the highest heaven, cannot contain You.
How much less the temples we build? **1 KINGS 8:27**

Author note: God is already with the believer so there is no need to pray for God's presence. However, when understood as a declaration, this prayer moves us to think about God's abiding presence in our lives.
Through every moment of this day: **You are with me Lord.**
Through every day of all this week: **You are with me Lord.**
Through every week of all this year: **You are with me Lord.**
Through every year of all this life: **You are with me Lord.**
So that when time is past,
> By grace I may at last be with you, Lord.
> **THE BOOK OF THE HOURS** *(1514)* [*BCP, 145* PD]

Almighty God, the giver of wisdom,
without whose help resolutions are vain,
without whose blessing study is ineffectual;
enable me, if it be your will, to attain such knowledge as may qualify me
> to direct the doubtful, and instruct the ignorant;
> to prevent wrongs and terminate contentions;
> and grant that I may use that knowledge which I shall attain to your
glory and my own *good*,
for Christ's sake.
> **SAMUEL JOHNSON**, *English author (1709–1784)* [*COS, 86* PD]

A PRAYER FOR TODAY

God, You are a God who is everywhere present.
There is nowhere that I can go that You are not there.
There is no place of danger beyond Your presence.
There are places where I am fearful today, . . . but You see.
There is no place of hiding beyond Your presence.
Although You are already present in every sphere of my life, I ask You to be obvious to me in . . .
Show me what would be different in my life if I were to live attentively in Your presence. . . .
Show me where and how to instruct the ignorant today by . . .
Show me where and how to prevent wrongs and terminate contentions today by . . . Amen.

PRAYERS *of* INTERCESSION

Lord, help me to give double honor to those who minister through preaching and teaching.   1 TIMOTHY 5:17

This was prayed during a service of ordination. Use it today to pray for your pastor or another you know and love.

Heavenly Father, we commit *(insert name)* to Your service today. My earnest prayer for him is that:

- all of his life and ministry he would be devoted to Your glory.
- the promises of Christ be trusted so fully that peace and joy and strength fill his soul to overflowing. . . .
- he be a man of the Book, who loves and studies and obeys the Bible in every area of its teaching; that meditation on biblical truth be the source of hope and faith; that he continue to grow in understanding through all the chapters of his life. . . .
- he be a man of prayer, so that the Word of God will be opened to him, so that the power of faith and holiness will descend upon him, that his spiritual influence may increase at home and at church and in the world. . . .
- he be totally committed to ministry, that he not fritter away his time on excessive recreation, unimportant hobbies or aimless ambition, but that he learn to redeem the time for Christ and His Kingdom.
- he love *his wife* the way Christ loves the church and gave Himself for her; . . . that he consistently grow in grace and knowledge so as never to quench her aspirations for spiritual advancement; . . .
- he not assume advancement and peer approval in ministry are the highest values in life.
- he see the biblical *vision for* ministry as a call from God to live a life that is radically different from the rest of society.
- he remember daily that he doesn't minister for the applause of others, but he ministers before an audience of one. . . . Amen.

RICK IGLESIAS, *Cuban-American pastor (1957–present day)*

A PRAYER FOR TODAY

Father, today I want to pray for those I know who are engaged in vocational ministry. . . .
Grant them joy, wisdom, passion, and courage. . . .
Grant them power through Your Holy Spirit. . . .
Grant them resolve to minister when it is difficult . . . and true friends. . . .
Provide for their needs both through Your miraculous provision and through the faithful and fair support of those involved in the local church. . . . Amen.

PRAYERS *of* SURRENDER

Lord, may my heart be devoted to Your ways;
may I remove the high places that idols have in my life.
   2 CHRONICLES 17:6

The dearest idol I have known,
whatever that idol be,
help me to tear it from thy throne,
and worship only Thee.
   WILLIAM COWPER, *English poet (1731–1800)* [BTP, 125 PD]

My Lord and my God, take from me all that keeps me from thee.
My Lord and my God, grant me all that leads me to thee.
My Lord and my God, take me from myself and give me completely to thee.
   NICOLAS OF FLUE, *Swiss hermit (1417–1487)* [CBP, 7 PD]

I ask you, Lord Jesus, to develop in me, your lover,
   an immeasurable urge toward you,
   an affection that is unbounded, longing that is unrestrained,
   fervor that throws discretion to the winds!
The more worthwhile our love for you, all the more pressing does it become.
   Reason cannot hold it in check,
   fear does not make it tremble,
wise judgment does not temper it.
   RICHARD ROLLE, *English author/Bible translator (1290–1349)* [GSG, 237]

A PRAYER FOR TODAY

God, You are a God who is worthy of my full allegiance.
Yet I often grant my attention, affection, and allegiance to things that are not as
worthy as You. . . .
Your Word calls this idolatry.
I surrender my idols to You. . . .
I surrender to You what I think my affection for these idols will give to me. . . .
I ask that I would be able to see the emptiness of my idols. . . .
Enlarge my desire for what is from You and for You. . . .

PRAYERS *of* THANKSGIVING

> Behold the Lamb of God, who takes away the sin of the world.
> **JOHN 1:29**

> *Lord Jesus Christ,*
> Can it be that I should gain an interest in my Savior's blood?
> Died He for me, who caused His pain? For me, who Him to death pursued?
> Amazing love! How can it be That Thou, my God, shouldst die for me?
> Amazing love! How can it be That Thou, my God, shouldst die for me!
>
> He left His Father's throne above, So free, so infinite His grace!
> Emptied Himself of all but love, and bled for Adam's helpless race!
> 'Tis mercy all, immense and free, For O my God, it found out me.
> Amazing love! How can it be That Thou, my God, shouldst die for me!
>
> No condemnation now I dread: Jesus, and all in Him is mine!
> Alive in Him, my living Head, and clothed in righteousness divine.
> Bold I approach the eternal throne, and claim the crown, thru Christ my own.
> Amazing love! How can it be That Thou, my God, shouldst die for me!
> "AND CAN IT BE?" **CHARLES WESLEY**, *English ,minister (1707–1788)*
> [*PSH, 61* PD]

> I give you glory, O Christ, because you, the Only Begotten, the Lord of all things, who alone are without sin, gave yourself to die for me, a sinner unworthy of such a blessing: you died the death of the cross to free my sinful soul from the bonds of sin. . . .
> Glory to you for your love.
> Glory to you for your mercy.
> Glory to you for your patience.
> Glory to you for forgiving us all our sins.
> Glory to you for coming to save our souls. . . .
> Glory to you for your crucifixion.
> Glory to you for your burial.
> Glory to you for your resurrection. . . .
> Glory to you who sit in great glory at the Father's right hand.
> **EPHRAIM**, *Syrian theologian (306–373)* [*COS, 6* PD]

A PRAYER FOR TODAY

Lord, I thank You for the depth and wonder of Your love in the passion and crucifixion of Jesus. . . .
I thank You for the depth and wonder of Your love in the resurrection and life of Jesus. . . . Amen.

PRAYERS *of* CONFESSION

Father, when I return to you, you see me in the distance and you are filled with compassion for me; you run to me, throw your arms around me and kiss me. Then I say, "Father, I have sinned, against heaven and against you."

But you say, "For this son or daughter of mine was dead and is alive again, has been lost and is found, so let's celebrate." LUKE 15:20–24

Note: You may want to read all of Luke 15:11–32 first:

Dear Father: How it must crush you when I turn my back on you and walk away. How you must weep when you see me disappear over a far horizon to squander my life in a distant country.

Thank you that although I have sometimes left home, I have never left your heart. Though I have forgotten about you, you have never forgotten about me.

Thank you for the financial crisis or the famine or the pigsty or whatever it took to bring me to my senses. And thank you that even though what brought me home were pangs of hunger instead of pangs of conscience, yet still, even on those terms, you welcomed me back.

Thank you for the forgiveness and the restoration you have lavished on me—me, the one who needed them most but deserved them least.

I confess that there is inside me not only a prodigal son but also a critical older brother.

How dutiful I have sometimes been, and yet so proud of the duties I have done. How generous I have been in my opinion of myself, and yet so judgmental in my opinion of others. How often I have entered into criticism, and yet how seldom I have entered into your joy.

Gather both the prodigal part of myself and the critical part of myself in your loving arms, O Lord. And bring them home.

KEN GIRE, *American author (1950–present day) [MW?, 247]*

A PRAYER FOR TODAY

God, You are my Father.
You are big, having more than enough for me.
You are gracious, allowing me to squander Your good gifts and still receiving me back.
I confess to You the times I have squandered what You have given me.
I have squandered relationships . . . opportunities . . . possessions . . . and my gifts and abilities. . . .
I have, figuratively speaking, gone to the far country by . . . Sometimes my pride keeps me there. But when I come to my senses, I return home to You.
Forgive me for all the times I have been the older brother. . . .
Thank You for Your incredible mercy and grace. Amen.

PRAYERS *of* AFFIRMATION

🍇 Lord Jesus Christ, You are worthy to take the scroll and to open its seals, for You were slain, and have redeemed us to God by Your blood out of every tribe and tongue and people and nation. REVELATION 5:9

🍇 Grant us purity of heart and strength of purpose, that no selfish passion may hinder us from knowing your will, and no weakness hinder us from doing it; but that in your light we may see light, and in your service find our perfect freedom; through Jesus Christ our Lord.
     AUGUSTINE, *bishop of Hippo (354–430)* [BTP, 33 PD]

🍇 I believe, O God, that you are
the Eternal Father of peace, the Eternal Father of power,
the Eternal Father of all people.
I believe, O God, that you are
The Lord and giver of longings, the Lord and giver of life,
The Lord and giver of love.
I believe, O God, that you are
the Spirit of all glory, the Spirit of all goodness
the Spirit of all grace.
I believe, O God, that you are here and with me now . . .
to protect me . . . to guide me . . .
to uphold me [and] to restore me.
     "AFFIRMATIONS," *Celtic prayer [PL, 11]*

🍇 O Jesus, You were chosen before the creation of the world, but were revealed in these last times for my sake.
Through You I believe in God the Father, who raised You from the dead and glorified You, so that my faith and hope are in Almighty God.
     1 PETER 1:20–21

A PRAYER FOR TODAY

I believe in Your greatness—Almighty God—Your greatness as seen in . . .
I believe in Your Son—Merciful God—as the redeemer of humanity.
And I believe in Your presence (the Holy Spirit) in my life—Omnipresent God—as seen in . . .
And I believe that You have worked in my life in these ways . . .
Keep me from selfish passions that would keep away my allegiance to You.
I rest in You because You are with me, You protect me, You enfold me and You uphold me, You are beside me, You guide me,
You heal me, and You restore me. Amen.

PRAYERS *of* PETITION

Jesus, You send me out like a sheep among wolves. Therefore I will seek to be as wise as a serpent while being as innocent as a dove.   MATTHEW 10:16

Dear Lord, you have sent me into this world to *proclaim* your word. So often the problems of the world seem so complex and intricate that your word strikes me as embarrassingly simple. Many times I feel tongue-tied in the company of people who are dealing with the world's social and economic problems.

But you, O Lord, said, "Be clever as serpents and innocent as doves." Let me retain innocence and simplicity in the midst of this complex world. I realize that I have to be informed, that I have to study the many aspects of the problems facing the world, and that I have to try to understand as well as possible the dynamics of our contemporary society. But what really counts is that all this information, knowledge, and insight allow me to speak more clearly and unambiguously your truthful word.

Do not allow evil powers to seduce me with the complexities of the world's problems, but give me the strength to think clearly, speak freely, and act boldly in your service. Give me the courage to show the dove in the world so full of serpents.

HENRI NOUWEN, *American priest (1932–1996) [HBP, 274]*

A PRAYER FOR TODAY

God, You are the God of truth.
You have given me a mission to be a person who stands for and proclaims Your truth.
I acknowledge that this is the context where You have placed me. I have a responsibility, a calling, and the privilege to be Your emissary here.
I ask for wisdom to understand the complexities and the potential snares around me. . . .
In other words, help me to think clearly.
I ask for the innocence and simplicity to have a voice that cuts through the chatter. For me, innocence would include . . .
In other words, help me to speak freely.
I ask for the courage to act on my convictions in these ways . . .
In other words, help me to act boldly.

PRAYERS *for* RENEWAL

⚜ You have taught us so that we may have a full measure of Your joy.
   JOHN 17:13

⚜ Let Your joy be in me, and make it complete in me.   **JOHN 15:11**

⚜ May I glory in Your holy name, O Lord.
   Let the hearts of all those who seek You be filled with rejoicing.
   May I seek You and Your strength.
   May I seek Your face at all times and in every situation.
   May I remember the wonderful things You have done,
   Your miraculous deeds, and Your timeless words.   **1 CHRONICLES 16:10–12**

⚜ God of goodness, give me yourself, for you are sufficient for me.
   To be worthy of you I cannot ask for anything less.
   If I were to ask less, I should always be in want, for in you alone do I have all.
   JULIAN OF NORWICH, *English mystic (1342–1416)* [BTP, 42 PD]

⚜ Grant, Lord, that I may not for one moment admit willingly into my soul
   any thought contrary to your love.
   EDWARD PUSEY, *English Bible professor (1800–1882)* [BTP, 49 PD]

A PRAYER FOR TODAY

Father, here is where I am experiencing joy . . .
Here is where I am experiencing sorrow . . .
Here is the sickness that I am facing . . .
Here is where I am enjoying health . . .
Here is the success that I am currently encountering . . .
Here is the failure that I am currently encountering . . .
Help me to understand and embrace that in You alone do I have all.
Help me to believe and receive that You are sufficient for me.
Help me to embrace life as Your student, not as fate's victim.
Help me to experience Your joy in both the highs and lows of life.

Prayers *of* Praise/Adoration

For You, Lord, are good and Your love endures forever,
Your faithfulness continues throughout all generations. **PSALM 100:5**

Blessing and honour, thanksgiving and praise, more than I can utter, more than I can understand, be yours, O most glorious Trinity, Father, Son and Holy Spirit, by all angels, all people, all creatures, now and for ever.
LANCELOT ANDREWES, *English minister (1555–1626)* [*BTP, 778* PD]

Jesus, You once said, "If you, then, though you are evil, know how to give good gifts to your children, how much more will your Father in heaven give good gifts to those who ask him!" **MATTHEW 7:11**

Lord, remind me that Your disposition toward me is goodness.
      Keep me from the dark suspicion that You are not good.
You act with generosity and benevolence.
      Keep me from believing that You are not for me.
You are gracious and compassionate.
      Keep me from the assumption that I am beyond Your grace.
You are faithful and steadfast.
      Keep me from the opinion that Your disposition toward me could change.
You are rich in love and never petty in Your anger.
      Keep me from doubting the richness of Your love for me.
      KURT BJORKLUND, *American minister (1968–present day)*

My God, I pray that I may so know you and love you that I may rejoice in you. And if I may not do so fully in this life, let me go steadily on to the day when I come to fullness of life.
Meanwhile let my mind meditate on your eternal goodness,
      let my tongue speak of it,
      let my heart live it,
      let my mouth speak it,
      let my soul hunger for it,
and my whole being desire it, until I enter into your joy.
      ANSELM, *bishop of Canterbury (1033–1109)* [*BTP, 44* PD]

A PRAYER FOR TODAY

Take a few minutes to recall God's goodness to you . . .
Lord God, I praise You for the goodness of Your character, . . .
and for the goodness in Your works. . . . Amen.

PRAYERS *for* CHRISTLIKE CHARACTER

My Lord, these three remain:
> faith, (Gk.=*pistis: holding fast, confident assurance*)
> hope, (Gk.=*elpis: confident expectation or solid assurance about the future*)
> and love. (Gk.=*agape: full of care and concern expressed without condition*)

But the greatest of these is love.   1 CORINTHIANS 13:13

Lord, as the apostles prayed, I too ask: Increase my faith.   LUKE 17:5

Prayed as he awaited trial for his part in a plot against Adolf Hitler
O Holy Spirit, give me faith that will protect me from despair,
from passions and vice;
give me such love for God and *people* as will blot out all hatred and
bitterness;
give me the hope that will deliver me from fear and faint-heartedness.
> DIETRICH BONHOEFFER, *German pastor (1906–1945) [BCP, 199]*

I will keep myself in Your love, God, as I wait for the mercy of my Lord Jesus
Christ to bring me to eternal life.   JUDE 21

O God . . .
> let no word cross my lips that is not your word,
> no thoughts enter my mind that are not your thoughts,
> no deed ever be done or entertained by me that is not your deed.
> MALCOLM MUGGERIDGE, *English journalist (1903–1990) [COS, 51]*

A PRAYER FOR TODAY

Father, in these ways I can be tempted toward despair . . .
In these ways I can be tempted toward vice . . .
Increase my faith.
Please grant me the steadfastness and assurance to persevere in faith.
In these ways I have felt bitterness toward situations and people . . .
In these ways I have felt hatred toward people . . .
Increase my love.
Please grant me the concern and compassion for others to persevere in love.
In these ways I at times feel fear . . .
In these ways I at times feel fainthearted . . .
Increase my hope.
Please grant me the solid assurance of the future to rise above fear. Amen.

PRAYERS *for* WISDOM/GUIDANCE

If from wherever I am, I will seek You Lord God,
I will find You if I look for You with all my heart and with all my soul.
DEUTERONOMY 4:29

I will look to You Lord and Your strength.
I will seek Your face always.   **PSALM 105:4**

O Lord my God, teach my heart this day
where and how to see you,
where and how to find you.
You have made me and remade me,
and you have bestowed on me all the good things I possess,
and still I do not know you.
I have not yet done that for which I was made.
Teach me to seek you,
for I cannot seek you unless you teach me,
or find you unless you show yourself to me.
Let me seek you in my desire, let me desire you in my seeking.
Let me find you by loving you, let me love you when I find you.
ANSELM, *Italian monk (1033–1109)* [*CPB, 147* PD]

Give us, O Lord,
open minds to seek your will,
soft hearts to receive your will,
and ready hands to do your will.
Through Jesus Christ our Lord, Amen
CORNELIUS PLANTINGA JR., *American seminary president (1946–present day)*
[*BDD, 67*]

A PRAYER FOR TODAY

What would it mean for you to seek God with all your heart and soul?
Would it mean setting more time apart for you to spend alone with God?
Would it mean serving Him in a tangible and systematic way?
Would it mean participating in a regular time of worship and teaching with others?
Would it mean giving up something else that is too important to you?
Father, today I purpose to seek You with all my heart by . . .
I will seek You with an open mind.
I will receive Your will with a soft and open heart.
I will do Your will with open hands. *(Open your hands physically in symbolic posture.)* Amen.

PRAYERS *of* INTERCESSION

Lord, we look forward to the day of the fullness of Your kingdom:
   When the wolf will dwell with the lamb,
   and the leopard will lie down with the goat,
   and the little child will lead them.
Then the cow will feed with the bear;
Their young will lie down together, and the lion will eat straw like the ox.
The infant will play near the hole of the cobra, and the young child will put
his hand into the viper's hole; they will neither harm nor destroy on all
Your holy mountain, for the earth will be full of the knowledge of You, O Lord,
as the waters cover the sea.   **ISAIAH 11:6–9**

For the peace of the world, that a spirit of respect and
forbearance may grow among many nations and peoples,
we pray to you, O Lord. Lord, hear our prayer.

For those in positions of public trust,
that they may serve justice and promote the dignity and freedom of every
person, **we pray to you, O Lord. Lord, hear our prayer.**

For a blessing upon all human labor, and for the right use
of the riches of creation, that the world may be freed from poverty, famine,
and disaster, **we pray to you, O Lord. Lord, hear our prayer.**

For the poor, the persecuted, the sick, and all who suffer;
for refugees, prisoners, and all who are in danger; that they may be relieved
and protected, **we pray to you, O Lord. Lord, hear our prayer.**
   "LITANY FOR SEVERAL OCCASIONS" [*BCP, 549–50* PD]

A PRAYER FOR TODAY

God, I ask You to bring about a taste of Your kingdom even now in these
situations . . . *(name a few current events)*
For those in positions of power, give them a concern for justice and equality.
For children under the yoke of slavery and sex trafficking, I ask that You would
free them.
Grant great effectiveness to those working on issues relating to freeing children. Let those who are responsible for this tragedy be convicted of the evil of
their ways.
Show me a tangible way that I can aid in bringing a taste of Your kingdom
today. . . .

PRAYERS *of* SURRENDER

O Lord, You are my strength and my shield; My heart trusts in You, and I am helped. **PSALM 28:7**

I will not let my heart be troubled. I will trust in You, Father, and also in Christ. **JOHN 14:1**

Lord God, I am no longer my own, but yours.
Put me to what you will, rank me with whom you will.
Put me to doing, put me to enduring;
Let me be employed for you, or laid aside for you,
Exalted for you or brought low for you; . . .
I freely and wholeheartedly yield all things to your pleasure and disposal.
And now, glorious and blessed God, Father, Son and Holy Spirit,
You are mine and I am yours. So be it.
    JOHN WESLEY, *English minister (1703–1791)* [BTP, 24 PD]

Gracious Father, be pleased to touch our hearts in time with trouble, with sorrow, with sickness, with disappointment, with anything that may hinder them from being hard to the end, and leading us to eternal ruin.
    THOMAS ARNOLD, *British educator/historian (1795–1842)* [COS, 102 PD]

Thank you, Lord Jesus, that you will be our hiding place whatever happens.
    CORRIE TEN BOOM, *Dutch Holocaust survivor (1892–1983)* [CBP, 41]
    Prayed while in a German concentration camp during World War II

A PRAYER FOR TODAY

Father, here is where I am troubled today . . .
Here is where I struggle to pray "rank me with whom You will" . . .
Here is where I struggle to pray "I'm willing to be laid aside or brought low" . . .
Here is where I struggle to pray "let me be empty, or let me have nothing" . . .
Here is where I struggle to pray "I yield all things to Your pleasure and disposal" . . .
I acknowledge that this is because I don't have full confidence in You as my strength and shield.
I acknowledge that this is because I value this life at times over eternity.
I surrender my fear to You. . . .
I now surrender to You all that I am withholding. . . . Amen.

PRAYERS *of* THANKSGIVING

🌸 Your lovingkindness, O Lord, reaches to the heavens,
Your faithfulness to the skies,
Your righteousness is like the mighty mountains;
Your justice like the ocean deep.
O Lord, You preserve people and beasts.
How priceless is Your lovingkindness, O Lord!
Both well-regarded and ill-regarded people find refuge in the shadow of
    Your wings. . . .
For with You is the fountain of life. PSALM 36:5–7, 9

🌸 We give you thanks, most gracious God, for the beauty of the earth and sky
and sea;
    for the richness of mountains, plains, and rivers;
    for the songs of birds and the loveliness of flowers.
We praise you for these good gifts. . . .
Grant that we may continue to grow in our grateful enjoyment of your
abundant creation, to the honor and glory of your Name, now and forever.
Amen.
    "PRAYER OF THANKSGIVING FOR THE BEAUTY OF THE EARTH" *[BCP, 840]*

🌸 Lord of all blessing, as we walk about your world,
Let us know ourselves blessed at every turn; . . .
Blessed in the turning of the world beneath our feet;
Blessed in silence;
Blessed in sleep;
Blessed in our children, our parents, and our friends;
Blessed in conversation and the human voice;
Blessed in waiting for the bus, or train or traffic lights;
Blessed in conversation and the human voices,
Blessed in the songs of birds;
Blessed in the cry that pierces the heart; . . .
Blessed in waiting and waiting and waiting.
Lord of all blessing, we bless you.
    HUGH DICKINSON, *English professor (twentieth century) [CBP, 34]*

Think about the most beautiful places you have ever been. . . .
Thank You, God, for what You have created. . . .
Thank You for how You preserve and provide through nature. . . .
Thank You for the ability to enjoy Your creation. . . . Amen.

PRAYERS *of* CONFESSION

- There is no temptation that has come upon me that is more intense than other people have faced. And You, my God, are faithful; You will not let me be tempted beyond what I can bear.   1 CORINTHIANS 10:13A

- Almighty God, . . . in asking for forgiveness I cannot claim a right to be forgiven but only cast myself upon thine unbounded love.
  I can plead no merit or desert:
  I can plead no extenuating circumstances:
  I cannot plead the frailty of my nature:
  I cannot plead the force of the temptations I encounter:
  I cannot plead the persuasions of others who led me astray:
  I can only say, for the sake of Jesus Christ thy Son, my Lord. Amen.
      JOHN BAILLIE, *Scottish theologian (1886–1960) [DPP, 79]*

- Lord, I sometimes wander away from you.
  But this is not because I am deliberately turning my back on you.
  It is because of the inconstancy of my mind.
  I weaken in my intention to give my whole soul to you.
  I fall back into thinking of myself as my own master.
  But when I wander from you, my life becomes a burden,
  and within me I find nothing but darkness and wretchedness, fear and anxiety.
  So I come back to you, and confess that I have sinned against you.
  And I know you will forgive me.
      AELRED OF RIEVAULX, *English monk (1110–1167) [BOP, 20]*

- But when I am tempted, You will provide a way for me so that I can stand strong while under the duress of that temptation.
      1 CORINTHIANS 10:13B

A PRAYER FOR TODAY

Father, I acknowledge the places where I have sinned this week. . . .
I acknowledge that I have excused myself in the following ways . . .
I acknowledge that there is not a single excuse that is convincing to You or me.
I acknowledge the ways my mind and heart wander from You. . . .
I acknowledge the places and ways I want to be my own master. . . .
I acknowledge that when I am my own master it leads me to darkness and fear by . . .
I ask You on the basis of Your love and goodness to forgive me. . . .
I ask You to show me Your already-given provision for resisting compromise. . . .
I ask You to aid me so that I can stand strong. Amen.

PRAYERS *of* AFFIRMATION

🌿 Jesus, You have said, "Everything is possible for the one who believes."
I do believe—help me overcome my unbelief! **MARK 9:23–24**

🌿 Lord, I want to love you, yet I'm not sure.
I want to trust you, yet I'm afraid of being taken in.
I know I need you, yet I'm ashamed of the need.
I want to pray, yet I'm afraid of being a hypocrite.
I need my independence, yet I fear to be alone.
I want to belong, yet I must be myself.
Take me, Lord, yet leave me alone.
Lord, I believe; help thou my unbelief.
　　　BERNARD, *(Unknown position, era) [OBP, 69]*

🌿 I will fear You, Lord, and serve You in truth with all my heart,
for I contemplate the great things You have done for me. **1 SAMUEL 12:24**

🌿 O Lord, how hard it is to accept your way. You come to me as a small,
powerless child born away from home. You live for me as a stranger in your
own land. You die for me as a criminal outside the walls of the city, rejected
by your own people, misunderstood by your friends, and feeling abandoned by your God.

　　I am trying to overcome the feelings of alienation and separation which
continue to assail me. But I wonder now if my deep sense of homelessness
does not bring me closer to you than my occasional feelings of belonging.

　　I do not have to run away from those experiences that are closest to
yours. Every time I feel this way I have an occasion to be grateful and to
embrace you better and taste more fully your joy and peace.

　　Come, Lord Jesus, and be with me where I feel poorest.
　　HENRI NOUWEN, *American priest (1932–1996) [BTP, 122]*

A PRAYER FOR TODAY

Lord, here is where it is hard for me to believe . . .
Here is where I feel alienated and alone . . .
Here is where I feel small and powerless . . .
Here is where I have felt rejected or misunderstood . . .
Remind me that this was the lot of Jesus on this earth
　　and allow me to meet You in my similar experiences.
I embrace the experiences of alienation today as a way to identify with You in
　　Your suffering. I affirm that with You anything and everything is possible.
Help my unbelief. Amen.

PRAYERS *of* PETITION

🌿 Woe to me when I seek assistance from those in the world, when I rely on methods, and resources, and expertise, but do not look to You the Holy One, or seek help from You, Lord.   ISAIAH 31:1

🌿 I am cursed when I trust in human strength and turn away from You, Lord. . . . But I am blessed when I trust in You, Lord, and when I place my confidence in You.   JEREMIAH 17:5, 7

🌿 O Lord, I do not pray for tasks equal to my strength:
I ask for strength equal to my tasks.
    PHILLIPS BROOKS, *American minister (1835–1893) [CBP, 323]*

🌿 This is my one incessant prayer to you, hour by hour, day upon day: It's yours. I am not fighting this battle for me. It is all yours, and I want whatever you have for me in this situation.

It is not my organization, it is yours, so I depend on your Spirit to show me what to do. These are not my people. I chose them and organize their efforts, but they do not belong to me. You entrusted them to my leadership, and they agreed to follow me. They deserve more and sometimes expect more of me than I can give them. What they really need is enormous. If I take their needs and hopes and fears on myself personally, I will be crushed instantly. They are yours. . . .

Yours is the kingdom, but we never seem to have enough resources! We are always lacking something, our dreams always mocking our reality, our vision always dancing around our poverty. You own everything, so what we need must seem small to you. Show me where to look for it, how to know it when I see it, how to get it, how to use it best, and especially how to be content with it. It is all yours. . . .

So this day is yours; I am yours; these people are yours; these resources are yours. The challenges we face are yours, as is anything we hope to accomplish. It's yours, God. It's not mine.
    RICHARD KRIEGBAUM, *American educator (twentieth century) [LP, 6–7]*

A PRAYER FOR TODAY

Father, here is what I am tempted to trust in today besides You . . .
I affirm that You care more about the organization I'm a part of and my family than I often realize. So, what I am concerned most about today is Yours. . . .
And I ask You, God, to work in these situations way beyond my abilities. . . .
And I ask for contentment whatever comes. . . .
And that I could live with the mind-set that says—it's Your deal! Amen.

PRAYERS *for* RENEWAL

❧ Father, You promise to bless me, if I hunger and thirst after righteousness. You have said that I would be filled. **MATTHEW 5:6**

❧ O lead my Spirit, O raise it from these weary depths, that ravished by your art, that it may strive upwards with tempestuous fire. For you alone have knowledge, you alone can inspire enthusiasm.
   LUDWIG VAN BEETHOVEN, *German composer (1770–1827)* [COS, 85 PD]

❧ O God, I have tasted thy goodness, and it has both satisfied me and made me thirsty for more.
   I am painfully conscious of my need of further grace.
   I am ashamed of my lack of desire.
   O God, the Triune God, I want to want thee;
   I long to be filled with longing; I thirst to be made more thirsty still.
   Show me thy glory, I pray, so that I may know thee indeed.
   Begin in mercy a new work of love within me.
   A. W. TOZER, *American minister (1897–1963)* [POG, 17]

❧ All the longing of my heart and soul lie before You, O Lord; what I really desire is not hidden from You. **PSALM 38:9**

❧ O Lord our God, grant us grace to desire you with our whole heart,
   so that desiring you, we may seek and find you;
   and so finding you, may love you;
   and so loving you, may hate those sins which separate us from you,
   for the sake of Jesus Christ our Lord.
   ANSELM, *bishop of Canterbury (1033–1109)* [BTP, 23 PD]

A PRAYER FOR TODAY

Father, this is honestly what I desire most right now . . . *(name those desires)*
I know there are things that I desire more than I desire You and Your ways.
Increase my desire for You.
Let me see Your beauty and goodness above all else.
Bring people and experiences into my life that ignite my desire for You.
Help me to see and embrace those people and experiences. . . .
Help me to be fully aware and present in those experiences. . . .
Bring enthusiasm to my tasks and relationships. . . .
Bring joy to my day. Amen.

PRAYERS *of* PRAISE/ADORATION

O Lord, our Lord, how majestic is Your name in all the earth!
You have set Your glory above the heavens.   PSALM 8:1

Great and marvelous are Your works, Lord God Almighty!
Righteous and true are Your ways, King of Nations!
Who will not fear You, O Lord, and glorify Your name?
For You alone are holy. All nations will come and worship before You,
For Your righteous acts have been revealed.   REVELATION 15:3–4

Praise God from whom all blessings flow,
Praise Him all creatures here below;
Praise Him above all ye heavenly host.
Praise Father, Son and Holy Ghost, Amen.
    "DOXOLOGY," THOMAS KEN, *English cleric (1637–1711)* [PD]

You are God; we praise you;
You are the Lord: we acclaim you;
You are the eternal Father: all creation worships you.
To you all angels, all the powers of heaven, . . . sing in endless praise:
Holy, holy, holy God, God of power and might,
Heaven and earth are full of your glory.
The glorious company of the apostles praise you.
The noble fellowship of the prophets praise you.
The white-robed army of martyrs praise you.
Through the world the holy Church acclaims you;
Father of majesty unbounded,
Your true and only Son, worthy of all worship,
And the Holy Spirit, advocate and guide.
You Christ, are the King of glory,
The eternal Son of the Father.
We believe that you will come to be our judge.
Come then, Lord, and help your people, bought with the price of your own
blood, and bring us with your saints to glory everlasting.
    PRAYER OF ADORATION *[BCP, 95–96]*

A PRAYER FOR TODAY

Add your own expressions of praise and thanksgiving for who God is and what He has done....
Father, I am grateful for the ways You have worked in my life. . . . Amen.

PRAYERS *for* CHRISTLIKE CHARACTER

But now I must rid myself of all such things as these:
anger, (Gk.=*orge: a deep-seated anger that simmers with resentment*)
rage, (Gk.=*thumos: an anger that burns with the intensity of a fire; a flare-up*)
malice, (Gk.=*kakia: a disposition to harm others; a vicious approach to others*)
slander, (Gk.=*blasphemos: an attempt to belittle and cause another to fall into disrepute*)
and filthy language from my mouth. (Gk.=*aischrologia: obscene or foul talk*)
I will not lie to others, since I have taken off my old self with its evil practices and have put on a new self which is being renewed in the knowledge of You, my Creator. COLOSSIANS 3:8–10

Lord, in my anger, I will not sin and I will not let the day end without dealing with my anger. . . . I will not let any unwholesome talk come out of my mouth, but only what is helpful for building others up according to their needs, so that my word would benefit those who listen.
EPHESIANS 4:26, 29

O God, we hold in your presence the anger that this day will bring forth. Teach us to really care, so that our anger is not occasioned by trifles to do with our comfort and status, but by what outrages your heart of love.
RICHARD HARRIES, *English bishop (1936–present day) [CBP, 230]*

May God grant us the wisdom to discover the right,
and the courage to choose it,
and the strength to make it endure.
KING ARTHUR, *mythical king of Camelot* [PD]

A PRAYER FOR TODAY

Think about the situations that you will face and the emotions you may feel. . . .
Where is it possible that you will become angry? . . .
Do you have anyone you wish to harm? Even if only through words. . . .
Now commit those situations to God, . . . and to only speaking words that are helpful.
Think about your motivation for speaking words that injure or mislead versus words that build up. . . .

Father, grant me, I ask, the perspective to see the power of my emotions and words for good or harm, and the desire to use them for Your glory and for the good of others. Amen.

Lord, You give wisdom; from Your mouth come knowledge and
understanding.
You store up sound wisdom for the upright; You are a shield to those who
walk in integrity,
guarding the paths of the just and protecting the way of Your saints.
Then I will understand righteousness and justice and honesty—every good
path, for wisdom will enter my heart, and knowledge will be pleasant
to my soul.
Discretion will protect me and understanding will guard me.

PROVERBS 2:6–11

O Lord, to be turned from you is to fall,
to turn to you is to rise, and to stand in your presence is to live for ever.
Grant us in all our duties your help,
in all our perplexities your guidance,
in all our dangers your protection,
and in all our sorrows your peace;
through Jesus Christ our Lord.

AUGUSTINE, *bishop of Hippo (354–450)* [*BTP, 67* PD]

Your foolishness, O God, is wiser than human wisdom,
and Your weakness is stronger than human strength.

1 CORINTHIANS 1:25

A PRAYER FOR TODAY

Lord, You do choose the things that seem foolish to the world and the things
that seem weak.
Where are You prompting me to trust Your wisdom over the wisdom of the
world? . . .
Where are You prompting me to trust Your strength over the strength of the
world? . . .
What changes do You want to prompt in me today? . . .
What course of action would please You this week? . . . Month? . . . Year? . . .
Help me to trust Your hand in Your leading. Allow my look at how You have
worked in the past to give me confidence to trust You again. Amen.

PRAYERS *of* INTERCESSION

I will remember those in prison as though I were in prison with them, and those who are mistreated as though I were suffering with them.
HEBREWS 13:3

This is pure and undefiled religion before You, my God and Father:
to visit orphans and widows in their affliction
and to keep oneself from being stained by the world. **JAMES 1:27**

Strengthen us, O God,
to relieve the oppressed, to hear the groans of poor prisoners,
to reform the abuses of all professions;
that many be made not poor to make a few rich; for Jesus Christ's sake.
OLIVER CROMWELL, *English soldier/statesman (1599–1658) [EOP, 364]*

Father, I have seen the commands of Scripture to care deeply about the plight of the oppressed.
I am often moved emotionally when oppression is before me.
I am often filled with good intentions about what I could do to help those who are oppressed.
Yet I seldom act.
I seldom visit the orphans and widows.
I seldom speak against the systematic oppression in our world.
Sometimes I don't act because I'm too consumed with the details of my life.
Sometimes I don't act because I don't want to complicate my life.
But today please strip away all my excuses, and let me practice pure religion:
by visiting the afflicted and comforting them, by working to stop injustice,
and by keeping myself from loving this world too much to act or pray.
KURT BJORKLUND, *American minister (1968–present day)*

A PRAYER FOR TODAY

Lord, I have recently seen oppression in these ways . . .
I have responded by or failed to respond by . . .
I have made the following excuses for my non-involvement . . .
Help me not to be comfortable in my excessive comforts while others struggle to just get by. . . .
Help me instead to act, even if only in ways that seem small to me. . . .
Today I ask You to provide for those without the basic necessities of life. . . .
I ask You to comfort the lonely . . . relieve the suffering of the hurting. . . .
I ask You to use me and Your church to meet these needs. . . . Amen.

PRAYERS of SURRENDER

● Lord, I know that unless a grain of wheat is buried in the ground, and dies to all, it will never come to life as more than a grain of wheat. But when it is buried, it sprouts to life and reproduces itself many times. In the same way if I hold on to my life, I will not really live. But when I let go, then I find everlasting and satisfying life.   JOHN 12:24–25

● Grant, O Lord, that I may not lavish away the life which Thou hast given me on useless trifles,
nor waste it in vain searches after things which Thou has hidden from me.
Enable me, by thy Holy Spirit, so to shun sloth and negligence,
that every day may discharge part of the task which Thou has allotted me;
and so further with thy help that labour which, without thy help, must be ineffectual,
that I may obtain, in all my undertakings, such success as will most promote thy glory,
and the salvation of my own soul, for the sake of Jesus Christ, Amen.
SAMUEL JOHNSON, *English minister (1709–1784)* [GMO, 274 PD]

● It is a comfort, Lord, to know that you did not entrust the fulfillment of your will to one so pitiable as me. . . . Although my will is still self-centered, I give it, Lord, freely to you.
TERESA OF ÁVILA, *Spanish nun (1515–1582)* [BTP, 27 PD]

A PRAYER FOR TODAY

Lord, help me to accept the dreams that have died as a path to new vision and life. . . .
Produce in me the approval of Your gifts even if I don't initially recognize them as gifts. . . .
Produce in me the approval of Your timing in the giving of gifts. Let me say with sincerity that You can do with me whatever pleases You most. . . .
Show me where I am prone to "lavish away my life on useless trifles". . . .
Enable me to invest my life, my days, and my hours in things that promote Your glory. . . .
Grant me the steadfast belief that what promotes Your glory will ultimately bring about my good. . . .
I want to want Your approval
more than the approval of those around me. Amen.

PRAYERS *of* THANKSGIVING

When I pray I want to always thank You, God the Father of my Lord Jesus Christ, for the friends You have given me who have a genuine faith in Christ Jesus and a love for Your people. This faith and love spring from the hope that is stored up in heaven.   COLOSSIANS 1:3–5

We give you thanks, O God, for those who mean so much to us—
> Those to whom we can go at any time.
> Those with whom we can talk and keep nothing back, knowing that they will not laugh at our dreams or our failures.
> Those in whose presence it is easier to be good.
> Those who by their warning have held us back from mistakes we might have made.
Above all we thank you for Jesus Christ, Lord of our hearts and Savior of our souls, in whose name we offer this thanksgiving.
> **WILLIAM BARCLAY,** *Scottish Bible professor (1907–1978) [COS, 8]*

Two are better than one, because they have a good outcome for their joint work. And if one falls down the other is there to help the first up. But it is sad when someone falls and there is no one there to help him or her up. Also, if two lie down together, they will keep warm. But how can one keep warm alone? Though one may be overpowered, two can defend themselves. A cord of three strands is not quickly broken.
> ECCLESIASTES 4:9–12

A PRAYER FOR TODAY

Lord, I thank You specifically for the family and best friends You have brought into my life. . . .
For those who bring joy and laughter. . . .
For those who bring insight to me and challenge me. . . .
For those who bring comfort and care. . . .
For those who bring stability and faithfulness. . . .
For those who bring acceptance and unhurried attentiveness. . . .
For those who bring inspiration and motivation to be what You created me to be. . . .
For those who believe in You and love people. . . .
For those who have picked me up when I've fallen down. . . .
For those who have pushed me to be more than I would have been without their encouragement or confrontation. . . .
For these, the best gifts in my life—I thank You, my God, the giver of all good things. Amen.

PRAYERS *of* CONFESSION

O my God, I am too ashamed and disgraced to lift up my face to You, my God, because my sins are higher than my head, and my guilt has reached the heavens. EZRA 9:6

I am bitterly ashamed, O God, that always I must be confessing to Thee my forgetfulness of Thee,
The feebleness of my love for Thee,
The fitfulness and listlessness of my desire.
How many plain commandments of Thine have I this day disobeyed!
How many little services of love have I withheld from Thee, O Christ, in that I withheld them from the least of these Thy brethren with whom I have had to do!
    JOHN BAILLIE, *Scottish theologian (1886–1960)* [AGP, 281]

Though I have been enslaved,
You have not deserted me.
You have shown kindness . . .
You have granted me new life. EZRA 9:9

O Lord Jesus Christ . . . save us from the error of wishing to admire you instead of being willing to follow you and to resemble you.
    SØREN KIERKEGAARD, *Danish philosopher/theologian (1813–1855)*
    [COS, 33 PD]

A PRAYER FOR TODAY

Lord, I confess that I too often do not even see the things that offend you and others.
Let me see the ways I have forgotten You. . . .
Let me see the ways my love has been feeble and my desire listless. . . .
Let me see the places I have offended. . . .
Let me see the things that are obvious, the plain commandments I have disobeyed. . . .
Let me see the things that are not so obvious, the little services I have withheld. . . .
Let me see the injustice I have ignored. . . .
Let me see the times I have walked past one I might have helped. . . .
Forgive me. Grant me eyes to see.
Enable me by Your Holy Spirit to amend my life to be pleasing unto You.
Amen.

PRAYERS *of* AFFIRMATION

I hope in You, O God, my hope is that there will be a resurrection for both the righteous and the wicked.

Because of this I strive to always keep my conscience blameless before You and before all people. **ACTS 24:15–16**

You, Lord God, will swallow up death forever, and You will wipe away the tears from every face;

You will remove the reproach of Your people from all the earth.

And it will be said in that day,

"Behold, this is our God; we have waited for Him and He will save us.

This is the Lord; we have trusted in Him.

Let us rejoice and be glad in His salvation." **ISAIAH 25:8–9**

Lord, You have promised that all people will rise (Matthew 22:29–32) from death, the righteous to everlasting life, and the wicked to everlasting torment.

Righteous here does not mean good—but declared righteous through Your Son.

For those of us who have come by faith to Your Son, the resurrection promises:

A new body—renewed and vigorous. (Philippians 3:20–21)

A new heaven and a new earth—beautiful and free from the corruption that dominates this world. (Revelation 21–22)

A new community—one focused on worship of You and love for one another. (Revelation 4:9–11; 5:11–12)

A new perspective—one without tears and pain. (Revelation 21:4–5)

Help me to live this life with a full awareness and anticipation of what is to come.

KURT BJORKLUND, *American minister (1968–present day)*

A PRAYER FOR TODAY

Lord, I affirm that I will rise from death.

Death is not the end of my existence.

This impacts how I live today in this way . . .

Let me not lose the confidence of this truth

due to the unseen nature of it . . .

due to the current pain I am experiencing that makes me numb . . .

due to routine and busyness. . . . Amen.

PRAYERS *of* PETITION

Lord, the fighting and quarrels that exist in my life are a result of wanting my own way, a deeply held desire that battles within me. I covet what I don't have, and I am sometimes willing to do destructive things to others to get what I want. When I want what is not rightfully mine, I am sometimes willing to quarrel and fight.   JAMES 4:1–2

Lord, remind me that a heart at peace gives life to the body, but that envy rots the bones.   PROVERBS 14:30

Father, give me the peace of mind that is truly rest.
Take from me
    all envy of anyone else
    all resentment for anything which has been withheld from me
    all bitterness against anyone who has hurt or wronged me
    all anger against the apparent injustice of life
    all foolish worry about the future
    and all futile regret about the past.
Help me to be
    at peace with myself
    at peace with my fellow human beings
    at peace with you
    so indeed may I lay myself down to rest in peace, through Jesus Christ.
    ANONYMOUS *[CBP, 326]*

A PRAYER FOR TODAY

Lord, Your Word teaches that the cause of my conflicts with others is my own covetousness and envy.
Show me where I covet. . . . *(Covetousness is wanting what someone else has.)*
Show me where I envy. . . . *(Envy is resenting what someone else has.)*
Show me where this has brought conflict. . . .
Show me where I have seen people, family, friends, and acquaintances as competitors. . . .
Show me where my anger is tied to my covetousness and envy. . . .
Show me how my envy has been a mask of my pride—wanting to be the one drawing praise. . . .
Show me how selfish my prayers can be. . . .
Please free me from the cycle of envy.
I know that freedom is not found in trying to envy less, but in wanting You my God to have all glory.

PRAYERS *for* RENEWAL

My God, I give You my heart and I fix my eyes on Your ways.
PROVERBS 23:26

O God, who has prepared for them that love thee such good things as pass
our understanding:
Pour into our hearts such love toward thee, that we,
loving thee above all things,
may obtain thy promises, which exceed all that we can desire;
through Jesus Christ our Lord.
BOOK OF COMMON PRAYER [PD]

Lord, help me to see how much I lose when I lose you. My perspective
on my life and all of life gets distorted when I don't make space for you,
obscuring your love for me. Your love is better than life, and truly, I long for
more tastes of that love. In Jesus' name, amen.
PETER SCAZZERO, *American minister (twentieth century)* [BJD, 3]

Your love, Lord, is better than life, therefore my lips will glorify You.
PSALM 63:3

This is how You, God, showed Your love among us: You sent Your one and
only Son into the world that we might live through Him. This is love: not
that we love You, but that You loved us and sent Your Son as an atoning
sacrifice for our sins.   1 JOHN 4:9–10

A PRAYER FOR TODAY

Find a chair you don't normally sit in and sit in it quietly contemplating God's love for
you.
Think about the sacrifice of Christ and how that expresses love....
Think about the privilege of being called God's child....
Think about the good things God has promised to you....
Imagine what God would say to you to express His love for you if He were seated nearby....
Today, pause several times to recall God's love, by praying, "Your love is better than life."

Lord, help me today and this week to fix my eyes on Your love,
    so that I may experience renewal,
so that I may experience clarity. Amen.

PRAYERS *of* PRAISE/ADORATION

Those who pursue righteousness will rejoice in You, O Lord;
praise is becoming to the upright.   PSALM 33:1

I will sing to You, Lord, for You are highly exalted.
You, O Lord, are my strength and my song;
You have become my salvation.
You are my God, and I will praise You, my parent's God,
and I will exalt You.
You, Lord, are a warrior; the Lord is Your name.   EXODUS 15:1–3

Dear Lord, help me keep my eyes on you.
You are the incarnation of divine love,
    you are the expression of God's infinite compassion,
    you are the visible manifestation of the Father's holiness.
    You are beauty, goodness, gentleness, forgiveness, and mercy.
In you all can be found. Outside of you nothing can be found.
Why should I look elsewhere or go elsewhere?
    You have the words of eternal life,
    you are food and drink, you are the Way, the Truth, and the Life.
    You are the light that shines in the darkness, the lamp on the
    lampstand, the house on the hilltop.
    You are the perfect icon of God.
In and through you I can see and find my way to the heavenly Father.
O Holy One, Beautiful One, Glorious One,
    be my Lord, my Saviour, my Redeemer,
    my Guide, my Consoler, my Comforter,
    my Hope, my Joy, and my Peace.
To you I want to give all that I am. Let me be generous, not stingy or
hesitant.
Let me give you all—all I have, think, do and feel.
It is yours, O Lord. Please accept it and make it fully your own.
    HENRI NOUWEN, *American priest (1932–1996) [CBP, 57]*

A PRAYER FOR TODAY

Lord, I offer my praise and adoration to You.
You are my . . . *(Pick phrases from above to pray as personal praise.)*
You are highly exalted and I will exalt You.
Giving You all I have today means . . .
Keep my awareness of You sharp all day long. Amen.

PRAYERS *for* CHRISTLIKE CHARACTER

Help me, God,
> to be joyful (Gk.=*chairo, imperative: rejoice, be joyful, full of joy*)
>> at all times, (Gk.=*pantote: always*)
> to pray (Gk.=*proseuchomai, imperative: a comprehensive word for prayer including all entreaties*)
>> continuously, (Gk.=*adialeiptos: without interruption, constantly*)
> and to be thankful (Gk.=*eucharisteo: imperative for give thanks*)
>> in all circumstances. (Gk.=*en tanti: in everything; includes hardships*)
> For this is Your will for me in Christ Jesus.   1 THESSALONIANS 5:16–18

O God, animate us to cheerfulness, may we have a joyful sense of our blessings, learn to look on the bright circumstances of our lot,
and maintain a perpetual contentedness under thy allotments.
Fortify our minds against disappointments and calamity.
Preserve us from despondency, from yielding to dejection.
Teach us that no evil is intolerable but a guilty conscience,
> and that nothing can hurt us,
> if with true loyalty of affection,
> we keep thy commandments and take refuge in thee;
> through Jesus Christ our Lord. Amen.
> > **WILLIAM ELLERY CHANNING**, *American minister (1780–1842) [EOP, 91]*

Lord, make us to walk in your way:
Where there is love and wisdom, there is neither fear nor ignorance;
Where there is patience and humility, there is neither anger nor annoyance;
Where there is poverty and joy, there is neither greed nor avarice;
Where there is peace and contemplation, there is neither care nor restlessness;
Where there is the fear of God to guard the dwelling, there no enemy can enter;
Where there is mercy and prudence, there is neither excess nor harshness;
This we know through your Son, Jesus Christ our Lord.
> **FRANCIS OF ASSISI**, *Italian monk (1567–1622) [CBP, 209 PD]*

A PRAYER FOR TODAY

God, grant me genuine joy in these situations that I am facing today. . . .
Allow me to sense blessing in the routines of life. . . .
Guard me against despondency in the midst of my disappointments. . . .
Remind me that I can pray constantly about anything as I do now. . . .
Remind me that Your joy is my strength. Amen.

- Since the creation of the world Your invisible qualities—Your eternal power and divine nature—have been clearly seen, being understood from what has been made, so that people are without excuse. For although they knew You, they neither glorified You as God nor gave thanks to You, but their thinking became futile and their foolish hearts were darkened. Although they claimed to be wise, they became fools and exchanged Your glory as the immortal God for images made to look like mere human beings and birds and animals and reptiles. Therefore, You gave them over to the sinful desires of their hearts. **ROMANS 1:19–24**

- The heavens declare Your glory, God,
  and the skies proclaim the work of Your hands. **PSALM 19:1**

- Lord, do not punish me, I beg you, by granting what I wish or ask,
  if it offends your love which should always live in me.
  Let me die to myself, that I may serve you:
  let me live for you, who in yourself are the true life.
  TERESA OF ÁVILA, *Spanish nun (1515–1582)* [COS, 48 PD]

A PRAYER FOR TODAY

If possible, go outside where you can observe nature.
Lord, I affirm that Your glory is evident in nature as I see . . .
Show me the ways that I exchange Your glory for lesser glory. . . .
Show me where I choose my ways instead of Your ways. . . .
Show me again today that Your way is the best way. . . .
Do not give me over to the desires of my heart that are askew from Your will.
Do not let my heart become darkened.
Do not let my thinking become futile.
Now slowly pray aloud the following prayer:

- Almighty God, Father of our Lord Jesus Christ,
  I commit all my ways unto you.
  I pledge my life to your service.
  Speak to me of duty and faithfulness.
  Show me my noble task, and strengthen me to walk in it. . . .
  My God, I give myself to you as a gift of love.
  I place my life in your hands to do with as you will.
  Only use me, my Lord, that my life be not wasted. Amen.
  RUEBEN JOB AND NORMAN SHAWCHUCK, *American authors (twentieth century)* [AGP, 72]

PRAYERS *of* INTERCESSION

🌿 I will not seek my own good, but rather I will seek the good of others.
1 CORINTHIANS 10:24

🌿 Far be it from me that I should sin against You, Lord, by failing to pray for those in my life. And I will teach them the ways that are right and good.
1 SAMUEL 12:23

A PRAYER FOR TODAY

Lord, I admit my prayers are often self-centered lists of things I think I need and want.

But today, I want to intercede for others. I pray for *(insert name and repeat process)*:

🌿 **Body** (physical). Pray that God will meet their needs "according to his glorious riches in Christ Jesus" (Philippians 4:19). Pray that the Father who sends "every good and perfect gift . . . from above" (James 1:17) will meet their needs.

Labor (work). Pray that they may live quiet lives, mind their own business, and work with their hands so that they may win the respect of others and not be dependent on anyone (1 Thessalonians 4:11–12). Pray that they may keep their lives "free from the love of money and be content with what they have" (Hebrews 13:5). Pray for diligence in work.

Emotional (inner life). Pray for those who are depressed, that they may have peace of heart and mind and may put their hope in God (Psalm 42:5). Pray that they may have "the unfading beauty of a gentle and quiet spirit, which is of great worth in God's sight" (1 Peter 3:4). Pray that they may have the Holy Spirit and his fruit . . . (Galatians 5:22–23).

Social (relational). Pray that they may have good friends who will stick by them at all times and family members who will stand by them in adversity. Pray that they will "bear with each other and forgive whatever grievances [they] may have against one another" (Colossians 3:13).

Spiritual. Pray that the kindness of God will lead them to repentance (Romans 2:4). Pray that they may confess Jesus as Lord, believe God raised him from the dead and be saved (Romans 10:9).
ALVIN VANDER GRIEND, *American minister/missionary (1946–present day)*
[*PCS, 25, 17, 13*]

PRAYERS *of* SURRENDER

God, I wouldn't think of robbing You. Yet You have said that is possible. How? By withholding my tithes *(10 percent of my income)* and offerings *(giving beyond the original 10 percent).* When we do that, we are robbing You. You have commanded me to bring the whole tithe into the storehouse, that there may be enough for Your work. You have challenged me to test You in this, and see if You will not throw open the floodgates of heaven and pour out so much blessing that I will not have room enough for it.
MALACHI 3:8–10

Lord, tithes are required as a matter of debt, and he who has been unwilling to give them has been guilty of robbery. Whosoever, therefore, desires a secure reward for himself, let him render tithes, and out of the nine parts let him seek to give alms.
AUGUSTINE, *bishop of Hippo (354–430)* [PD]

Lord, I know that the tithe can become an idol to set upon a pedestal to admire. It is often a dangerously tempting resting place rather than a minimal starting place. Much of the Christian community thinks of tithing as a high and lofty perch that only a few fanatical radicals have reached after years of struggle, rather than seeing it at the bottom or beginning place.
DON MCLANEN, *American author (unknown era)* [MPE, 187]

A PRAYER FOR TODAY

God, You are a generous God who wants to open the floodgates to me.
Yet I am often stingy with the resources entrusted to me. I surrender money and giving to You.
I commit today to tithe (give 10 percent of my income) to the local church.
I renounce my excuse of calling tithing legalism, or debating the biblical call. . . .
I renounce my excuse of waiting until I'm in a financially more stable place and can afford it. . . .
I renounce my excuse of saying "I'll work toward it". . . .
I renounce my excuse of saying it is unclear rather than acting in faith. . . .
I renounce giving to causes where I am recognized rather than giving money to my local church. . . .
I renounce my tithing or giving to clear my conscience so I can do what I want with the other 90 percent. . . .
I know that if all Christians practiced tithing, the task of world evangelism and feeding the hungry would be possible in our lifetimes. . . .
I will seek to not only tithe, but to give above and beyond to worthy causes. . . .
Amen.

PRAYERS *of* THANKSGIVING

🍂 Lord, I have set You always before me.
Because I have set You at my right hand, *(connotes idea of choice)*
I will not be shaken. (Heb.=*mot: to fall, totter, or stagger; used in Ps. 13:4; 15:5; 17:5*)
Therefore my heart is glad,
   and my tongue rejoices;
   my body also will rest in hope,
because You will not abandon me in my death,
nor will You allow those who are faithful to You to experience decay.
You will make known to me the path of life;
in Your presence is fullness of joy;
in Your right hand are pleasures forever. **PSALM 16:8–11**

🍂 God our creator, our centre, our friend, we thank you for our good life,
for those who are dear to us, . . . and for all who have helped and influenced
us.
We thank you for the measure of freedom we have,
And the extent to which we control our lives;
And most of all we thank you for the faith that is in us,
for our awareness of you and our hope in you.
Keep us, we pray you, thankful and hopeful and useful until our lives shall
end.
    NEW ZEALAND PRAYER BOOK [*CBP, 31* PD]

🍂 I thank you O God, for the pleasures you have given me through my senses;
   for the glory of thunder, for the mystery of music,
    the singing of the birds and the laughter of children.
I thank you for the delights of *color,*
   the awe of the sunset,
   the wild roses in the hedgerows, . . .
I thank you for the sweetness of flowers and the scent of hay.
Truly, O Lord, the earth is full of your riches!
    EDWARD KING, *English bishop (1829–1910)* [*BTP, 87* PD]

A PRAYER FOR TODAY

Lord, I thank You today for who You are. . . .
I thank You for the grandeur of creation. . . .
I thank You for the simple pleasures of this life. . . .
I thank You for what You have done for me. . . .
I thank You for what You have given to me. . . .
I thank You for what You have promised to me. . . .

PRAYERS *of* CONFESSION

O Lord, do not rebuke me in Your anger
    or discipline me in Your wrath.
Be gracious to me, Lord, for I am weary;
O Lord, heal me, for my bones ache.
My soul is in terror.
How long will it be this way? How long?
Turn, O Lord, and rescue me;
Save me because of Your unfailing love. . . .
You have heard my cry for mercy,
You accept my prayer.   PSALM 6:1–4, 9

Lord Jesus,
My soul and body are defiled by so many sinful deeds.
My tongue and my heart have run wild without restraint,
    causing misery to others and shame to myself.
My soul bleeds with the wounds of wrongdoing, and my body is *a
    playground of selfish indulgence.*
If I was to come before you as a judge, you could only condemn me to
    eternal torment, for that is what I deserve.
Yet I come before you, not as a judge, but as a saviour.
I depend not on your justice, but on your mercy.
As you look upon the wretched creature that I am,
I ask that your eyes be filled with compassion and forgiveness.
And as I sit at your table, I beg you to renew within me a spirit of holiness.
    AMBROSE, *governor of Milan (339–397)* [BOP, 26 PD]

A PRAYER FOR TODAY

Lord, I have felt Your rebuke and discipline in this . . .
I ask You to rebuke me and discipline me without anger.
I have been weary in this . . .
I have felt terror in this way . . .
Today I appeal to Your mercy—
    not giving me what my sins deserve. . . .
Today I appeal to Your grace—
    granting me what I do not deserve and what I have not earned. . . .
Today I appeal to Your unfailing love—
    showering me with Your affection. . . .
Today I appeal to Your glory—
    deliver me that I may proclaim Your greatness.

PRAYERS *of* AFFIRMATION

I know that You can do all things and that no purpose of Yours can be thwarted.   JOB 42:2

Jesus, You have given me eternal life, and I will never perish;
    no one can snatch me out of Your hand.
My Father, who has given me to You, is greater than all
    and no one can snatch me out of His hand.   JOHN 10:28–29

Lord, through weariness and hurt,
through disaster on the news,
through headaches and depression,
I am still yours.
I do not understand,
but I believe that you are here in the dark places of human life,
and that nothing can take us out of your hands.
    ANGELA ASHWIN, *American author (twentieth century) [BTP, 96]*

I know that when the stress has grown too strong, you will be there.
I know that when the waiting seems so long, you hear my prayer.
I know that through the crash of falling worlds, you're holding me.
I know that life and death are yours eternally.
    JANET STUART, *English author (1857–1914) [BTP, 101]*

A PRAYER FOR TODAY

Take something small and hold it in your hand. Consider how you can control what is in your hand. . . .
Ponder the affirmation—that no one can snatch you out of Jesus' hand. . . .
Lord, here is where my life does not feel like it is in Your hand . . .
Sometimes I fear national and international events. . . .
Sometimes I fear personal disaster. . . .
Sometimes I experience darkness and dread. . . .
Remind me that none of this is outside Your control.
Let me live in the reality that I am safely in Your hand
and that You control my life as easily as I control what I now hold in my hand.
I know that You are good, so anything that passes by Your hand into my life is
for my ultimate good, even if right now I can't understand how. Amen.

PRAYERS *of* PETITION

In the same way, the Spirit helps us in our weakness.
We do not know what we ought to pray for,
but the Spirit Himself speaks to You for us through wordless groans.
And You who knows our hearts knows the mind of the Spirit,
because the Spirit intercedes for us in accordance with Your will.
      ROMANS 8:26–27

Give us, O God, what is good,
    whether we pray for it or not;
and avert us from the evil,
    even if we pray for it.
      ANONYMOUS *[US]*

May all Your people love You, O Lord!
You preserve the faithful and fully repay the proud.
We will be of good courage, for You will strengthen the hearts of those who
hope in You.   PSALM 31:23–24

Dear Father, I don't want to treat you like Santa Claus, but I do need to ask
things of you.
Give me, please, food to eat today.
I'm not asking for tomorrow, but I am asking for today. . . .
And in my ignorance if I have asked for things that would really be
destructive,
    please, do not give them to me—do not lead me into temptation.
Do protect me from the evil one. . . . Amen.
      RICHARD FOSTER, *American author (1942–present day) [PHH, 190]*

A PRAYER FOR TODAY

God, You are the God who provides.
Often, I don't even know how to pray—I thank You for the Spirit's intercession
    in these times.
Right now, this is what I don't know how to pray about . . .
Please have the Holy Spirit intercede for me right now. . . .
Please grant me the best things even when I don't ask for them. . . .
Please avert things that are destructive even if I ask for them and plead for them
    in my ignorance. . . .
Please provide for my necessities, and help me to differentiate between my
    needs and wants. . . .
Please strengthen my resolve when I don't understand what is happening.
Please place hope in You deep within my heart.
I am only asking for the grace and provision for today. Amen.

PRAYERS *for* RENEWAL

O God, You give strength to the weary
and increase the power of the weak.
Even though young people grow tired and weary, and stumble and fall;
those of us who wait for You, O Lord, will renew our strength.
We will mount up with wings like eagles;
we will run and not grow weary;
we will walk and not be faint.   ISAIAH 40:29–31

O God, quicken to life every power within me, that I may lay hold of eternal
things.
Open my eyes that I may see; give me acute spiritual perception;
Enable me to taste Thee and know that Thou art good.
Make heaven more real to me than *any* earthly thing has ever been. Amen.
A. W. TOZER, *American pastor (1897–1963) [POG, 56]*

Lord, let me not become weary in doing good,
for at the proper time I will reap a harvest if I do not give up.
GALATIANS 6:9

Lord, give us grace to hold to you
when all is weariness and fear
    and sin abounds within, without
    when love itself is *tested* by the doubt . . .
Lord, give us grace that we may know
    that in the darkness pressing round
    it is the mist of sin that hides your face, that you are there
    and you do know we love you still
    and our dependence and endurance in your will is our gift of love.
GILBERT SHAW, *American minister (1886–1967) [OBP, 124]*

You are never weary of doing us good. Let us never be weary of serving
you. But as you have pleasure in the prosperity of your servants, so let us
take pleasure in *our* service, and abound in your work, and in your love and
praise.
JOHN WESLEY, *English minister (1703–1791) [COS, 75 PD]*

A PRAYER FOR TODAY

Lord, where I feel weary renew my soul through . . .
Let me cling to You by . . .
Allow me to take pleasure in serving You. Amen.

PRAYERS *of* PRAISE/ADORATION

Father, a time is coming and is now here,
when true worship will be offered to You in spirit and in truth.
The worshipers that You seek are those that offer such worship.
God, You are spirit, therefore I will worship You in spirit and in truth.
JOHN 4:23–24

Lord God, let me join with the living creatures who day and night never
stop saying:
Holy, holy, holy, is the Lord God Almighty, who was, and is, and is to come.
Lord God, let me join with the living creatures and worship You who lives
forever and ever . . . saying:
You are worthy, our Lord and God, to receive glory and honor and power,
for You created all things, and by Your will they were created
and have their being.   REVELATION 4:8–9, 11

Eternal God, my sovereign Lord,
I acknowledge all I am, all I have is yours.
Give me such a sense of your infinite goodness
that I may return to you all possible love and obedience.
JOHN WESLEY, *English minister (1703–1791)* [COS, 7 PD]

O Almighty God, who pourest out on all who desire it, the Spirit of grace;
deliver us, when we draw nigh to thee,
from coldness of heart
and wanderings of mind;
that with steadfast thoughts and kindled affections, we may worship thee
in spirit and in truth, through Jesus Christ, our Lord.
WILLIAM BRIGHT, *English historian (1824–1901)* [OBP, 122 PD]

A PRAYER FOR TODAY

I praise You that You are beyond explanation, and that You are worshiped in
Spirit.
Spirit brings passion.
I also praise You that You are knowable, and that You are worshiped in truth.
Truth brings direction.
You are worthy, God, of all . . . *(Insert words of honor here.)*
I join the host of heaven in proclaiming that You are holy.
I praise You for Your infinite goodness as seen in . . .
You are worthy of all my devotion and obedience.
I worship You. Amen.

PRAYERS *for* CHRISTLIKE CHARACTER

🌸 Above all, Lord, I will guard (Heb.=*nasar: to watch over something that will likely be attacked*) my heart, because from it everything I do flows like a spring. **PROVERBS 4:23**

🌸 Lord, I will guard (Gk.=*thulasso, imperative: to guard, to protect, to keep watch over—used in military sense*) the good deposit that was entrusted to me with the help of the Holy Spirit who lives in me. **2 TIMOTHY 1:14**

🌸 Guard for me my eyes, Jesus, . . . lest seeing another's wealth makes me covetous.
Guard for me my ears, lest they hearken to slander, lest they listen constantly to folly in the sinful world.
Guard for me my heart, O Christ, in thy love, lest I ponder wretchedly the desire of any iniquity.
Guard for me my hands, that they be not stretched out for quarrelling, that they may not, after that, practice shameful supplication.
Guard for me my feet upon the gentle earth . . . lest, bent on profitless errands, they abandon rest.
TRADITIONAL IRISH PRAYER [*OBP, 125* PD]

🌸 We pray, O Lord, for deliverance from all that weakens faith in you:
from pompous solemnity;
from mistaking earnestness for trust in you;
from seeking easy answers to large questions;
from being overawed by the self-confident;
from dependence upon mood and feelings;
from despondency and the loss of self-respect;
from timidity and hesitation in making decisions. Amen.
WILLARD SPERRY, *seminary dean (1882–1954)* [*COS, 25*]

A PRAYER FOR TODAY

Lord, I don't often think about my heart being the object of an attack,
or the vigilance with which You command me to guard my heart.
Let me see today where my heart can be attacked. . . .
(Reread the prayers above seeing what strikes you as a place of vulnerability.)
Remind me that no measure of action I take is too severe to guard my heart . . .
because it is what produces the reality of the choices I make.
Show me how to protect my heart:
Grant me the vigilance of a military sentry. Amen.

Day 158
PRAYERS for WISDOM/GUIDANCE

🌿 Jesus, You are the way, and the truth, and the life. No one comes to God except through You.   JOHN 14:6

🌿 O Lord our God, you know who we are;
> people with good consciences and with bad,
> persons who are content and those who are discontent,
> the certain and the uncertain,
> Christians by conviction and Christians by convention,
> those who believe and those who half-believe, those who disbelieve.

And you know where we have come from:
> from the circle of relatives, acquaintances and friends,
> or from the greatest loneliness; from a life of quiet prosperity,
> or from manifold confusion and distress;
> from family relationships that are well-ordered or from those disordered . . .
> from the inner circle of the Christian community or from its outer edge.

But now we all stand before you,
> in all our differences,
> yet alike in that we are all in the wrong with you and with one another,
> that we must all one day die,
> that we would be lost without your grace,

but also in that your grace is promised and made available to us all in your dear Son, Jesus Christ.

KARL BARTH, *German theologian (1886–1968) [CBP, 248]*

🌿 Lord, You know me,
You see me and You test my thoughts about You.   JEREMIAH 12:3

A PRAYER FOR TODAY

Lord, here is who I am . . . Here is where I come from . . .
I now stand before You seeking Your way, . . .
Seeking Your truth, . . .
Seeking Your life, . . .
I look to You to guide my coming and going.
I give You the decisions I am facing, asking for Your wisdom and guidance. . . .
You see me and my thoughts even when I can't see myself.
If I am living in a past decision assuming that it is still right and You have a new direction for me, please reveal that to me now. . . .
If I am unaware of a decision that needs to be made, I ask You to reveal that to me now. . . . In Jesus' name, amen.

PRAYERS *of* INTERCESSION

- O Lord, nothing is too difficult for You.   **GENESIS 18:14**

- Wherever You went, Jesus, whether in villages, towns, or the countryside, the sick were brought to You. People begged You to let them touch even the edge of Your coat, and all who touched You were healed.   **MARK 6:56**

- Faith to be healed I surely have (and faith can all things do);
Thou are Omnipotent to save, and Thou art willing too.
   CHARLES WESLEY, *English minister (1707–1788)* [GSG, 315 PD]

- *Prayed for his sick and dying wife in 1727*
Almighty and most gracious Lord God, extend we beseech Thee, Thy pity and compassion toward this Thy languishing servant:
teach her to place her hope and confidence entirely in Thee;
give her a true sense of the emptiness and vanity of all earthly things;
make her truly sensible of all the infirmities of her life past,
and grant her such a true sincere repentance as is not to be repented of.
Preserve her, O Lord, in sound mind and understanding during this Thy visitation;
keep her from both the sad extremes of presumption and despair.
If Thou shalt please to restore her to her former health, give her grace to be ever mindful of that mercy,
and to keep those good resolutions she now makes in her sickness,
so that no length of time nor prosperity may entice her to forget them.
Let no thought of misfortunes distract her mind. . . .
   JONATHAN SWIFT, *Irish satirist (1667–1745)* [EOP, 221 PD]

A PRAYER FOR TODAY

Father God, when it comes to healing, I'm not always certain how to pray.
Some people seem to discount the possibility that You can and do heal today
—I don't want to miss the miraculous due to doubt.
Some people seem to presume upon and even demand that You heal according to their faith—
I don't want to presume upon You and Your ways.
I acknowledge that You are good and that You love Your people.
Help me to neither presume upon You nor to be timid about this issue.
I bring these health concerns of mine or someone I love to You . . .
I trust You to bring physical healing if this is Your highest good in this situation.
I trust You to bring good out of this situation. Amen.

PRAYERS *of* SURRENDER

Lord my God, You have commanded me to love You
with all my heart and with all my soul and with all my mind.
This is the first and greatest commandment You have given.
The second is like it: To love my neighbor as myself.
All of the law and the prophets hang on these two commandments.
   MATTHEW 22:37–40

Lord, I am yours and I must belong to no one but you.
My soul is yours, and must live only through you.
My will is yours, and must love only for you.
I must love you as my first cause, since I am from you.
I must love you as my goal and rest, since I am for you.
I must love you more than my own being, since my being comes from you.
I must love you more than myself, since I am all yours and all in you. Amen.
   FRANCIS DE SALES, *French minister/author (1567–1622)* [*EOP, 30* PD]

I give you my hands to do your work.
I give you my feet to go your way.
I give you my eyes to see as you do.
I give you my tongue to speak your words.
I give you my mind that you may think in me.
I give you my spirit that you may pray in me.
Above all,
I give you my heart that you may love in me, your Father and all *humanity*.
I give you my whole self that you may grow in me, so that it is you, Lord
Jesus, Who live and work . . . in me.
   "THE GRAIL," *unknown author* [*CPB, 150*]

A PRAYER FOR TODAY

Lord, at times I love myself and my agenda more than You and Your agenda.
Although this is natural, it is not how I want to live.
I want to love You with all that I am above all else and I want to love others well.
Show me the things that obstruct my love for You and others. . . .
Show me the things that spark my love for You and others. . . .
Help me to direct more of myself to what sparks my love for You than what
obstructs it. . . . Amen.

PRAYERS *of* THANKSGIVING

🌵 Every good and perfect gift comes from above, coming down from You, the
Father of heavenly lights.
You do not change like the shifting shadows.   **JAMES 1:17**

🌵 Lord, I can receive only what You give to me from heaven.   **JOHN 3:27**

🌵 O God our Father, we would thank thee for all the bright things of life.
Help us to see them, and to count them, and to remember them,
that our lives may flow in ceaseless praise;
for the sake of Jesus Christ our Lord.
> **J. H. JOWETT**, *English minister (1846–1923) [CBP, 34]*

🌵 Father, at times I focus on what others have been given and wish I had their
gifts.
Help me today to appreciate and enjoy the gifts You have graciously given
to me,
> gifts that were perfectly selected for me,
> gifts that have made my life richer.
Remind me that these gifts are but a taste of what is ahead.
> **KURT BJORKLUND**, *American minister (1968–present day)*

🌵 O Lord, that lends me life,
Lend me a heart replete with thankfulness.
> **WILLIAM SHAKESPEARE**, *English author (1564–1616)* [CBP, 213 PD]

Father, today I want to thank You for all the good gifts You have given me:
> Gifts of heritage . . . gifts of family . . .
> Gifts of health . . . gifts of home . . .
> Gifts of community . . . gifts of friendship . . . gifts of laughter . . .
> Gifts of education . . . gifts of vocation . . .
> Gifts of affection . . . gifts of encouragement . . . gifts of opportunity . . .
> Gifts of provision . . . gifts of abundance . . .
> Gifts of mentors . . .
> Gifts of travel . . . gifts of recreation . . . gifts of unique experiences . . .
> Gifts of kindnesses received . . .
> Gifts of ambition . . .
> Gifts of contribution (where I have been able to contribute to the good of
> the world) . . .

PRAYERS *of* CONFESSION

O Lord, remember not the sins of my youth and my rebellious ways;
   according to Your love remember me, for You are good.
Lord, You are good and upright; therefore You instruct sinners in Your ways.
You guide the humble in what is right and teach them Your ways.
All Your ways are loving and faithful for those who keep the demands of
   Your covenant.
For the sake of Your name, O Lord, forgive my iniquity, though it is great.
   PSALM 25:7–11

Forgive me my sins, O Lord;
   forgive me the sins of my youth and the sins of my age,
   the sins of my soul and the sins of my body,
   my secret and my whispering sins,
   my presumptuous and my crying sins,
   the sins that I have done to please myself,
   and the sins I have done to please others.
Forgive me the sins which I know,
   and those sins which I know not;
forgive them, O Lord, forgive them all *because* of thy great goodness.
   LANCELOT ANDREWES, *English minister/translator of* KJV *(1555–1626)*
   [*CBP, 244* PD]

A PRAYER FOR TODAY

Lord, today I confess and turn from:
My insensitivity to those in need . . .
My prejudgments of people . . .
My fear of embracing Your vision for my life . . .
My resentments toward those who have hurt me . . .
My desire to name the terms under which I will follow You . . .
My impatience toward those that believe and act in different ways than me . . .
My unwillingness to humbly listen . . .
My willful choices to do things my own way . . .
My attempts to hide my foolish and sinful thoughts and actions . . .
My efforts to please myself at the expense of what is good and true . . .
My efforts to please others at the expense of what is good and true . . .
I acknowledge that Your ways are good and true, and that it is best to submit to You.
Instruct me in Your ways. Amen.

PRAYERS *of* AFFIRMATION

God, You have breathed all Scripture and it is useful for teaching, rebuking, correcting, and training in righteousness, so that all Your people may be thoroughly equipped for every good work.   **2 TIMOTHY 3:16–17**

God, the authority of Scripture is a key issue for the Christian church in this and every age. Those who profess faith in Jesus Christ as Lord and Savior are called to show the reality of their discipleship by humbly and faithfully obeying *Your* written word. To stray from Scripture in faith or conduct is disloyalty to *You*, our Master. Recognition of the total truth and trustworthiness of Holy Scriptures is essential to a full grasp and adequate confession of its authority.
> **THE CHICAGO STATEMENT** on Biblical Inerrancy of 1978 [PD]

For all who in every generation have taught and explained and expounded and preached the word of Scripture: We thank you, O God.
Grant, O God, that no false teaching may ever have any power to deceive us or to seduce us from the truth.
Grant, O God, that we may never listen to any teaching which would encourage us to think sin less serious, vice more attractive, or virtue less important;
Grant, O God, that we may never listen to any teaching which would dethrone Jesus Christ from the utmost place;
Grant, O God, that we may never listen to any teaching which for its own purposes perverts the truth.
O God, our Father, establish us immovably in the truth.
So grant that all our lives we may know, and love, and live the truth; through Jesus Christ our Lord. Amen.
> **WILLIAM BARCLAY,** *Scottish Bible professor (1907–1978) [PCY, as quoted in GMO, 75]*

A PRAYER FOR TODAY

I affirm that the Scriptures are fully Your Word, containing all I need for salvation and life.
I affirm that to disbelieve or disobey any word of the Bible is to disbelieve or disobey You. . . .
I choose today to surrender to all revelation contained in Your Word.
Amen.

PRAYERS *of* PETITION

You are the Lord Almighty. (Heb.=*El Shaddai*: *eternal and all-powerful God*)
I will seek to walk before You and be blameless. **GENESIS 17:1**

God, You are a mighty fortress, a bulwark never failing.
Our helper *You* amid the flood of mortal ills prevailing;
For still our ancient foe doth seek to work us woe—
His craft and power are great, and armed with cruel hate, on earth is not His equal. . . .
The Spirit and the gifts are ours through *You* who with us sideth.
Let goods and kindred go, this mortal life also, the body they may kill;
Your truth abideth still: *Your* kingdom is forever.
    "A MIGHTY FORTRESS IS OUR GOD," MARTIN LUTHER, *German theologian (1483–1546)* [PD]

Infinite God, our base problem is unbelief. Failing to trust in You, we live anxiously, restlessly, always trying to secure and extend ourselves with finite goods that can't take the weight we put on them. We climb social ladders, buy securities, try to make a name for ourselves or leave a legacy. We put others in our debt. We strive for raw power or for intellectual transcendence or for moral superiority. Alternatively, we try to escape all these strivings, calming our restlessness with flights into lust or drunkenness or gluttony. Unbelief yields anxiety, which yields alternating pride and sensuality.
    REINHOLD NIEBUHR, *American minister (1892–1971)* [NTW, 61]

Grant, O God, that amidst all the discouragements, difficulties, and dangers, distress and darkness of this mortal life,
I may depend upon thy mercy, and on this build my hopes, as on a sure foundation.
Let thine infinite mercy in Christ Jesus deliver me from despair,
both now and at the hour of death.
    THOMAS WILSON, *Anglican theologian (1663–1755)* [PD]

A PRAYER FOR TODAY

God, You are the eternal and all-powerful God.
Here is where I am struggling . . .
Here is where I am anxious . . .
Here is where I am indulgent . . .
I need Your help today in this way . . .
Help me to trust You entirely.
You are my Lord, Almighty. Amen.

PRAYERS *for* RENEWAL

Jesus, You declared that anyone who is thirsty can come to You and drink. You and the Scriptures have said that whoever believes in You will experience rivers of water flowing from within them.   JOHN 7:37–38

My spirit has become dry because it forgets to feed on you.
JOHN OF THE CROSS *(1541–1591)* [*OBP, 139* PD]

We have forgotten (Heb.=*sakah: forget, ignore, wither, to disregard*)
You, our Maker,
while we have tried to build our own good lives.   **HOSEA 8:14**

Ah, Lord, my prayers are dead,
    my affections dead,
    and my heart is dead:
but thou art a living God and I bear myself upon thee.
WILLIAM BRIDGE, *English minister (1600–1670)* [*CBP, 250* PD]

I will love Thee, O Lord, my strength.   **PSALM 18:1**

A PRAYER FOR TODAY

Lord, I come to You thirsty.
Sometimes I am unaware of my need for You. . . .
Here is where I am dry . . .
Sometimes my prayers, my affections, or my heart is dead toward . . .
This deadness and dryness is because I have not come to You as my source of life.
It is because I have forgotten You by . . .
It is because I have ignored You by . . .
It is because I have disregarded You by . . .
But I come to You today asking You to renew me by . . .
You are the living God, who has promised rivers of living water.
I come to You now for renewal.
Please draw me to Yourself once again.
May I find my deepest satisfaction in You.
May I be empowered for Your service, emboldened by Your joy, and carried along by Your favor.

PRAYERS *of* PRAISE/ADORATION

Blessed be Your name, O God, for ever and ever, for wisdom and power
belong to You.
You change the times and the seasons;
You raise up kings and depose them.
You give wisdom to the wise and knowledge to those who have under-
standing.
You reveal deep and hidden things;
You know what is in the darkness, and light dwells with You.
   DANIEL 2:20–22

You are an omnipotent God!
You indeed do have power!
You can do anything!
Nothing is too hard for You!
There is no sickness that You cannot heal.
There is no problem that You cannot solve.
There is no challenge that You cannot meet. . . .
There is no committee that can thwart Your work in the church of Jesus
Christ.
You are the all-powerful, magnificent, amazing, beyond comprehension,
God!
Lord, You are more than anything that I could say about You.
There are no words to describe *Your* greatness and glory and majesty.
   DAVID JEREMIAH, *American pastor (1946–present day) [PGA, 80]*

In darkness and in light, in trouble and joy,
help us, heavenly Father,
     to trust your love,
     to serve your purpose
     and to praise your name
through Jesus Christ our Lord.
   THE DAILY OFFICE [*cited in BTP, 123* PD]

A PRAYER FOR TODAY

Lord, You are more powerful than:
The leaders of the world's most powerful militaries and nations . . .
The financial markets and the economy . . . The ecosystem and nature . . .
The illnesses that strike the body . . .
The individuals with weapons, whether of mass destruction or concealed in
their coats . . .
The challenges and problems I am facing today . . . *or* tomorrow.
Therefore, I can trust Your love, serve Your purposes, and praise Your name.
Amen.

PRAYERS *for* CHRISTLIKE CHARACTER

You have shown me what is good, O Lord, and what You require of me:
To act justly (Heb.=*mispat: justice, laws, judgment, right, regulation*)
and to love mercy (Heb.=*hesed: unfailing loyal love, devotion, kindness*)
and to walk humbly (Heb.=*sana: unassuming, deferential, not prideful*)
with You, My God.   MICAH 6:8

Dear Lord, help us to direct all our living—what we think, say and do—
so that your name will never be blasphemed because of us,
but always honored and praised. . . . Amen.
HEIDELBERG CATECHISM, Answer 122 [*BDD, 65* PD]

God, stay with me, let no word cross my lips that is not your word,
no thoughts enter my mind that are not your thoughts,
no deed ever be done or entertained by me that is not your deed.
MALCOLM MUGGERIDGE, *English journalist (1903–1990)* [*CBP, 210* PD]

Grant us, O Lord, to know that which is worth knowing,
to love that which is worth loving,
to praise that which can bear with praise,
to hate what in thy sight is unworthy,
to prize what to thee is precious,
and, above all, to search out and to do what is well-pleasing unto thee;
through Jesus Christ our Lord.
THOMAS Á KEMPIS, *German theologian (1380–1471)* [*CBP, 212* PD]

You have given me a new heart and put a new spirit within me;
You have removed from me my heart of stone and given me a heart of flesh.
EZEKIEL 36:26

A PRAYER FOR TODAY

Lord, You have given me new life so I am alive to You.
Lead me to search out what is well-pleasing to You by . . .
Lord, what would it mean for me to act justly? . . .
What would it mean for me to love mercy? . . .
What would it mean for me to walk humbly with You? . . .
Show me the old patterns I still embrace that bring reproach to Your name . . .
Show me the new patterns I can embrace that bring honor and praise to Your name . . .
Lord, I commit today to grasp the experiences that draw me to You. . . . Amen.

PRAYERS for WISDOM/GUIDANCE

Show me, O Lord, my life's end and the number of my days;
   let me know how fleeting is my life.
You have made my days a mere handbreadth;
   the span of years is as nothing before You.
Each person's life is but a breath. Selah *(pause to consider)*
People are a mere phantom as they go to and fro:
bustling about, but only in vain;
they heap up wealth, not knowing who will get it.
But, now Lord . . . my hope is in You.   PSALM 39:4–7

Almighty God, lead us in thine own way, and the end will be rest.
We know nothing of the way ourselves,
   except that it is often long and weary,
   and much trying to every failing power;
but thou knowest the road—all of it;
it is not one mile too long.
Lead thou us, and we shall be safe;
carry us when we are weary,
and give us rest according to thine own will and the measure of our need.
   JOSEPH PARKER, *English minister (1830–1904)* [BUP, 16 PD]

Lord, you put twenty-four hours in a day, and gave me a body which gets
tired and can only do so much. Show me which tasks you want me to do,
and help me to live prayerfully as I do them.
Sharpen my senses, that I may truly
   see what I am looking at,
   taste what I am eating,
   listen to what I am hearing, face what I am suffering,
   celebrate the ways I am loved, and offer to you whatever I am doing,
so that the water of the present moment may be turned into wine.
   ANGELA ASHWIN, *English author (twentieth century)* [BTP, 109]

A PRAYER FOR TODAY

Lord, I ask for the confidence to cease worrying and enjoy the journey. . . .
(Imagine what you will do today and see yourself enjoying it thoroughly.)
I ask for enjoyment to dispel the weariness I sometimes feel. . . .
(Imagine not being weary, but being full of life in your day's activities.)
Remind me that much of what I worry about will cease to matter. . . .
(Imagine your wealth and achievements and positions 100 years from now.)
Remind me that You are my hope! Amen.

PRAYERS *of* INTERCESSION

⚜ Lord Jesus, You have said that You will build Your church
and that the gates of death and Hades will not stand against it.
MATTHEW 16:18

⚜ Gracious Father, we pray for your Church.
Fill it with your truth, and keep it in your peace.
Where it is corrupt, purge it;
where it is in error, direct it;
where it is right, strengthen and confirm it;
where it needs help, provide for it;
where it is divided, heal it,
and unite it in your love, through Jesus Christ our Saviour.
WILLIAM LAUD, *English bishop (1573–1645)* [*BTP, 22* PD]

⚜ Infinite Lord and eternal God, rouse your church in this land,
restore your people's sense of mission, and revive your work . . . and
strength.
By your Spirit, teach us to give our energy, our time, our money, our service
and our prayer,
that your kingdom may be advanced here and in all the world;
In the name of Jesus Christ our Lord.
PRAYER FROM THE CHURCH IN WALES [*CBP, 434* PD]

A PRAYER FOR TODAY

*Pray for your church, and repeat the prayers for other churches in your area or that you
care about. . . .*
Father God, You have made the church Your instrument for good in this world.
Please work in *(name church)* in a powerful way by empowering:
the leaders with wisdom, conviction, and perseverance . . .
all of the people with unity around Your mission . . .
passionate worship centered on You, not around personalities . . .
powerful life-changing teaching and receptive hearers of the Word . . .
deep relationships that testify to the world what Christian community is . . .
people to put aside petty hurts and insults for the sake of Your kingdom . . .
the people to give generously and sacrificially to Your cause . . . and
the church to have a relevant voice to its culture. . . .
At the same time, cause the fervor for the lost and the least to never wane . . .
and cause love for the poor and resources to flow toward them . . .
all the while preserving doctrinal purity . . .
So that *(name church)* can be a prevailing church used for Your eternal purposes.
Amen.

PRAYERS *of* SURRENDER

O God, let us be
> steadfast, (Gk.=*hedraios: firm, settled, constant in character*)
> immovable, (Gk.=*ametakinetos: not capable of being moved from its place*)
> abounding (Gk.=*perisseuo: to be in abundance above what is expected*) in
the work of Jesus Christ, always aware that, in Him, our labor is not in vain.
> **1 CORINTHIANS 15:58**

Use me, then, my Saviour, for whatever purpose, and in whatever way, thou
may require.
Here is my poor heart, an empty vessel; fill it with thy grace.
Here is my sinful and troubled soul; quicken it and refresh it with thy love.
Take my heart for thine abode;
my mouth to spread abroad the glory of thy name;
my love and all my powers for the advancement of your believing people;
and never suffer the steadfastness and confidence of my faith to abate.
> **DWIGHT L. MOODY**, *American evangelist (1837–1899)* [*CBP, 52–53* PD]

But thanks be to You, God, who leads us in Christ's triumphal procession
and uses us to spread the fragrance of the knowledge of Him everywhere.
> **2 CORINTHIANS 2:14**

Prayed daily by Mother Teresa and the workers at her charity
Dear Jesus, help us to spread your fragrance everywhere we go.
Flood our souls with your spirit and life.
Penetrate and possess our whole being so utterly that our lives may only be
a radiance of yours.
Shine through us, and be so in us, that every soul we come in contact with
may feel your presence in our soul.
Let them look up and see no longer us but only Jesus! . . .
Let us preach you without preaching, not by words but by our example, by
the catching force, the sympathetic influence of what we do.
> **JOHN HENRY NEWMAN**, *English clergy (1801–1890); credited to Mother Teresa*
> [*CBP, 56* PD; *also in OBP/COS*]

A PRAYER FOR TODAY

Lord, You have placed me where You have a design to use me. . . .
I surrender all that I am and do to You. . . .
Help me to be steadfast, immovable, and abounding in Your work, convinced
that it is not in vain. Amen.

PRAYERS *of* THANKSGIVING

I will give thanks to You, Lord,
    for You are good and Your love endures forever. . . .
I will give thanks to You, Lord,
for Your unfailing love and Your wonderful deeds done for humanity.
I will offer my thanksgiving to You through sacrifice,
and I will tell of Your works in songs of joy.   **PSALM 107:1, 21–22**

Lord of all mercy and goodness, suffer us not by any ingratitude or hardness of heart to forget the wonderful benefits that thou hast bestowed upon us this and every day; but grant that we may be mindful all the days of our life of the incomparable gifts which thou ever givest us.
EARLY SCOTTISH PRAYER [*CBP, 212* PD]

Jesus, help me to have the thankful heart of the one who praised You for being healed, rather than the indifferent heart of the nine who were healed and didn't praise You.   **LUKE 17:17–18**

A PRAYER FOR TODAY

God, You have been good to me. I will offer You thanks because of:
    Your goodness and love (Psalms 36:5–8) to me . . .
    Your wonderful deeds (Psalm 107) to me and others . . .
    Your gift of Jesus Christ (2 Corinthians 9:15) . . .
    Your drawing of others to Yourself (Romans 6:17) . . .
    Your available power to combat indwelling sin now (Romans 7:23–25) . . .
    Your daily provisions (Philippians 4:19) for me . . .
    Your protecting hand (Psalm 56:12–13) seen and unseen . . .
    Your grace (1 Corinthians 1:4) to me . . .
    Your victory over sin and death (1 Corinthians 15:57) . . .
    Your provision of friends (Philippians 1:3–6) . . .
    Your spurring others on to love (2 Thessalonians 1:3) . . .
    Your power and reign (Revelation 11:17) . . .
    Your provision of everything (1 Thessalonians 5:18) . . .
God, You have been good to me. I will offer You thanks by:
    Singing to You (Psalm 28:7) . . .
    Giving financial offerings beyond the tithe (2 Corinthians 9:12–15) . . .
    Praying (1 Corinthians 1:4–9) . . .
    Worshiping in public (Psalm 35:18) . . .
    Worshiping in private (Daniel 6:10) . . .
    Speaking about Jesus to others (Luke 2:38) . . .
    Living a holy life (Romans 12:1) . . . Amen.

PRAYERS *of* CONFESSION

Lord, be merciful to me;
Heal my soul, for I have sinned against You. . . .
I know that You are pleased with me, for my enemy does not triumph over me.
In my integrity You uphold me and set me in Your presence forever.
    PSALM 41:4, 11–12

O God, we confess to you that we have seen ourselves as others see us;
we have seen ourselves as we would like to be.
Now, in your grace, change us into the likeness of Christ,
and then let us see ourselves as we really are.
    CORNELIUS PLANTINGA JR., *American seminary president (1946–present day)*
    [BDD, 103]

Almighty and most merciful Father,
    we have erred and strayed from thy ways like lost sheep,
    we have followed too much the devices and desires of our own hearts,
    we have offended against thy holy laws,
        we have left undone those things which we ought to have done,
    and we have done those things we ought not to have done.
But thou, O Lord, have mercy upon us,
spare thou those who confess their faults,
restore thou those who are penitent,
according to thy promises declared unto *humankind* in Christ Jesus our Lord.
    "CONFESSION," BOOK OF COMMON PRAYER *[BCP, 41–42 PD]*

We beseech thee, good Lord,
that it may please thee to give us true repentance;
to forgive us all our sins, negligences, and ignorances;
and to endue us with the grace of thy Holy Spirit,
to amend our lives according to thy holy word.
    THOMAS CRAMER, *English minister (1489–1556) [EOP, 52 PD]*

A PRAYER FOR TODAY

Take a few moments and ask God to reveal any areas of unconfessed sin. . . .
Lord, as You have brought to mind my sin, I ask for mercy. . . .
Grant me true repentance. . . .
Amend my life to be in accordance with Your Word. . . .
Allow me to feel Your pleasure in me despite my sinful choices, actions, and thoughts. . . .
I abandon all efforts at image management. . . . Amen.

PRAYERS *of* AFFIRMATION

- God, good standing with You does not depend on my desire or effort, but entirely on Your mercy. **ROMANS 9:16**

- Jesus Christ, *you are the* God whom we approach without pride, and before whom we humble ourselves without despair.
  BLAISE PASCAL, *French philosopher (1623–1662) [AGP, 267]*

- O God, Giver of Life, Bearer of Pain, Maker of Love,
  you are able to accept in us what we cannot even acknowledge:
  you are able to name in us what we cannot bear to speak of;
  you are able to hold in your memory what we have tried to forget;
  you are able to hold out to us the glory that we cannot conceive of.
  Reconcile us through your cross to all that we have rejected in ourselves,
  that we may find no part of your creation to be alien or strange to us, and
  that we ourselves may be made whole. Through Jesus Christ, our love and
  our friend.
  JANET MORELY, *(unknown era) [CBP, 165]*

- God, You presented Christ as a sacrifice of atonement, through the shedding of His blood—to be received by faith. You did this to demonstrate Your justice, because in Your forbearance You had left the sins committed before-hand unpunished. You did it to demonstrate Your justice at the present time, so as to be just and the one who justifies those who have faith in Jesus.
  Where, then, is boasting? It is excluded. (Note: *Greek for "sacrifice of atonement"=hilasterio: propitiation, to assuage wrath, so Christ takes the wrath others deserve*) **ROMANS 3:25–27**

A PRAYER FOR TODAY

God, You are a God of justice and mercy.
I know that justice in my case would demand punishment.
For I have violated Your precepts, Your ways, and Your heart by . . .
It is because of my sin that the cross was necessary.
I am such a sinner that I cannot garner Your favor through my efforts.
But Your mercy and grace sent Christ to the cross in my place.
He is the one who took the punishment I deserve.
So I no longer need to hide or deny my sinfulness . . .
Through faith it is covered by what Christ did on the cross.
So I can come to You without fear or despair.
So I affirm that giving an account to You is not dreadful because of Jesus.
And it is no occasion for pride, because of Jesus. Amen.

PRAYERS *of* PETITION

Lord God, . . . I will train myself to be godly.
For physical discipline has some value, but godliness is valuable for all
things, holding a promise both for this life and the life to come.
This is truth, and I accept it as such. That is why I will labor and strive,
because I have put my hope in You, the living God.
(Note: *Greek for "train"=gymnaz: to train in gymnastic discipline; to discipline
oneself for athletic purposes*)
(Note: *Greek for "labor"=kopiao: to work hard, even to the point of exhaustion*)
(Note: *Greek for "strive"=agonizomai: to agonize, to struggle, to exert oneself to the
maximum*)   1 TIMOTHY 4:7–10

Father lead me and help me:
To try to learn to be thoroughly poor in spirit, meek and ready to be silent
when others speak.
To learn from everyone.
To try to feel my own insignificance.
To believe *Your enablement to work through me,* and the powers with which I
am entrusted.
To try to make conversation more useful and therefore to store my mind
with facts, yet to be on guard against a wish to shine.
To try to despise the principle of the day, "every man his own trumpeter";
and to feel it a degradation to speak of my own doings, as a poor braggart. . . .
To speak less of self, and think less *of self.* . . .
To try to fix attention on Christ, rather than on the doctrines of Christ. . . .
To fix my thoughts on prayer, without distraction. . . .
To contend, one by one, against evil thoughts.
To watch over a growing habit of uncharitable judgments.
FREDRICK W. ROBERTSON, *English theologian (1816–1853) [GMO, 382]*

A PRAYER FOR TODAY

*There is a tension between trying to be godly and training to be godly. It is nearly impos-
sible to simply will ourselves to more godly behaviors and attitudes. But spiritual training
enables us to do what we cannot do now through direct effort. However, 1 Timothy 4
shows that our training is to be characterized by great effort.*
Lord, in what areas do You want me to train for godliness? . . . *(Select an area from
Robertson.)* How do You want me to train? . . .
How do You want me to labor and strive toward this end? . . .
Help me to do this by relying upon Your Spirit. Amen.

PRAYERS *for* RENEWAL

God, when I consider our present sufferings, I see that they are not worth comparing with the glory that will be revealed in us. The creation waits excitedly for Your children to be revealed.

We know that the whole creation has been groaning like a lady giving birth right up to the present time. Not only so, but we ourselves, who have the first part of Your promise in the Holy Spirit, groan inwardly as we wait eagerly for our adoption, the redemption of our bodies. For in this hope we were saved.

ROMANS 8:18-24

O Holy Spirit, Giver of light and life,
impart to us thoughts higher than our own thoughts,
and prayers better than our own prayers
and powers beyond our own powers
that we may spend and be spent in the ways of love and goodness,
after the perfect image of our Lord and Savior Jesus Christ.

ERIC MILNER-WHITE AND G. W. BRIGGS, *American authors (twentieth century) [OBP, 155]*

Come, my Light, and illumine my darkness.
Come, my Physician, and heal my wounds.
Come, Flame of divine love, and burn up the thorns of my sins,
kindling my heart with the flame of thy love.
Come, my King, sit upon the throne of my heart and reign there.
For thou alone art my King and my Lord.

DIMITRII OF ROSTOV, *monk (seventeenth century) [OBP, 4 PD]*

Thou knowest *my* inward and outward state. Whatever it be that holds *me* back from self-surrender, unto Thee, grant that it may be taken out of the way, that there may be a free and open intercourse between *me* and Thee. Thou hast spoken the "everlasting *affirmation*" that puts to flight our every care. Grant *me* the victory over every besetting doubt; and patience while any darkness remains, that *I* may glorify Thee, through Jesus Christ our Lord.

SAMUEL MCCOMB, *Irish minister (1864–1938) [MOP, 95]*

A PRAYER FOR TODAY

Lord, remind me in periods of doubt and darkness that You will yet reveal Your glory.
Help me to never doubt in the dark what You have shown me in the light.
Open my eyes to see You as You are. . . .
Take from me the dread of evils and besetting doubts. . . . Amen.

PRAYERS *of* PRAISE/ADORATION

❦ Now to You the King eternal, immortal, invisible, the only wise God, be honor and glory for ever and ever. Amen.   1 TIMOTHY 1:17

❦ O God, our help in ages past,
our hope for years to come,
still be our guard while troubles last,
and our eternal home. Amen.

> "O GOD, OUR HELP IN AGES PAST," ISAAC WATTS, *English hymn writer (1674–1748)* [BDD, 207 PD]

❦ Lord, You are omniscient.
You know what will happen tomorrow and the day after that.
You see eternity and You know how all these things fit into Your plan!
I can only see today and only feel the pain of this moment.
I have no concept of eternity except to know You are eternal.
Lord, You know what You are doing with me—I do not!
I must trust Your judgment and Your all-knowing wisdom to show me what to do every moment of each day.
If I thought You did not know as I do not know, I would really have reason for fear and despair.

> DAVID JEREMIAH, *American pastor (1941–present day)* [PGA, 181]

❦ Immortal, invisible, God only wise, in light inaccessible hid from our eyes;
most blessed, most glorious, the Ancient of Days; Almighty, victorious, Thy great name we praise.
To all life Thou givest, to both great and small; in all life Thou livest, the true life of all;
we blossom and flourish as leaves on the tree, and wither and perish, but naught changeth Thee.
Great Father of glory, pure Father of light; Thine angels adore Thee, all veiling their sight;
all praise we would render, O help us to see, 'tis only the splendor of light hideth Thee.

> "IMMORTAL, INVISIBLE," WALTER CHALMERS SMITH, *Scottish hymn writer (1824–1908)* [PSH, 55]

A PRAYER FOR TODAY

What does it mean to you that God is eternal, and beyond time?...
What does it mean to you that God is omniscient or all wise?...
Lord, I offer my praise to You today because You are eternal.
I offer my praise to You today because You are wise.

PRAYERS *for* CHRISTLIKE CHARACTER

God, I will not let anyone look down on me because I am young,
but I will set an example for all believers
in my words, in my conduct, in my love,
in my faith, and in my purity. . . .
I will not neglect the gift that is within me. . . .
I will be diligent in these things and give myself wholly to them. . . .
I will watch my life and my doctrine closely.
I will persevere in them. . . .   1 TIMOTHY 4:12, 14–16

Make me, O my God,
humble without pretence,
cheerful without levity,
serious without dejection,
grave without moroseness,
active without frivolity,
truthful without duplicity,
fearful of thee without despair,
trustful of thee without presumption,
chaste without depravity,
able to correct my neighbor without angry feeling,
and by word and example to edify him without pride,
obedient without gainsaying, *and* patient without murmuring.
THOMAS AQUINAS, *Italian theologian (1225–1274)* [*EOP, 72* PD]

A PRAYER FOR TODAY

Lord, I want my character to reflect You.
I realize that I will either be an example or an excuse.
I want to be an example
In my words by . . .
Where am I prone to tear down rather than build up? (Ephesians 4:29) . . .
In my conduct by . . .
Where does my life not reflect You? (Philippians 2:1–4) . . .
In my love by . . .
Where could I grow in my love for You and others? (1 Corinthians 13:4–7) . . .
Where am I at risk of not living in purity? (1 Thessalonians 4:3–8) . . .
In my attitudes by . . .
Choose expressions from Aquinas's prayer to pray. . . . Amen.

God, You give generously without finding fault.
You have said that if we seek wisdom, (Gk.=*sophia: wisdom, ability to act in accordance with understanding*)
asking in faith (Gk.=*pistis: here not constancy in faith but confidence God will heed request or deny it in His superior wisdom*)
without doubting (Gk.=*diakrino: to be divided, internal conflict, to waver*)
that You will give it.
For the one who doubts is like the waves of the sea that are driven anywhere by the wind.   JAMES 1:5–6

Heavenly Father, in you we live and move and have our being:
We humbly pray you so to guide and govern us by your Holy Spirit,
That in all the cares and occupations of our life we may not forget you,
But may remember that we are ever walking in your sight;
Through Jesus Christ our Lord. Amen.
"A COLLECT FOR GUIDANCE" [*BCP, 100* PD]

Give me, O God, . . . a strong and vivid sense that Thou are by my side.
In multitude and solitude,
> in business and leisure,
> in my downsitting and in my uprising
> may I ever be aware of Thine accompanying presence. . . .
By Thy grace I will let no thought enter my heart that might hinder my communion with Thee. . . .
JOHN BAILLIE, *Scottish theologian (1886–1960) [DPP, 69]*

A PRAYER FOR TODAY

Father, I seek Your wisdom now concerning . . .
I seek Your wisdom by asking the following questions:
- Is the decision I'm considering in line with what the Bible teaches? (2 Timothy 3:16–17)
- Does the decision I'm considering reflect the character and priorities of Christ? (1 Corinthians 10:27–33)
- Am I moving through open doors or pushing doors open? (Acts 16:6–10)
- What would spiritually astute counselors say? (Proverbs 13:10; 20:5)
- Do I have peace about this decision? (Philippians 4:7; James 1:5)

I forsake my own way of doing things—the ways I have doubted. . . .
You call such hedging being double-minded—I set my mind fully on You.

PRAYERS *of* INTERCESSION

Lord God, if Your people who are called by Your name
   will humble themselves
   and pray
   and seek Your face
   and turn from their wicked ways,
then You will hear from heaven and forgive their sin and heal their land.
   2 CHRONICLES 7:14

Almighty God, our heavenly Father, to forget *You* is to stumble and fall,
to remember *You* is to rise again: we pray thee to draw the people of this
country to thyself. Prosper all efforts to make known to them thy truth,
that many may learn their need of thee and thy love for them; so that thy
Church and kingdom may be established among us to the glory of thy
Name.
   RANDAL T. DAVIDSON, *English minister (1848–1930) [CBP, 168]*

O God, the Father of all humanity,
   we beseech thee so to inspire the people of this land
   with the spirit of justice, truth, and love,
   that in all our dealings one with another
   we may show forth our brotherhood in thee,
   for the sake of Jesus Christ our Lord.
   SOUTH AFRICAN BOOK OF COMMON PRAYER [PD]

A PRAYER FOR TODAY

You are the God of the nations, all of them.
I pray for my nation today, Lord, asking You to bring a fresh work of Your Spirit
to this land. I ask that it would start with Your people.
May we humble ourselves by . . .
May we pray for . . .
May we seek You by . . .
May we turn from our wicked ways. . . .
Then may the witness of Your people inspire all people of this land to long for
You and Your ways.
Free us from national pride. . . .
Free us from oppressing other nations. . . .
Free us from oppressing the poor within our own land. . . .
Please bring to justice now those who tyrannize others. . . .
Please bring to justice now those holding positions of power who practice
corruption. . . .
Please bring this about so that we are spared Your national judgment. Amen.

PRAYERS *of* SURRENDER

Then You, King, will say to those on Your right, "Come, you who are blessed of my Father; take for your inheritance the kingdom prepared for you since the creation of the world.

> For I was hungry and you gave me something to eat,
> I was thirsty and you gave me something to drink,
> I was a stranger and you invited me in,
> I needed clothes and you clothed me,
> I was sick and you looked after me,
> I was in prison and you came to visit me."

Then the righteous will answer him, "Lord, when did we . . . ?"
Then You, King, will reply, "Truly I tell you, whatever you did for one of the least of these brothers and sisters of mine, you did for me."

MATTHEW 25:34–37, 40

At the end of our lives, *Lord,* we will not be judged by
> How many diplomas we have received
> How much money we have made
> How many great things we have done.

We will be judged by
> "I was hungry and you gave me to eat
> I was naked and you clothed me
> I was homeless and you took me in."

MOTHER TERESA, *Albanian nun (1910–1997)* [AGP, 300]

O Lord, let me not henceforth desire health or life except to spend them for thee and with thee.
Thou alone knowest what is good for me; do therefore what seemeth best.
Give to me or take from me; conform my will to thine; and grant that, with humble and perfect submission, and in holy confidence,
I may receive the orders of thine eternal providence; and may equally adore all that comes from thee, through Jesus Christ our Lord.

BLAISE PASCAL, *French philosopher (1623–1662)* [PD]

A PRAYER FOR TODAY

Lord, I don't want to be like those who ignore the needs around them.
I want to be like those who respond to the needs of the least.
Help me to see where I may ignore the needs of people. . . .
Help me not to seek my own success while ignoring the needs of others. . . .
Amen.

PRAYERS *of* THANKSGIVING

It is good to give thanks to You, O Lord, and to sing praises to Your name,
O Most High,
to declare Your lovingkindness (Heb.=*hesed*: *unfailing love, kindness, devotion, loyal love*)
   in the morning
and Your faithfulness (Heb.=*emuna*: *steadiness, trustworthiness, reliability*) at
night.   PSALM 92:1–2

You have given so much to me,
Give one thing more, a grateful heart.
   GEORGE HERBERT, *English minister (1593–1633)* [*COS, 3* PD]

I will enter Your gates with thanksgiving and Your courts with praise.
I will give thanks to You and praise Your name.
For You, O Lord, are good, and Your love endures into all eternity.
Your faithfulness is throughout all generations.   PSALM 100:4–5

God, our Father,
   in a world where many are lonely, we thank you for friendship.
   In a world where many are despairing, we thank you for hope.
   In a world that many find meaninglessness, we thank you for faith.
   In a world where many are hungry, we thank you for this food.
   TRADITIONAL CANADIAN GRACE [*EOP, 258* PD]

A PRAYER FOR TODAY

Lord, I thank You for the great expressions of "loving-kindness" You have
shown to me. . . .
I thank You for the seemingly little things I often take for granted that are expressions of Your "faithfulness". . . .
*To give thanks—Psalm 92:1 connotes the idea of a public thanks or proclamation as a
way to praise God today—look for an opportunity to speak of God's love or faithfulness to
someone in your life. Consider it a moment of public praise.*

PRAYERS *of* CONFESSION

Who is a God like You, who pardons iniquity and forgives the transgressions of the remnant of Your inheritance?
You do not stay angry forever but delight to show mercy.
You will have compassion on Your people; You will tread their iniquities underfoot and hurl all their sins into the depths of the sea.   MICAH 7:18–19

Father eternal, giver of light and grace,
we have sinned against you and against our neighbour,
in what we have thought, in what we have said and done,
through ignorance, through weakness, through our own deliberate fault.
We have wounded your love, and marred your image in us.
We are sorry and ashamed, and repent of all our sins.
For the sake of your Son Jesus Christ, who died for us, forgive us all that is past;
and lead us out from darkness to walk as children of light.
1980 ALTERNATIVE SERVICE BOOK *[BTP, 141–42]*

Forgive me, Lord, my sins—the sins of my youth, the sins of the present;
the sins I laid upon myself in an ill pleasure,
the sins I cast upon others in an ill example;
the sins which are manifest to all the world,
the sins which I have *labored* to hide from mine acquaintance,
and labored to hide from mine own conscience, and even from my memory;
my crying sins and my whispering sins,
my ignorant sins and my willful sins;
sins against my superiors, equals, *subordinates*,
against my lovers and benefactors,
sins against myself, mine own body, mine own soul,
sins against thee,
O almighty Father, O merciful Son, O blessed Spirit of God.
Forgive me, O Lord, through the merits of thine anointed, my Saviour, Jesus Christ.
JOHN DONNE, *English poet (1572–1631)* [CBP, 251 PD]

A PRAYER FOR TODAY

Lord, I confess my willful sins to You. . . .
Reveal to me my sins of ignorance. . . . I confess these to You also. . . .

PRAYERS *of* AFFIRMATION

O Christ, You have appeared once for all at the end of the ages to do away with sin by sacrificing Yourself. And as it is appointed for people once to die and after that to face judgment, so You were offered once to bear the sins of many; and You will appear a second time, not to bear sin but to bring salvation to those who eagerly wait for You. HEBREWS 9:26–28

God, I affirm that . . . in each of us there is something growing, which will be Hell unless it is nipped in the bud. . . . There are only two kinds of people—those who say, "Thy will be done to You" or those to whom You in the end say, "Thy will be done." All that are in Hell choose it. Without that self-choice it wouldn't be Hell.
      C. S. LEWIS, *English professor (1898–1963) [quoted in RFG, 78–79]*

Some people think of hell as a place where sinners will be crying out for another chance, begging for the opportunity to repent, with *You,* God, somehow taking a tough guy stance and declaring, "Sorry. You had your chance. Too late." But the reality is infinitely more sobering. There is no evidence anywhere in the Bible that there is any repentance in hell. The biblical pictures suggest that evil and self-centeredness persist and persist—and so does the judgment. Men and women wantonly refuse to acknowledge *You* as God; they will not confess essential righteousness; they will not own *Your* just requirements; they will not give up their perpetual desire to be the center of the universe; they will not accept that they are guilty of rebellion; they will not accept forgiveness on the ground that *You* Yourself make provision for sinners in the sacrifice of *Your* own Son, *Jesus Christ.*
      D. A. CARSON, *Canadian professor (1946–present day) [HCG, n.p.]*

A PRAYER FOR TODAY

Lord, I affirm the reality of hell.
Although I do not understand exactly what it is, I know from Your Word that it
      is terrible.
This affirmation makes me see how seriously You take Your righteousness . . .
      and how hard the human heart becomes. . . .
Save me from internal hell. . . .
Save me from eternal hell. . . .
I affirm that when You appear again it will be to bring salvation to those who
      eagerly wait for You.
I long for that day. . . . Amen.

PRAYERS *of* PETITION

I will rejoice in You, Lord, always. Again I say it, I will rejoice.
I will allow my gentleness to be evident to all. For You are near.
I will not be anxious about anything, but rather in everything, with thanks-
giving, I will present my requests to You.
Then Your peace, God, the peace that transcends understanding,
will guard my heart and my mind in Jesus Christ. **PHILIPPIANS 4:4–7**

All I ask from you, provided I ask it with faith and confidence, that you
will give, that I shall obtain. That is, of course, I must not ask anything that
would be harmful, or something mean that, though it seems great in my
eyes, is really much less than what you wish to give me. You are a Father,
all powerful and infinitely wise and good and tender. You say to us as your
children, so frail we are and hardly able to walk except with our hand in
yours, "all that you ask I will give you if only you ask in confidence." And
you do give it, so willingly . . . when our petitions are . . . in accord with
your desires . . . and in conformity with all that you yourself desire.

If we ask you for dangerous playthings, you refuse them in goodness
for us, and you console us by giving us other things for our good. If we ask
you to put us where it would be dangerous for us to be, you do not give us
what is not for our good, but you give us something really for our welfare,
something that we would ask for ourselves if our eyes were open. You take
us by the hand and lead us, not here where we would wish to go, but there
where it is best for us to be.
    CHARLES DE FOUCAULD, *Algerian priest (1858–1916)* [GMO, 370–71]

Father, give to us, and to all your people,
In times of anxiety, serenity;
In times of hardship, courage;
In times of uncertainty, patience;
And at all times, a quiet trust in your wisdom and love;
through Jesus Christ our Lord.
    CHARLES SPURGEON, *British pastor (1834–1892)* [CBP, 189 PD]

A PRAYER FOR TODAY

Lord, here is what I have a tendency to be anxious about right now . . .
I will choose today to be thankful and to present my request to You for . . .
I thank You in advance for not granting me my harmful or selfish requests . . .
I will anticipate Your peace.
I will anticipate bearing much fruit.
I will seek to remain in You today by . . . Amen.

PRAYERS *for* RENEWAL

Father, I don't want to be lukewarm in my faith. . . .
I know that You stand at the door and knock.
If I hear Your voice and open the door, You will come in and have fellowship with me. **REVELATION 3:15, 20**

Deliver me, O God,
    from a slothful mind,
    from all lukewarmness,
    and all dejection of spirit.
I know these cannot but deaden my love to thee;
give me a lively, zealous, active, and cheerful spirit
that I may vigorously perform whatever thou commandest, and
thankfully suffer whatever thou choosest for me,
    JOHN WESLEY, *Anglican minister (1703–1791)* [CBP, 58 PD]

Lord Jesus, our Saviour, let us now come to thee:
Our hearts are cold; Lord, warm them with thy selfless love.
Our hearts are sinful; cleanse them with thy precious blood.
Our hearts are weak; strengthen them with thy joyous Spirit.
Our hearts are empty; fill them with thy divine presence.
Lord Jesus, our hearts are thine; possess them always and only for thyself.
    AUGUSTINE, *bishop of Hippo in North Africa (354–430)* [CBP, 228 PD]

Father God, I do not want to be indifferent in my faith, yet that is often
exactly what I am. I am indifferent because:
    I get so busy doing necessary things that I neglect the essential things.
    I get so focused on myself and my hurts to see much else.
    I get too complacent with what already is.
    I get too immersed in the amusements of life.
    I get too detached from the pain of others.
    I get too comfortable not being near to You.
    I choose to be passionate. Renew my passion and love for You. Amen.
    KURT BJORKLUND, *American minister (1968–present day)*

A PRAYER FOR TODAY

Lord, show me the reasons for my indifference. . . .
Do not let me be satisfied with a lukewarm faith.
Grant me a renewed focus upon You, which I will seek by eliminating . . .
Grant me a fresh vision of what faith could be like in my life. . . .
Grant me a renewed fellowship with You which I will seek by . . . Amen.

Day 186
PRAYERS *of* PRAISE/ADORATION

To You, God, belong wisdom and power;
    counsel (Heb.=*esa: advice, consultation; i.e., learn what to do*)
    and understanding. (Heb.=*tebuna: ability, insight, discernment, wisdom—
i.e., learn how to do it*) JOB 12:13

You, O Lord, are the true God;
You are the living God and the everlasting King.
At Your wrath the earth trembles, and the nations cannot endure Your indignation. JEREMIAH 10:10

I am giving thee worship with my whole life,
I am giving thee assent with my whole power,
I am giving thee praise with my whole tongue,
I am giving thee *honor* with my whole utterance,
I am giving thee reverence with my whole understanding,
I am giving thee offering with my whole thought, . . .
I am giving thee humility in the blood of the Lamb.
I am giving thee love with my whole devotion.
I am giving thee kneeling with my whole desire, . . .
I am giving thee my soul, O God of all gods.
    EARLY SCOTTISH PRAYER [*CBP, 48* PD]

Glory be to you, O God, the Father, the Maker of the world:
Glory be to you, O God, the Son, the Redeemer of humankind:
Glory be to you, O God, the Holy Spirit, the Sanctifier of your people.
    F. B. WESTCOTT, *bishop of Durham/Bible scholar (1825–1901)* [*EOP, 301* PD]

A PRAYER FOR TODAY

Lord, I affirm Your wisdom, counsel, and understanding over the circumstances of my life. . . .
Lord, I affirm Your power over the circumstances of my life. . . .
Since You are wise and powerful, I can freely praise You.
I give You my . . . *(Pick a phrase from the Early Scottish Prayer to offer to God.)*
I will give You glory by . . . *(Giving glory means to give weight to or make much of.)*
My soul will cling to You throughout this day and night. Amen.

PRAYERS *for* CHRISTLIKE CHARACTER

⚜ You are the Lord who brought Your people up out of Egypt to be their God, therefore I will be holy because You are holy. (Note: *Hebrew for "holy"=qados: set apart, consecrated, holy, sacred*) **LEVITICUS 11:45**

⚜ O Lord, give us more charity,
> more self-denial,
> more likeness to thee.
Teach us to sacrifice our comforts to others,
> and our likings for the sake of doing good.
Make us kindly in thought, gentle in word, generous in deed.
Teach us that it is better to give than to receive;
> better to forget ourselves than to put ourselves forward;
> better to minister than to be ministered unto.
And unto thee, the God of love, be glory and praise for ever.
> **HENRY ALFORD**, *English theologian (1810–1871)* [PD]

⚜ Breathe in me, Holy Spirit, that I may think what is holy.
Move me, Holy Spirit, that I may do what is holy.
Attract me, Holy Spirit, that I may love what is holy.
Strengthen me, Holy Spirit, that I may guard what is holy.
Guard me, Holy Spirit, that I may keep what is holy.
> **AUGUSTINE**, *bishop of Hippo in North Africa (354–430)* [BTP, 355]

A PRAYER FOR TODAY

To be holy means to be set apart for God's purposes. In one sense, all believers are holy in Christ. In another sense, holiness is the result of actual lifestyle choices that move us to more fully reflect God's character and to pursue God's agenda.

Lord, the internal struggle for holiness is generally not in knowing what is holy—it is in choosing what is holy.

Draw me and attract me to Yourself.

Show me again how much better Your character is than the character I am naturally drawn to. . . .

Show me again how much sweeter Your agenda is than my agenda is. . . .

To be kindly in thought today would be to . . .

To be gentle in word today would include . . .

To be generous in deed today is to . . .

I can give today by . . .

I will not seek to put myself forward in this setting today. Instead,

I will gladly sacrifice my rightful comforts for a greater good. . . . Amen.

PRAYERS *for* WISDOM/GUIDANCE

Lord, let me not boast *(or have confidence)* in my wisdom
> or in my strength
> or in my riches,

but let me boast *(or have confidence)* in this, that I understand and know You, that You are the Lord who exercises kindness, justice, and righteousness on earth, for in these You delight.
You have declared this to be true. **JEREMIAH 9:23–24**

Lord of my heart, give me vision to inspire me, that, working or resting, I may always think of you.
Lord of my heart, give me light to guide me, that, at home or abroad, I may always walk in your way.
Lord of my heart, give me wisdom to direct me, that, thinking or acting, I may always discern right from wrong.
Lord of my heart, give me courage to strengthen me, that, amongst friends or enemies, I may always proclaim your justice.
Lord of my heart, give me trust to console me, that, hungry or well fed, I may always rely on your mercy.
Lord of my heart, save me from empty praise, that I may always boast of you.
Lord of my heart, save me from worldly wealth, that I may always look to riches of heaven. . . .
Lord of my heart, save me from vain knowledge, that I may always study your word. . . .
Heart of my own heart, whatever befall me, rule over my thoughts and feelings, my words and actions.
> **ANONYMOUS** *[CBP, 179]*

Blessed are those who find wisdom and those who gain understanding,
> for wisdom's profit is greater than that of silver, and her gain is more than fine gold.

She is more precious than jewels, and nothing I desire can compare with her.
> **PROVERBS 3:13–15**

A PRAYER FOR TODAY

Lord, show me the limits of my current wisdom or the wisdom I might gain. . . .
Show me the limits of my current strength or the strength I might yet get. . . .
Show me where I have been relying on human benefits and abilities. . . .
Help me to understand and know Your kindness, justice, and righteousness.
Help me to rely upon Your wisdom and strength. . . . Amen.

PRAYERS *of* INTERCESSION

* You, Lord God, said, "It is not good for the man to be alone. I will make a helper suitable for him." **GENESIS 2:18**

* Lord, who can find a wife of noble character? (Heb.=*khayil: wealth, strength, virtue, nobility*) She is worth far more than rubies. **PROVERBS 31:10**

* We thank You, O God, for the love You have implanted in their hearts. May it always inspire them to be kind in words, considerate in feelings, and concerned for each other's needs and wishes. Bless their marriage for Your glory and their joy. Amen.
  ANONYMOUS *[US]*

A PRAYER FOR TODAY

If you are married, pray this for friends, relatives, or children, who are unmarried.
If you are unmarried, pray this for yourself; then pray for others.
Lord, I ask, according to Your will, that You would bring a spouse to *(insert name)*.
Bring a person of godly character, and Christlike virtue, who is led by Your Spirit.
Bring a person who loves You more than anything in this world.
Bring a person who is focused on Your mission in the world.
Bring a person who will love *(insert name)* fully and selflessly.
Bring a person who will see *(insert name)*'s gifts and talents, celebrate him/her, and give all of himself or herself to help *(insert name)* thrive.
Bring a person who will draw *(insert name)* out, and be a safe place for his/her heart and soul.
Bring a person who will share the deepest places with *(insert name)* and tenderly love him/her there.
Bring a person that is fun and joyful.
Bring a person that deals with his/her negative emotions well.
Bring a person who will continue to mature throughout his/her life.
Bring a person who will serve *(insert name)*.
Lord, we thank You that You care more about the future spouse of *(insert name)* than I do.
I ask that You would give *(insert name)* the patience to wait,
    not to settle for less than Your best,
    not to compromise in order to feel loved and attractive today,
    not to be discouraged in the waiting.

PRAYERS *of* SURRENDER

❧ Lord Jesus, whoever wants to be Your disciple must deny themselves and take up their cross daily and follow You. For whoever wants to save their life will lose it, but whoever loses their life for You will save it. What good is it for us to gain the whole world, and yet lose or forfeit our very selves? If any of us are ashamed of You and Your words, then You, the Son of Man, will be ashamed of them when You come in all Your glory.
LUKE 9:23–26

❧ O Lord, prepare us for all the events of the day; for we know not what a day may bring forth.
Give us grace to deny ourselves;
to take up our cross daily,
and to follow in the steps of our Lord and Master.
MATTHEW HENRY, *English Bible commentator (1662–1714) [EOP, 244]*

❧ Grant, O Lord, that your love may so fill our lives that we may count nothing too small to do for you,
nothing too much to give,
and nothing too hard to bear,
for Jesus Christ's sake.
IGNATIUS, *Spanish hermit (1491–1556) [CBP, 64 PD]*

❧ Therefore, we who share in the heavenly calling will fix our thoughts on You, Jesus. HEBREWS 3:1

A PRAYER FOR TODAY

Get a picture of a cross or an actual cross; then contemplate Jesus on the cross.... Consider what it would be like for you to be crucified....

Lord, right now this part of my following You can at times seem small. . . .
Right now this part of my following You can at times seem too costly. . . .
Right now this part of my following You can at times seem too hard to bear. . . .
Help me to fix my eyes on You, and what You have endured. . . .
So that what is naturally pleasing to me will not gain my heart. . . .
Rather, let what is pleasing to You be what garners my affections. . . .
Lord, in what area of my life would self-denial be most pleasing to You? . . .
Lord, what cross am I currently carrying that I am resenting? . . .
Lord, what would full surrender to You look like in my current situation? . . .
I give myself, my life, my time, my talent, my treasure to You. . . . Amen.

PRAYERS *of* THANKSGIVING

❧ I will give thanks to You Lord, I will call on Your name and make known among the nations what You have done. I will sing to You, I will sing my praises to You and tell of all Your wonderful acts. PSALM 105:1–2

❧ I thank thee, O Lord, my Lord, for my being, my life, my gift of reason;
for my nurture, my preservation, my guidance;
for my education, my civil rights, my religious privileges;
for thy gifts of grace, of nature of this world;
for my redemption, my regeneration, my instruction in the Christian faith;
for thy forbearance and long-suffering, thy prolonged forbearance, many a time, and many a year;
for all the benefits I have received, and all the undertakings wherein I have prospered;
for any good I may have done;
for the use of the blessings of this life;
for thy promise, and my hope of the enjoyment of good things to come;
for all these and also for all other mercies, known and unknown, . . .
I praise thee, I bless thee, I thank thee,
all the days of my life.
    LANCELOT ANDREWES, *English minister (1555–1626)* [*CBP, 32* PD]

❧ For the beauty of the earth, for the glory of the skies,
for the love which from our birth over and around us lies,
Lord of all, to thee we raise this our hymn of grateful praise.
For the joy of ear and eye, for the heart and mind's delight,
for the mystic harmony linking sense to sound and light,
Lord of all, to thee we raise this our hymn of grateful praise.
For the joy of human love, brother, sister, parent, child,
friends on earth, and friends above, for all gentle thoughts and mild,
Lord of all, to thee we raise this our hymn of grateful praise.
    "FOR THE BEAUTY OF THE EARTH," FOLLIOTT S. PIERPOINT, *hymn writer (written 1864)* [PD]

A PRAYER FOR TODAY

Thank You Lord, for every blessing You have granted. . . .
Thank You for general graces granted to all people. . . .
Thank You for specific graces granted to me. . . .
Thank You for forgotten graces unrecognized by me.
Thank You for future graces yet to be received. Amen.

PRAYERS *of* CONFESSION

And the wages of that sin is spiritual death,
But Your gift is eternal life through Jesus Christ our Lord.
ROMANS 6:23

We do not presume to come to *you*, merciful Lord,
trusting in our own goodness, but in your unfailing mercies.
We are not worthy that you should receive us,
but give your word and we shall be healed,
through Jesus Christ our Lord. Amen.
FROM THE METHODIST BOOK OF WORSHIP *(UMW, 7–8)*

If we have worshipped you as a relic from the past, a theological concept, a religious novelty, but not as *the* living God: **Lord forgive us.**
If we have confused your will with our understanding of it, if we have preferred divergence to unity: **Lord forgive us. . . .**
If we have identified the misuse of power, but failed to *speak* against it, and refused to empower the weak: **Lord forgive us. . . .**
Lord, *you have said*: "I will bring my people back to me.
I will love them with all my heart. No longer am I angry with them.
I will be to the people like rain in a dry land."
This is the promise of God.
Amen. Thanks be to God.
WORSHIP RESOURCES, *World Conference on Mission and Evangelism*
[BTP, 143]

Lord and Master of our lives, take from us the spirit
of laziness, half-heartedness, selfish ambition and idle talk.
Give us rather the spirit
of integrity, purity of heart, humility, faithfulness and love.
Lord and King, help us to see our own errors, and not to judge our *neighbors'*;
for your mercy's sake.
TRADITIONAL LITURGY DURING LENT [*BTP, 140* PD]

A PRAYER FOR TODAY

Lord, reveal to me the areas of unconfessed sin in my life. . . .
Having seen my sin, grant me the desire to turn from it.
Grant me the desire and ability to acknowledge You as my Master in all of my life. . . .

PRAYERS *of* AFFIRMATION

I know that You, Lord God, are God and that You are the faithful God,
keeping Your covenant of love to a thousand generations
of those who love You and keep Your commandments.
DEUTERONOMY 7:9

New every morning is your love, great God of light,
And all day long you are working for good in the world.
Stir up in us the desire to serve you, to live peacefully with our neighbors,
And to devote each day to your Son, our Savior, Jesus Christ the Lord.
THE WORSHIP BOOK: SERVICES AND HYMNS *[TAL, 206–207]*

O Lord, Thou knowest what is the better way;
let this or that be done as Thou shalt please.
Give what Thou wilt, and how much Thou wilt, and when Thou wilt.
Deal with me as Thou knowest, and best pleaseth Thee, and is most for Thy honor.
Set me where Thou wilt and deal with me in all things as Thou wilt.
I am in Thy hand; turn me round and turn me back again, even as a wheel.
Behold I am Thy servant, prepared for all things; for I desire not to live unto myself, but unto Thee; and Oh that I could do it worthily and perfectly!
THOMAS Á KEMPIS, *German theologian (1386–1471)* [GSG, 122–23 PD]

Let me hold unswervingly to the hope I profess, for You who has promised is faithful. **HEBREWS 10:23**

I believe in the sun, even when it isn't shining.
I believe in love, even when I feel it not.
I believe in God, even when He is silent.
ANONYMOUS, *Saying found on wall of Nazi concentration camp during World War II [CDP, 693]*

A PRAYER FOR TODAY

Lord, You are utterly reliable, steadfastly loyal, and constant in character and promises.
Yet here is where it is hard for me to believe that You are faithful . . .
Lord, please help my unbelief. . . .
I will proclaim Your faithfulness when the sun is shining and I will shout it in the dark. You are faithful to me! Amen.

PRAYERS *of* PETITION

This is the confidence I have in approaching You, God:
that if I ask anything according to Your will, You will hear me.
And if I know that You hear my prayer—and whatever I ask—then I know I
will receive it.   1 JOHN 5:14–15

Prayer is given and ordained for the purpose of glorifying *You*, God.
Prayer is the appointed way of giving Jesus an opportunity to exercise His
supernatural powers of salvation.
And in so doing *You* desire to make use of us. . . .
If we will make use of prayer, not to wrest from *You* advantages for ourselves or our dear ones, or to escape from tribulations and difficulties,
but to call down upon ourselves and others those things which will glorify
the name of God,
then we shall see the strongest and boldest promises of the Bible about
prayer fulfilled also in our weak, little prayer life, if it will glorify thy name.
    O. HALLESBY, *Norwegian theologian (1879–1961) [OHP, 127–28]*

Almighty God, from whom every good prayer cometh, deliver us when we
draw nigh to thee,
    from coldness of heart and wanderings of mind,
      that with steadfast thought and kindled desire we may worship thee
      in the faith and spirit of Jesus Christ our Lord.
    WILLIAM BRIGHT, *English historian (1824–1901) [CBP, 12]*

Lord, thou knowest what I want,
    if it be thy will that I have it, and if it be not thy will, good Lord, do not be
displeased, for I want nothing which you do not want.
    JULIAN OF NORWICH, *English mystic (1342–1416) [CBP, 55 PD]*

A PRAYER FOR TODAY

Reread Julian of Norwich's prayer; can you pray it with sincerity?
Lord, I bring to You my concerns about . . .
Show me what in this concern is for my advantage rather than Your glory. . . .
Allow me to see what would bring You glory in my concerns and
circumstances. . . .
As I pray about these things, I am reminded that You will favorably answer any
request according to Your will.
Help me to discern and yearn for Your will. Amen.

PRAYERS *for* RENEWAL

❧ I will be still and know that You are God.
You will be exalted among the nations.
You will be exalted in all the earth.   PSALM 46:10

❧ You will keep in perfect peace those whose mind is steadfast, because they
trust in You. I will trust in You Lord, forever, for You are the Rock eternal.
ISAIAH 26:3–4

❧ In the name of Jesus Christ, who was never in a hurry,
we pray, O God, that thou wilt slow us down, for we know that we live too
fast.
With all of eternity before us, make us take time to live—
time to get acquainted with thee,
time to enjoy thy blessings, and time to know each other.
PETER MARSHALL, *chaplain of U.S. Senate (1902–1949) [CBP, 224]*

❧ Almighty God, Who art the giver of every good gift,
send into my heart Thy Holy Spirit
to make me feel how much I owe to Thee,
and to make me love Thee more than I have ever yet done.
O Lord! Teach me to value
earthly enjoyments less, and heavenly things more
and show me the folly of giving my affections to this changing world,
and the wisdom of seeking a home in that better world where there
shall be no more change.
JW, *(unknown author) [JWP, 13]*

A PRAYER FOR TODAY

Sit and be completely still for several minutes....
Try to think only about the character of God....
Lord, I often allow myself to be defined by my tasks and achievements....
But my higher calling is to be a person who relates to and reflects You.
When I live at a frenetic pace, it is hard to sense You.
I need slowness and stillness—I will seek slowness and stillness today by . . .
I will seek slowness and stillness this week by . . .
In my stillness let me know that You are God.
In my stillness show me the folly of giving my affections to this changing
world.
And in this stillness make me love You more than I have ever yet done.
Let me trust You fully so that I may be kept in perfect peace. Amen.

You, Lord Jesus, are the first and the last and the Living One;
You were dead, and behold, You are alive forevermore;
and You hold the keys of death and of Hades. **REVELATION 1:17–18**

Lord, You are great and greatly to be praised; You are to be feared above all gods.
For all the gods of the nations are idols, but You made the heavens.
Splendor and majesty are before You; strength and joy are in Your place.
I will ascribe to You, O Lord, glory and strength. **1 CHRONICLES 16:25–29**

O Lord Jesus Christ, Wisdom and Word of God,
dwell in our hearts, we beseech thee, by thy most Holy Spirit,
that out of the abundance of our hearts, our mouths may speak thy praise.
CHRISTINA ROSSETTI, *English poet (1830–1894)* [*CBP, 238* PD]

Praise ye the Lord, the Almighty, the King of creation!
O my soul, praise Him, for He is thy health and salvation!
All ye who hear, now to His temple draw near; join me in glad adoration!
Praise to the Lord, whoe'er all things so wondrously reigneth,
shelters thee under His wings, yea, so gently sustaineth!
Hast thou not seen how thy desires e'er have been granted in what He ordaineth?
Praise to the Lord, O let all that is in me adore Him!
All that hath life and breath, come now with praises before Him!
"PRAISE YE THE LORD, THE ALMIGHTY," JOACHIM NEANDER, *German theologian/hymn writer (1650–1680)* [*PSH, 3* PD]

A PRAYER FOR TODAY

Lord, You are great. You are beyond the time and space in which I live. . . .
You hold the reality of what is beyond death. . . .
I praise You. . . .
You are above all other objects of affection (gods). . . .
The things that capture my affection besides You will never ultimately satisfy my soul. . . .
The things that capture my affection besides You will not endure beyond this life. . . .
Therefore You are to be revered above all other objects of my affection (gods).
So today as an act of my will I ascribe to You all my affection and worship. . . .

PRAYERS *for* CHRISTLIKE CHARACTER

This is how I know what love is: Jesus Christ laid down His life for me. And I ought to lay down my life for my brothers and sisters.   1 JOHN 3:16

Father in heaven! You have loved us first;
Help us never to forget that you are love so that this sure conviction might triumph in our hearts over the seduction of the world,
> over the disquiet of the soul,
> over the anxiety for the future,
> over the fright of the past,
> over the distress of the moment.

But grant also that this conviction might discipline our soul so that our heart might remain faithful and sincere in the love which we bear
to all those whom you have commanded us to love as we love ourselves.
SØREN KIERKEGAARD, *Danish philosopher (1813–1855)* [COS, 56 PD]

O most tender and gentle Lord Jesus, teach me so to contemplate you that I may become like you and love you sincerely and simply as you have loved me.
JOHN HENRY NEWMAN, *English clergy (1801–1890)* [COS, 72 PD]

Teach me, good Lord:
Not to murmur at multitude of *busyness* or shortness of time. . . .
Not to gather encouragement from appreciation by others, lest this should interfere with purity of motive.
Not to seek praise, respect, gratitude, or regard from superiors or equals on account of age or past service.
Not to let myself be placed in favorable contrast with another.
EDWARD WHITE BENSON, *English bishop (1829–1896)* [GMO, 356 PD]

A PRAYER FOR TODAY

Lord, when I remember Your love for me, it prompts an overwhelming sense of trust and confidence.
This trust and confidence lead me to surrender my thoughts and actions to You.
But when I forget Your love for me, I am overwhelmed with anxiety and disquiet.
This anxiety and disquiet lead me to seek control through my thoughts and actions.
Now remind me of Your deep love for me. . . . Affirm me with Your love. . . .
In this security, grant me the grace not to . . . (*Pray lines from Benson.*)
From the basis of Your love, grant that I may love others. . . . Amen.

❀ I will make every effort to do what leads to peace and aids in building others up in their faith. . . . Lord, as far as it depends on me, I will live in peace with everyone.   ROMANS 14:19; 12:18

❀ Show us, good Lord,
    the peace we should seek,
    the peace we must give,
    the peace we can keep,
    the peace we must forgo,
    and the peace you have given
in Jesus Christ our Lord.
    CARYL MICKLEM, *Irish minister (twentieth century) [BTP, 202]*

❀ Lord Jesus, since I have been justified through faith, I have peace with God through You, and through You have gained access by faith into this grace in which I now stand. And I rejoice in the hope of the glory of God.
    ROMANS 5:1–2

❀ Lord, make me willing to be used by you.
May my knowledge of my unworthiness never make me resist being used by you.
May the need of others always be remembered by me, so that I may ever be willing to be used by you.
And open my eyes and my heart that I may this coming day be able to do some work of peace for you.
    ALAN PATON, *South African writer/anti-apartheid activist (1903–1988)*
    [HBP, 286]

❀ Jesus, You have said that You did not come to bring peace but division . . .
and that father will be against son and son against father,
mother against daughter and daughter against mother,
mother-in-law against daughter-in-law and daughter-in-law against
mother-in-law.   LUKE 12:51, 53

A PRAYER FOR TODAY

Lord, I want to be about Your peace.
Show me where and how to seek peace. . . .
Show me where and how "peace" would mean compromise. . . .
Thank You for the peace I enjoy as a result of justification through faith. Amen.

PRAYERS *of* INTERCESSION

❦ God: Marriage is an honorable commitment; therefore, whether single
   or married,
I will seek to be honorable by keeping the marriage bed pure.
For I know that You, God, will judge the adulterer and all the sexually
   immoral. **HEBREWS 13:4**

❦ O God, you have so consecrated the covenant of Christian marriage that in
   it is represented the covenant between Christ and his church. Send therefore your blessing upon *(Name* and *Name)*, that they may surely keep their
   marriage covenant, and so grow in love and godliness together that their
   home may be a haven of . . . peace; through Jesus Christ our Lord. . . .
   Bless *(Name* and *Name)*, that their love for each other may reflect the love of
   Christ on us and grow from strength to strength as they faithfully serve you
   in the world. Defend them from every enemy. Lead them into all peace. Let
   their love for each other be a seal upon their hearts.
   UNTITLED, UNKNOWN AUTHOR *[UMW, 25, 28]*

A PRAYER FOR TODAY

*If you are married or engaged, pray this for your own marriage first, then for your friends
and family.*
If you are single, pray this for your friends and family.
Lord, I ask today that *(we/they)* would seek You before anything else, including
   their commitment to one another. . . .
I ask that *(we/they)* would give preference to one another. . . .
I ask that You would highlight to *(us/them)* where there is triangulation in the
   relationship. . . .
   (Note: Triangulation *is allowing a third party, whether a person, work, a hobby,
   children, or anything else, to be on equal footing with one's spouse.)*
I ask that You would give *(us/them)* the strength to neutralize triangulating
   influences. . . .
I ask that You would help *(us/them)* to resolve conflict quickly and well. . . .
I ask that You would show *(us/them)* where there is false peace. . . .
I ask that You would grant sexual purity in *(our/their)* minds and actions. . . .
I ask that You would protect *(us/them)* from wandering eyes and thoughts. . . .
I ask that You would help *(us/them)* to be honest with one another. . . .
I ask that You would help *(us/them)* to be gentle with one another. . . .
I ask that You would help *(us/them)* to laugh together and to find joy
   consistently. . . .
Help *(us/them)* to lavish grace and forgiveness on one another. . . .
Grant *(us/them)* the ability to change unhealthy patterns. . . .
I ask that You would allow *(our/their)* love to grow deeper and fuller with time. . . .
Amen.

PRAYERS *of* SURRENDER

God, I have died to my old way of life and my life is now hidden in Christ, in You.   COLOSSIANS 3:3

O God be all my love, all my hope, all my striving:
Let my thoughts and words flow from you,
my daily life be in you,
and every breath I take be for you.
JOHN CASSIAN *(360–435)* [*BTP, 26–27* PD]

God, You are worthy of my whole life.
I surrender my life to You today.
Help me to love You primarily rather than loving myself primarily.
Help me to love others freely rather than always looking for others to love me.
Help me to serve You rather than looking for You to improve my life.
Help me to serve others rather than seeking to be served.
Help me to give affirmation rather than seeking to be affirmed.
Help me to reach out when there is relational strife rather than waiting the other person out.
Help me to overlook offenses rather than noting and nursing my hurts.
Help me to give grace rather than expecting grace to be given to me after I have given it to others.
Help me to encourage others rather than waiting for encouragement to be given to me.
Help me to be genuinely interested in others rather than desiring their interest in me.
Help me to count all I gain in this world as loss rather than seeking to gain more of the world.
Help me to truly enjoy what You enjoy rather than enjoying earthly trifles.
Help me to be joyful rather than anxious and despondent.
Help me to be present in every situation rather than preoccupied and aloof.
When I say "help me" I am asking for the divine enablement of Your Holy Spirit.
I surrender my life to You today. Amen.
KURT BJORKLUND, *American minister (1968–present day)*

A PRAYER FOR TODAY

Add your own prayers of surrender or pray through one or more of the lines above specifically naming the ways you need to surrender in the situation prayed about.

Lord, help me to . . . rather than . . . Amen.

PRAYERS *of* THANKSGIVING

Lord Jesus, You were oppressed and afflicted,
    yet You did not open Your mouth;
You were led like a lamb to the slaughter,
    and as a sheep before her shearers is silent,
    so You did not open Your mouth. . . .
It was the Lord's will to crush You and cause You to suffer.
Though the Lord made You a guilt offering . . .
You who are God's righteous servant will justify many by Your knowledge.
And You will bear their iniquities.
Therefore, God will give You a portion among the great,
    and You will divide the spoils with the strong,
    because You poured out Your life unto death,
    and were numbered with the transgressors.
For You bore the sin of many,
    and made intercession for the transgressors. **ISAIAH 53:7, 9–12**

God, I ponder *Your* achievement.
You don't condone *my* sin, nor do *You* compromise *Your* standard.
You don't ignore *my* rebellion, nor do *You* relax *Your* demands.
Rather than dismiss *my* sin, You assume *my* sin, and incredibly sentence
    Yourself.
Your holiness is honored. *My* sin is punished . . . and *I* am redeemed.
You have done what *I* cannot do—so *I* can be what *I* dare not dream—
    Perfect before *You.*
    MAX LUCADO, *American minister (1955–present day) [GOC, 16]*

As a needle turns to the north when it is touched by the magnet, so it is fitting, O Lord, that I, your servant, should turn to love and praise and serve you; seeing that out of love *for* me you were willing to endure such grievous pangs and sufferings.
    RAYMOND LULL, *Spanish philosopher (1235–1315) [BTP, 75]*

A PRAYER FOR TODAY

Father, I focus my prayers of thanksgiving on the sufferings of Christ . . .
And on the accomplishments of Christ . . .
And on the reality of my redemption . . .
And on the lengths to which Jesus went to achieve this . . .
And on what You will accomplish in the future . . .
On my behalf and on the behalf of all You have called to Yourself.

* Let me fear You Lord my God, who gives autumn and spring rains in season and who assures us of the regular weeks of harvest. My wrongdoings keep me from experiencing Your blessings, and my sins deprive me of the good.
    JEREMIAH 5:24–25

* *God, my* freedom from the dominion of sin is not the end of *my* struggle against sin. In fact it is the beginning of a new conflict with it. For while *I* have died to sin, sin has not died in *me*. . . . It remains, and it is still sin. What has changed is not its presence within *my* heart, but its status (it no longer reigns) and our relationship to it (*I am* no longer its slave).
    SINCLAIR FERGUSON, *Scottish theologian (twentieth century)* *[KCL, 125, 138]*

* My sins, Lord, are dulling my conscience.
    I get used to evil very quickly:
    A little self-indulgence here,
    a small unfaithfulness there,
    an unwise action farther on
    and my vision becomes obscured;
    I no longer see stumbling-blocks, I no longer see other people on my road.
    Lord, I beseech you, keep me young in my efforts,
    Spare me the bondage of habit, which lulls to sleep and kills.
    MICHAEL QUOIST, *French author (1921–1997)* *[BTP, 133]*

* We have not seen and savored You as we ought.
    We have not worshiped You with the white-hot affections You deserve.
    Forgive us, O Lord, our merciful God.
    And lead us now into lasting joy.
    Enthrall us with Yourself.
    And break the power of all lesser pleasures.
    In Jesus' name, amen.
    JOHN PIPER, *American pastor (1946–present day)* *[LAV, 163]*

A PRAYER FOR TODAY

Lord God, I bring my sin to You. . . .
Spare me the bondage of habitual sin.
Let the tenderness of Your mercies incline me toward virtue.
Let the pleasures found in You dwarf all lesser pleasures. Amen.

PRAYERS *of* AFFIRMATION

⚜ God, I know that in all things You are working for my good, as one who loves You and has been called according to Your purpose.
For those You foreknew, You also predestined to be conformed to the likeness of Your Son, that He might be the firstborn among many siblings.
And those You predestined, You also called;
those You called, You also justified;
those You justified, You also glorified.   ROMANS 8:28–30

⚜ God, *You* permit what *You* hate to accomplish that which *You* love.
JONI EARECKSON TADA, *American author (1949–present day) [PGP, as cited in IGG, 387]. Joni was paralyzed in a diving accident at age seventeen.*

⚜ *You care* most God not about making us comfortable—
but about teaching us to hate our sins, grow up spiritually, and to love *You*.
To do this, *You* give us salvation's benefits only gradually, sometimes painfully gradually.
In other words, You let us continue to feel much of sin's sting while we're headed for heaven . . . where at last, every sorrow we taste will one day prove to be the best possible thing that could have happened.
JONI EARECKSON TADA, *American author (1949–present day) [WGW, as cited in IGG, 56]*

⚜ O Heavenly Father, I praise and thank you for all your goodness and faithfulness throughout my life.
You have granted me many blessings.
Now let me accept tribulation from your hand.
You will not lay on me more than I can bear.
You make all things work together for good.
For your children.
DIETRICH BONHOEFFER, *German pastor/martyr (1906–1945) [BTP, 38]*
As he awaited his trial in Nazi Germany for speaking out for his faith

A PRAYER FOR TODAY

Lord, You have allowed . . . in my life that I would not have chosen.
Father, I know that my character is a higher priority to You than my comfort.
Yet I long for comfort often more than I desire character formation.
I affirm that all things are working together for my good—
although I may not see how at the moment.
I affirm that You love me—and that is why You prioritize my greater good.
I affirm that being conformed to the likeness of Your Son is my greatest good.
I affirm that I am foreknown, predestined, called, justified, and glorified.
Help me to see through an eternal lens rather than a temporal lens.
Help me to prize what You prize. Amen.

PRAYERS *of* PETITION

Whatever I do, I will work at it with all my heart, as if I am working for You.
COLOSSIANS 3:23

O God, your Word tells me that, whatever my hand finds to do, I must do it with might.
Help me today to concentrate with my whole attention on whatever I am doing, and keep my thoughts from wandering and my mind from straying.
When I am *working*, help me to *work* with my whole mind.
When I am playing, help me to play with my whole heart.
Help me to do one thing at a time and to do it well. This I ask for Jesus' sake.
WILLIAM BARCLAY, *Scottish Bible professor (1907–1978) [CBP, 834]*

Lord, let me not live to have lazy hands that only make a man poor,
but give me diligent hands that bring productivity. . . .
For the sluggard craves and yet gets nothing,
but the desires of the diligent are fully satisfied. **PROVERBS 10:4; 13:4**

Father, it should never be said of *me as a worker*, that *I am* half-hearted, care-less, tardy, irresponsible, whiney, or negligent. Behavior like that embar-rasses *You*. It brings reproach on *You*. At work, *I* should epitomize character qualities like self-discipline, perseverance, and initiative. *I* should be self-motivated, prompt, organized, and industrious. *My* efforts should result in work of the very highest quality.
BILL HYBELS, *American pastor (twentieth century) [CDP, 669]*

May my work be faithful; May my work be honest;
May my work be blessed; May my work bless others; May my work bless you.
May the wealth and work of the world be available to all and for the exploitation of none.
CELTIC PRAYER *[EOP, 210 PD]*

May Your favor, O Lord my God, rest upon me.
Establish the work of my hands. **PSALM 90:17**

A PRAYER FOR TODAY

Lord, I ask You to reveal to me the type of effort I have given to my work. . . .
Help me to see my work as bringing order out of chaos, thus seeing the dignity of my work. . . .
I ask for diligence in the tasks . . . single-minded focus . . . and favor from You.
Establish the work of my hands, for Your glory. . . . Amen.

PRAYERS *for* RENEWAL

When I live according to my natural instincts, I set my mind on natural things; but when I live according to Your Spirit, O God, I set my mind on the things of the Spirit.
The mind set on natural things is death, but the mind set on Your Spirit is life and peace.   ROMANS 8:5–6

Breathe on me, Breath of God,
     fill me with life anew, that I may love what Thou dost love,
     and do what Thou wouldst do. . . .
Breathe on me, Breath of God,
     till I am wholly Thine,
     until this earthly part of me glows with the fire divine.
       "BREATHE ON ME, BREATH OF GOD," EDWIN HATCH, *hymn writer*
       (1835–1884) [MGH, 90 PD]

For Your name's sake, O Lord, preserve my life;
in Your righteousness bring me out of trouble.   PSALM 143:11

Lord, I am poured out, I come to you for renewal.
Lord, I am weary, I come to you for refreshment.
Lord, I am worn, I come to you for restoration.
Lord, I am lost, I come to you for guidance.
Lord, I am troubled, I come to you for peace.
Lord, I am lonely, I come to you for love.

Come Lord,
Come revive me
Come reshape me
Come mold me in your image
Recast me in the furnace of your love.
       "THE FURNACE OF GOD'S LOVE," CELTIC PRAYER *[PL, 57]*

A PRAYER FOR TODAY

Father, today I come to You and present this need . . .
I acknowledge that often I am led by my natural instincts
and I have these feelings . . . *(see Celtic prayer above)*
Here is what I think I need from You . . .
Please meet me in this need in whatever way You choose.
I will not demand that You meet my needs my way—I trust Your wisdom and goodness.
I choose today to fix my gaze upon You. . . . Amen.

PRAYERS *of* PRAISE/ADORATION

Lord my God, You are the God of all the heavens above and the earth below.
JOSHUA 2:11

Alleluia! Salvation and glory and honor and power belong to You
my God. . . .
I will praise You along with all your servants and those who fear You, both
the small and the mighty. **REVELATION 19:1, 5**

Joyful, joyful we adore Thee, God of glory, Lord of love;
Hearts unfold like flowers before Thee, hail Thee as the sun above.
Melt the clouds of sin and sadness, drive the dark of doubt away;
Giver of immortal gladness, fill us with the light of day!

All Thy works with joy surround Thee, earth and heaven reflect Thy rays,
Stars and angels sing around Thee, center of unbroken praise.
Field and forest, vale and mountain, flowery meadow, flashing sea,
Chanting bird and flowing fountain call us to rejoice in Thee.

Mortals join the mighty chorus which the morning stars began;
Father love is reigning over us, brother love binds man to man.
Ever singing, march we onward, victors in the midst of strife;
Joyful music lifts us sunward in the triumph song of life.
"JOYFUL, JOYFUL, WE ADORE THEE," **HENRY VAN DYKE,** *American author/*
minister (1852–1933) [PSH, 53 PD]

Now to You, the One who is able to establish us by the gospel and proclamation of Jesus Christ . . . O eternal God, and has been made known so
that all nations might believe and obey You—to You, the only wise God,
through Jesus Christ, be the glory forever. Amen. **ROMANS 16:25–27**

We worship you, O Lord God, and give thanks to you for your great glory
and power, which you show to your servants in your wonderful world. All
the things which we enjoy are from your mighty hand, and you alone are to
be praised for all the blessings of the life that now is. Make us thankful to
you for all your mercies and more ready to serve you with all our heart; for
the sake of Jesus Christ. Amen.
FROM THE NARROW WAY, *1869* [EOP, 57 PD]

A PRAYER FOR TODAY

Lord, I am moved to joy and wonder by . . .
I offer You my praise and glory. . . .
And this praise that I offer now—that I will offer forever and ever. Amen.

PRAYERS *for* CHRISTLIKE CHARACTER

⚜ Christ Jesus, I do not believe that I have already obtained all this, or that I have arrived at the goal, but I press onward to take hold of that for which You have taken hold of me. . . . I will forget what is in the past and I will strain forward to what is ahead. I will press on toward the goal to win the prize for which God has called me heavenward through my relationship with You.
    PHILIPPIANS 3:12–14

⚜ Loving Father, . . . I'm so grateful I can come to You with confidence. . . . I acknowledge You as Lord of my desires, my plans, my successes, my failures, my place in the world, my friendships, my popularity. You are Lord of my present and future relationships, health, money, possessions, and human approval. How good it is to yield to You, knowing that You withhold no good thing from Your obedient children who trust You and call on You. . . .
Give me grace not to let the world squeeze me into its mold—its desire to indulge . . . its desire to possess . . . its desire to impress.
    WARREN AND RUTH MYERS, *American missionaries (twentieth century)* *[MGH, 72]*

⚜ Teach me, O God, so to use all the circumstances of my life today that they may bring forth in me the fruits of holiness rather than the fruits of sin.
Let me use disappointments as material for patience:
Let me use success as material for thankfulness:
Let me use suspense as material for perseverance:
Let me use danger as material for courage:
Let me use reproach as material for longsuffering:
Let me use praise as material for humility:
Let me use pleasure as material for temperance:
Let me use pains as material for endurance.
    JOHN BAILLIE, *Scottish theologian (1886–1960) [DPP, 101]*

A PRAYER FOR TODAY

Lord, I think that pressing on for me today would look like . . .
I think that Your goal for my life could be expressed as . . .
Let me use . . . *(what I am facing today)*
as material for . . . *(what God wants it to become)*
Help me believe that being like You is greater than any earthly comfort.
Help me to forget what is behind and to press on. Amen.

PRAYERS *for* WISDOM/GUIDANCE

God, no eye has seen, no ear heard, no mind has conceived
    what You have prepared for those who love You,
    but You have revealed it to us by Your Spirit.
The Spirit teaches us all things, even the deep things of God.
      1 CORINTHIANS 2:9–10

There are four ways in which *You* reveal *Your* will to us—
    through the Scriptures,
    through providential circumstances,
    through the convictions of our own higher judgment,
    and through the inward impressions of the Holy Spirit on our minds.
Where these four harmonize, it is safe to say that *You* speak.
(Note: *There are more than four ways God can speak represented in the Bible, but
clearly any sense of God's speaking must be filtered through Scripture as this is the
primary and authoritative way that God speaks*)
      HANNAH WHITALL SMITH, *American author (1832–1911)* [GMO, 360]

Holy Spirit, think through me till your ideas are my ideas.
      AMY CARMICHAEL, *American missionary (1868–1951)* [CBP, 236 PD]

A PRAYER FOR TODAY

Lord, it is easy when making decisions to assume that I have Your mind on the
    matter when in reality, I may simply be making my decision and hoping it
    is of You.
Certainly, You have given me a mind to make decisions.
I never want to use seeking You as an excuse to forgo clear and diligent
    thinking.
But I also never want to use my thinking as an excuse to forgo the process of
    seeking Your direction.
So today, I bring these issues before You . . .
As I search the Scriptures, I find direction for my life in this . . .
As I look at circumstances, I see evidence of Your leading in this . . .
As I consider my convictions, they lead me to see Your direction this way . . .
As I respond to inward impressions of Your Spirit, I am prompted to . . .
As I think about the things people have recently said to me, knowingly or
    unknowingly, I sense Your voice in these words . . .
As I ponder the previous commitments I have made, I sense Your leading to . . .
When I take these together, I get a sense of how You may be leading me today.
. . . Amen.

PRAYERS *of* INTERCESSION

Lord, it is a calling for all of us to see to it that none of us has a sinful, unbelieving heart that turns away from You, the living God.
Therefore, I will encourage others as long as it is still called Today,
so that no one will be hardened by sin's deceitfulness.   **HEBREWS 3:12–13**
(Note: *Greek for "encourage"=parakaleo: to encourage or comfort, to come alongside, to beseech. This verb appears in the present imperative mood, meaning it is a continually commanded action*)

God, You are not the God of despair and discouragement.
Yet discouragement grips the hearts of many. I see many
    discouraged by perceived failures,
    discouraged by troubled finances,
    discouraged by relational friction,
    discouraged by consistent fear,
    discouraged by unrealized dreams.
Encourage the disheartened, Lord, and let me be a means of encouragement.
    KURT BJORKLUND, *American minister (1968–present day)*

Lord Jesus, take my mind and think through me,
    take my hands and bless through me,
    take my mouth and speak through me,
    above all, Lord Jesus, take my spirit and pray in me;
so that it is you who move and have your being in me.
    BOOK OF THE HOURS *(sixteenth century) [BTP, 33]*

A PRAYER FOR TODAY

Lord, let me be encouraged in Your truth. . . .
Show me the ways that I can be an instrument of encouragement . . .
and keep me from any discouraging actions or statements today. . . .
Let me see where those in my life are discouraged. . . .
Encourage the hearts of my family. . . .
Encourage the hearts of my friends. . . .
Encourage the hearts of spiritual leaders (Deuteronomy 3:28). . . .
Encourage the hearts of the oppressed (Isaiah 1:17). . . .
Encourage the hearts of the persecuted (1 Thessalonians 3:1–3). . . .
Encourage the hearts of all Christians (Acts 20:1).
Keep them from discouragement.
Keep discouraging people far from them.

PRAYERS *of* SURRENDER

Lord, just as I once presented the members of my body as slaves to impurity and ever-increasing lawlessness, so I now present my members as slaves of righteousness, leading to holiness.   ROMANS 6:19

Written January 12, 1723
I have been before *You* God, and have given myself, all that I am and have, to *You*, so that I am not in any respect my own. I can challenge no right in this understanding, this will, these affections, which are in me. Neither have I any right to this body or any of its members—no right to this tongue, these hands, these feet, no right to these senses, these eyes, these ears, this smell or this taste. I have given myself clear away, and have not retained anything as my own. . . . And I pray God, for the sake of Christ, to look upon it as a self-dedication and to receive me now as entirely *Your* own and deal with me in all respects as such, whether *You* afflict me or prosper me or whatever *You are pleased* to do with me.
      JONATHAN EDWARDS, *American pastor (1703–1758) [PFG, 166–67]*

God, Let me put right before interest,
let me put others before self,
let me put things of the spirit before things of the body.
Let me put the attainment of noble ends above the enjoyment of present pleasures.
Let me put principles above reputations.
Let me put thee before all else.
      JOHN BAILLIE, *Scottish theologian (1886–1960) [DPP, 61]*

Lord, I am willing
to receive what You give
to lack what You withhold
to relinquish what You take
to suffer what You inflict
to be what You require. Amen.
      NELSON MINK *(unknown era) [TTO, 552–53]*

A PRAYER FOR TODAY

Lord, whatever You ask of me, I will do. . . .
Whatever You send or allow in my life, I will accept. . . .
With Your help I will endeavor to put the best things before good things. . . .
I present all that I am to You as a slave to Your purposes. . . .
I surrender it all to You. Amen.

PRAYERS *of* THANKSGIVING

🌿 In You, God, we have redemption through Christ's blood, the forgiveness of sins, in accordance with the riches of Your grace. EPHESIANS 1:7

🌿 God, You raised us up with Christ and seated us with him in the heavenly realms in Christ Jesus, in order that in the coming ages You might show Your incomparable riches of grace, expressed in Your kindness to us in Christ Jesus. For it is by grace that we are saved, through faith; this is not something we can muster up, it is Your gift—not by our good works, so that no one can boast. EPHESIANS 2:6–9

🌿 *Newton wrote this hymn after realizing the sin of slavery and renouncing it completely.*
Amazing grace, how sweet the sound, that saved a wretch like me!
I once was lost, but now am found, was blind, but now I see.

'Twas grace that taught my heart to fear, and grace my fears relieved;
how precious did that grace appear the hour I first believed!

Through many dangers, toils and snares, I have already come;
'tis grace hath brought me safe thus far, and grace will lead me home.

When we've been there ten thousand years, bright shining as the sun,
we've no less days to sing *Your* praise, than when we first begun.
   "AMAZING GRACE," JOHN NEWTON, *English minister (1725–1807)* [PD]

🌿 Jesus, You have told us that in this world, we will have trouble.
But we can take heart! For You have overcome the world. JOHN 16:33

Joy does not come from positive predictions about the state of the world.
It does not depend on the ups and downs of the circumstances of our lives.
Joy is based on the spiritual knowledge that, while the world in which we
live is shrouded in darkness, *You God, have* overcome the world. . . .
   The surprise is not that, unexpectedly, things turn out better than
expected. No, the real surprise is that . . . *Your* love is stronger than death.
   HENRI NOUWEN, *American priest (1932–1996) [GSG, 358]*

A PRAYER FOR TODAY

Lord, I thank You for the experiences, the realities, and the promises of grace. . . .
I thank You for the reality that You have overcome the world. . . .
Let me catch a glimpse of how Your love and truth overcome what is seen. . . .
Let me rest in You. I worship You as my overcoming God. Amen.

PRAYERS *of* CONFESSION

Lord, I know that from everyone who has been given much, much will be required;
and from the one who has been entrusted with much, much will be asked.
LUKE 12:48

O Lord, our *Savior*, who hast warned us that thou wilt require much of those to whom much is given, grant that we, whose lot is cast in so goodly a heritage, may strive together the more abundantly by prayer, by almsgiving, by fasting, and by every other appointed means, to extend to others what we so richly enjoy . . . through Jesus Christ our Lord.
AUGUSTINE, *bishop of Hippo in North Africa (354–430) [PL, 109]*

Lord, I know the good I ought to do. But when I choose not to do what is good, I sin. **JAMES 4:17**

Lord, we demonstrate our evil not just by what we do,
but by what we fail to do and what we stand by and allow others to do.
Fathers abuse their children while mothers look the other way.
Nazis rounded up Jews in Germany while most citizens did nothing.
Slaves picked cotton while those who wore cotton garments created the demand for slave labor.
RANDY ALCORN, *American pastor, author (twentieth century) [IGG, 74]*

A PRAYER FOR TODAY

Lord, show me where I have been entrusted with much. . . .
I confess there are places where I have been entrusted with much and have not given much, such as . . .
It is not right for me to see things as mine, rather than a trust given to me by You.
I confess there are things I know to do and I have not done them, such as . . .
It is sin for me to not do the good I know to do.
Show me where I have turned a blind eye to injustice around me. . . .
I confess that sometimes I don't want to get entangled in the pressing issues of my day. Forgive me.
I confess that I often do only what is expected, seeing it as the minimum requirement.
I know that You ultimately want my affection, not merely my conformity.

PRAYERS *of* AFFIRMATION

I am confident of this, that You, the One who began a good work in me, will carry it on to completion until the day of Christ Jesus. **PHILIPPIANS 1:6**

I believe that you created me: let not the work of your hands be despised.
I believe that I am after your image and likeness: let not your own likeness be defaced.
I believe that you saved me by your blood: let not the price of the ransom be squandered.
I believe that you proclaimed me a Christian in your name: let not your namesake be scorned.
I believe that you hallowed me in rebirth: let not that consecration be despoiled.
I believe that you engrafted me into the cultivated olive tree: let not the limb of your mystical body be cut out. Amen.
LANCELOT ANDREWES, *English minister (1555–1626)* [*EOP, 93* PD]

Lord, even to my old age, You are the same,
and even when my hair is gray, You will carry me.
You have made me, and You will bear me;
You will sustain me, and You will deliver me. **ISAIAH 46:4**

O my God, I do believe in you. . . .
I believe in you as the Father, infinite in your love and power;
and as the Son, my Redeemer and my Life;
and as the Holy Spirit, Comforter and Guide and Strength.
Three-*in*-One God, I have faith in you. I know and am sure that all that you are, you are to me, that all you have promised you will perform.
Lord Jesus, increase this faith. Teach me to take time, to wait and worship in the holy presence until my faith takes in all there is in my God for me.
Let it see Him as the fountain of all life, working with almighty strength to accomplish His will in the world and in me. . . . Amen.
ANDREW MURRAY, *South African minister (1828–1917)* [*BSP, 73*]

A PRAYER FOR TODAY

Lord, I believe that You will work in me until Your work is done.
When I don't believe that I am sufficient, I believe that You will carry me. . . .
When I don't believe that I can continue, I believe that You will sustain me. . . .
When I don't believe there is a way out, I believe that You will deliver me. . . .
Increase my faith in You so I can walk confidently in Your promises. Amen.

PRAYERS *of* PETITION

God, it is not those who merely hear the law whom You declare righteous in Your sight.
It is those who obey the law whom You declare righteous.   ROMANS 2:13

Give me grace, good Lord, to count the world as nothing,
to set my mind firmly on you and not to hang on what people say;
to be content to be alone, not to long for worldly company,
little by little to throw off the world completely and rid my mind of all its business;
not to long to hear of any worldly things;
gladly to be thinking of you, . . .
to depend on your *help and* comfort, . . .
to suffer adversity patiently . . . to be joyful in troubles;
to walk the narrow way that leads to life,
to bear the Cross with Christ, . . .
to have always before my eyes my death, which is always at hand,
to make death no stranger to me,
to foresee and consider the everlasting fire of hell,
to pray for pardon before the judge comes;
to keep continually in mind the passion that Christ suffered for me,
for his benefits unceasingly to give him thanks;
to buy back the time that I have wasted before,
to refrain from futile chatter, to reject idle frivolity, to cut out unnecessary entertainments,
to count the loss of worldly possessions, friends, liberty and life itself as absolutely nothing for the winning of Christ.
> THOMAS MORE, *English political leader and clergy (1478–1535)* [*EOP, 101–102* PD] *Beheaded for his opposition to King Henry VIII*

We most humbly beg you to give us grace
not only to be hearers of the Word, but doers also of the same;
not only to love, but also to live your gospel;
not only to favor, but also to follow your godly doctrine;
not only to profess, but also to practice your blessed commandments,
to the honor of your Holy Name, and the health of our souls.
> THOMAS BECON, *English Reformer (1511–1567)* [*COS, 50* PD]

A PRAYER FOR TODAY

God, please work in these situations today in this way . . .
God, please work in my character in this way . . . Amen.

PRAYERS *for* RENEWAL

Lord God Almighty, I call You Lord. It is a name of renown.
May I seek to return to You, my God, and maintain love and justice,
and wait for You always. (Hebrew for *"wait"=qawa: to hope, to wait until hope
is fulfilled*) HOSEA 12:5–6

Jesus, *You* sought me when a stranger wandering from the fold of God;
You, to rescue me from danger, interposed *Your* precious blood.
O to grace how great a debtor daily I'm constrained to be!
Let Thy goodness like a fetter bind my wandering heart to Thee.
Prone to wander, Lord, I feel it. Prone to leave the God I love.
Here's my heart, O take and seal it, seal it for Your courts above.
    "COME THOU FOUNT," ROBERT ROBINSON, *hymn writer (1735–1790)*
    [*PSH, 35* PD]

Let no riches make me ever forget myself,
    no poverty make me to forget thee:
Let no hope or fear, no pleasure or pain, no accident without, no weakness
    within, hinder or discompose my duty,
    or turn me from the ways of thy commandments.
O let thy Spirit dwell with me forever, and make my soul just and charitable,
    full of honesty, full of *devotion to You . . .*
    JEREMY TAYLOR, *English clergy (1613–1667)* [OBP, 121 PD]

O Lord, reassure me with your quickening Spirit;
    without you I can do nothing.
Mortify in me all ambition, vanity, vainglory, worldliness, pride,
    selfishness, and resistance from God, and fill me with love, peace and
    all the fruits of the Spirit.
O Lord, I know not what I am, but to you I flee for refuge.
I would surrender myself to you, trusting your precious promises and
    against hope believing in hope.
    WILLIAM WILBERFORCE, *English abolitionist (1759–1833)* [COS, 84 PD]

A PRAYER FOR TODAY

Lord, I am prone to wander by . . .
Draw me to return to You.
Cause me to maintain love by . . .
Cause me to maintain justice by . . .
Cause me to wait for You by . . .
Bind my heart to Your goodness like a fetter. Amen.

Be exalted, O God, above the heavens; let Your glory be over all the earth. . . .

I will praise You, O Lord, among the nations; I will sing of You among the peoples.

For great is Your love, reaching to the heavens; Your faithfulness reaches to the skies.

Be exalted, O God, above the heavens; let Your glory be over all the earth.

PSALM 57:5, 9–11

You alone are holy, Lord God, Worker of Wonders.

You are mighty. You are great. You are the Most High.

You are omnipotent, our holy Father, King of heaven and earth.

You, Lord God, three in one, are our every good.

You, Lord God, all good, our highest good—Lord God living and true.

You are charity and love.

You are wisdom. You are humility.

You are patience.

You are security. You are peace.

You are joy and gladness.

You are justice and temperance.

You are riches altogether sufficient.

You are beauty. You are meekness.

You are our protector. You are our strength.

You are our refreshment.

You are our hope. You are our faith.

You are our most profound sweetness.

You are our eternal life, great and admirable Lord, omnipotent God, merciful Savior!

CARLO CARRETTO, *Italian cardinal (1454–1514) or minister (1910–1988)* *[GMO, 264–65]*

A PRAYER FOR TODAY

Lord, I praise You for how You have been mighty in my life. . . .

I praise You for loving me even when others do not. . . .

I praise You for the patience You have shown me. . . .

I praise You for the security You bring into my life. . . .

I praise You for the joy and gladness that is in You. . . .

I praise You for the justice that You do and will deliver. . . .

I praise You for the protection born out of Your strength in my life. . . .

I praise You for the refreshment, hope, and faith that is in You. . . .

I praise You for . . . *(add your own statements of praise)* Amen.

PRAYERS *for* CHRISTLIKE CHARACTER

Jesus, You taught that everyone who exalts himself or herself will be humbled,
and that the one who humbles himself will be exalted.
> **LUKE 14:11**

Dear Father . . . let us be peacemakers:
> more ready to call people friends than enemies
> more ready to trust than to mistrust
> more ready to love than to hate
> more ready to respect than despise
> more ready to serve than be served
> more ready to absorb evil than to pass it on.

Dear Father . . . let us be more like Christ.
> **MOTHER'S UNION ANTHOLOGY OF PUBLIC PRAYERS** *[BTP, 155]*

O Lord and Master of my life, grant that I may not have a spirit of idleness,
of discouragement, of lust for power, and of vain speaking.
But bestow on me, your servant, the spirit of chastity,
of meekness, of patience and of love.
> **EPHRAIM**, *Syrian theologian (306–378)* [EOP, 72 PD]

A PRAYER FOR TODAY

Lord, free me from my need to exalt myself.
Where I am prone to seek things for myself, help me to seek the best things for You and others. . . .
Where I am prone to make enemies, help me to make friends. . . .
Where I am prone to mistrust, help me to trust. . . .
Where I am prone to hate, help me to love. . . .
Where I am prone to despise, help me to respect. . . .
Where I am prone to seek being served, help me to serve. . . .
Where I am prone to speak evil, help me to speak words of life. . . .
Where I am prone to be idle, help me to choose action. . . .
Where I am prone to discouragement, help me to be encouraged and to give encouragement. . . .
Where I am prone to a lust for power, help me to yield power. . . .
Where I am prone to feel entitled, help me to relinquish my rights. . . .
Where I am prone to speak boastfully, help me to choose meekness. . . .
Where I am prone to impatience, help me to choose patience. . . .
Where I am prone to be demanding, help me to choose love. . . .
All for Your glory. Amen.

PRAYERS *for* WISDOM/GUIDANCE

❦ Before the mountains were born or You brought forth the entire world,
from everlasting to everlasting You are God.
You turn men and women back to dust, saying, "Return to dust, you
mortals." . . .
The length of our days is seventy or eighty years, if we have the strength;
yet their span is but trouble and sorrow, for they quickly pass and we fly
away. . . .
Teach me to number my days, that I may gain a heart of wisdom.
   PSALM 90:2–3, 10, 12

❦ So teach us to number our days that we may apply our hearts to wisdom.
Lighten, if it be your will, the pressure of this world's care,
and above all, reconcile us to your will,
and give us a peace which the world cannot take away;
through Jesus Christ our Lord. Amen.
   THOMAS CHALMERS, *Scottish pastor (1780–1847)* [COS, 90 PD]

❦ Lord, I will be very careful how I live, not as unwise, but as wise,
making the most of every opportunity, because the days are evil.
I will not be foolish about my life, but I will seek to understand what Your
will is.   **EPHESIANS 5:15–17**

❦ Father, teach us to number our days and to get a heart of wisdom.
Forbid that we should join the world in forgetting the certainty of our
death.
Don't let us play with the preciousness of life.
Make us ready to die well by helping us to live well by helping us to trust
You well.
Don't let us be surprised by our suffering.
Don't let us be surprised by being cut off early from this life.
Don't let us balk at the betrayal of friends and the blast of enmity.
Help us to embrace our lot and count it all joy . . . Amen.
   JOHN PIPER, *American pastor (1946–present day)* [PBW, 129]

A PRAYER FOR TODAY

Lord, show me the best use of this day. . . .
Show me the best use for this week. . . .
Show me the best use for this month. . . .
Show me the best use for this year. . . .
Show me the best use for this life. . . .
Please grant me the courage
   to order my day, my week, my month, my year, my life
   in accord with what You have shown me. Amen.

PRAYERS *of* INTERCESSION

🌸 I will discipline my children while there is hope and not be a willing party
to their death. **PROVERBS 19:18**

🌸 As a father *or mother*, help me not to embitter my children,
so they do not become discouraged. **COLOSSIANS 3:21**

🌸 O God, our heavenly Father, grant that these children, as they grow in
years, may also grow in grace and knowledge of the Lord Jesus Christ, and
that by the restraining and renewing influence of the Holy Spirit they may
ever be true children of thine, serving these faithfully all their days.
FROM THE METHODIST BOOK OF WORSHIP *[UMW, 16]*

A PRAYER FOR TODAY

*Pray for your own children or grandchildren each by name, or pray for the children of your
friends and relatives.*
God, You love Your people and want their best.
You entrust children to their earthly parents. We ask that *(insert parents' names)*
would parent well.
But we know that even when parents do things well, unless You work in a
child's life, it is only human effort that is at work.
We ask that *(insert child's name)* would come to know Jesus as his Savior early in
life.
We ask that all of *his/her* life would be devoted to Your glory.
We ask that Your promises be trusted so fully that peace and joy and strength
would fill *his/her* soul.
We ask that *he/she* would be a person of the Book, one who loves, studies, and
obeys Your Word in every area of its teaching.
We ask that *he/she* would be a person of prayer, so that the power of faith and
holiness would be upon *him/her* and that *his/her* spiritual impact would be
great.
We ask that *he/she* would give *himself/herself* to Your service, and not fritter away
his/her time on excessive recreation, unimportant hobbies, or aimless
ambition.
We ask that You would remove the influences that would lead *him/her* away
from You and from all that is good and right and true.
We ask that You would protect *him/her* from damaging experiences and people.
We ask that You would grant *him/her* positive relationships with the significant
people in *his/her* life.
We ask that *he/she* would live *his/her* life for Your approval alone. Amen.

PRAYERS *of* SURRENDER

Those who do not take up their cross and follow You, Jesus, are not worthy of You.
Those who find their lives will lose them, and those who lose their lives for Your sake will find them. **MATTHEW 10:38–39**

Dear God,
I am full of wishes, full of desires, full of expectations.
Some of them may be realized, many may not,
but in the midst of all my satisfactions and disappointments, I hope in you.
I know that you will never leave me alone and will fulfill your divine promises.
Even when it seems that things are not going my way,
I know that they are going your way and that in the end your way is the best way for me.
O Lord, strengthen my hope,
especially when my many wishes are not fulfilled. Amen.
HENRI NOUWEN, *American priest (1932–1996) [BHE, 88]*

Eternal and most glorious God, suffer me not so to undervalue myself
as to give away thy soul . . . thy dear and precious soul, for nothing;
and all the world is nothing, if the soul be given for it.
Preserve therefore my soul, O Lord, because it belongs to thee,
and preserve my body because it belongs to my soul.
JOHN DONNE, *English poet (1573–1631) [BTP, 125 PD]*

Father, I am not a fool to give the things I cannot keep to gain what I can never lose.
JIM ELLIOT, *American missionary/martyr (1927–1956) [JJE, 10/28/1949]*

Lord, humanly speaking, we know that no one likes to suffer physically.
But I know that if *You* lead me into it, *You* will give me the strength to survive it.
LI DE XIAN, *Chinese Christian pastor/martyr (died 2002) [JFM, 144]*
During time of persecution against Christians in China

A PRAYER FOR TODAY

Lord, I know intellectually that my desires and Your desires do not need to be at odds.
But often it seems like giving my life for You means losing it for me.
Help me to see that giving what I cannot keep is to gain what I can never lose.
It is the best investment I can make of my one and only life.
I choose to give my life to You again today by . . . Amen.

PRAYERS *of* THANKSGIVING

- Lord, I will consider it pure joy whenever I fall into various kinds of trials (or temptations),
  because I know that the testing of my faith develops perseverance,
  and perseverance develops maturity and completeness. JAMES 1:2–4

- Though the fig tree does not bud and there are no grapes on the vines,
  though the olive crop fails and the fields produce no food,
  though there are no sheep in the pen and no cattle in the stalls,
  yet I will rejoice in You, Lord; I will be joyful in You my Savior.
  You, Sovereign Lord, are my strength. HABAKKUK 3:17–19

- I will sing of Your strength; yes, I will sing of Your mercy in the morning,
  for in times of trouble.
  You are my stronghold, (Heb.=*misgab: fortress, a placed secured by might*) my place of safety. (Heb.=*manos: escape, place to run for safety, refuge*)
  To You, O my strength, I will sing praises, for You are my fortress, my loving God. PSALM 59:16–17

A PRAYER FOR TODAY

Lord, I do not see many people who are happy.
I see more people who are vexed by troubles and overcome with anguish at their difficulties. . . .
Sometimes, I too am derailed by trials. . . .
I am tempted to see trials as only negative because I like to think I'm in control. . . .
I am tempted to see trials as negative because I tend to think that this life matters most. . . .
Remind me that there is a limit to my perspective and wisdom. . . .
I do not see all there is to see.
Remind me that Jesus suffered and He was completely innocent. . . .
If He suffered, I too may experience suffering.
Remind me that this world is temporary. . . .
I will not be fully satisfied in this life.
So I thank You today for the trials You have allowed in my life. . . .
I thank You for being my fortress and strength . . .
and for giving me perseverance. . . .
Thank You for what these trials are doing in me—
developing maturity and completeness. . . . Amen.

PRAYERS *of* CONFESSION

O God, I will be diligent to present myself to You as one approved,
(Greek for diligent=spoudazo: persistent passion or zeal, making every effort)
(Greek for approved=dokimos: approved after a testing or examination)
a worker who does not need to be ashamed
and who correctly handles the word of truth.   **2 TIMOTHY 2:15**

O Father, how we need mercy. We sin every day.
We fall short of your command to love you with all our heart and soul and mind and strength.
We are lukewarm in our affections. All our motives, even at their best, are mixed.
We murmur.
We are anxious about tomorrow.
We get angry too quickly.
We desire what ought not be desired.
We get irritated at the very attitudes in others that we have displayed five minutes before.
If you do not show mercy to us, we are undone.
O God, let us see the mercy of Christ and savor it for what it is.
Grant us power to comprehend his love.
Incline us to read and ponder the stories of the mercy of Jesus in the Gospels.
Let us so admire what he did that we imitate him.
But let it be much more than external imitations.
Let it come from the heart where we have been broken for our sins and where we have come to cherish mercy and live by mercy and hope in mercy and long for mercy. . . .
Fulfill in us the command to do justice and love mercy. Let us love showing mercy.
Make it so much a part of us that it is who we are.
So unite us to Christ that his mercy is our mercy, . . .
He is all we have to give in the end. . . .
      JOHN PIPER, *American pastor (1946–present day) [SJC, 96–97]*

A PRAYER FOR TODAY

Lord, I want to be an approved worker for You. Yet I often choose another path by . . .
I will choose today to be diligent in my efforts to serve You by . . .
Let this choice not be merely external conformity to Your standards, but an internal transformation. Breathe in me the taste of Your goodness and mercy so You are my passion. Amen.

PRAYERS *of* AFFIRMATION

Jesus, You did many miraculous things in the presence of the disciples that are not recorded in the Scriptures. What is written, is given so that we may believe that You are the Christ, the very Son of God.   JOHN 20:30–31

God, where are you!?
What have I done to make you hide from me?
Are you playing cat and mouse with me, or are your purposes larger than my perceptions?
I feel alone, lost, forsaken.
You are the God who majors in revealing yourself.
You showed yourself to Abraham, Isaac, and Jacob.
When Moses wanted to know what you looked like, you obliged him.
Why them and not me?
I am tired of praying.
I am tired of asking.
I am tired of waiting.
But I will keep on praying and asking and waiting because I have nowhere else to go.
Jesus, you, too, knew the loneliness of the desert and the isolations of the cross.
And it is through your forsaken prayer that I speak these words. Amen.
    RICHARD FOSTER, *American author (1942–present day) [PHH, 24–25]*

O Lord our God, we know you are not only good but also great.
We know you are able to do strange and wonderful things.
Let us not be so skeptical that we fail to see them.
But neither let us be so greedy for signs that we fail to see the slow steady wonder of creation and providence all around us. In Jesus' name, Amen.
    CORNELIUS PLANTINGA JR., *American seminary president (1946–present day) [BDD, 45]*

A PRAYER FOR TODAY

Lord, when I don't see how You are working I tend to:
    work harder to try to control the outcomes by . . .
    try to reproduce what others are doing where You are working by . . .
    lose heart to the point of quitting or coasting. . . .
Help me to believe You are at work even when I don't see it.
Allow that affirmation and belief to comfort me . . .
    and to spur me on to courageous action . . .
    and to a confidence that nothing is beyond Your reach. . . . Amen.

Day 224
PRAYERS *of* PETITION

⚜ Lord, I am learning to be content (Gk.=*autarkes*: *sufficient, adequate, independent of external conditions*)
in whatever circumstances I am in.
I know what it is to be in need, and I know what it is to have plenty.
I have learned the secret of being content in every situation,
whether well fed or hungry, whether living in plenty or want.
PHILIPPIANS 4:11–12

⚜ For godliness when accompanied with contentment equates to real gain,
for we brought nothing into this world and we can take nothing out of it.
1 TIMOTHY 6:6–7

⚜ Two things have I required of thee, O Lord, deny thou me not before I die;
remove far from me vanity and lies; give me neither poverty nor riches,
feed me with food convenient for me; lest I be full and deny thee and say,
who is the Lord?
Or lest I be poor and steal, and take the name of my God in vain.
Let me learn to abound, let me learn to suffer need,
in whatsoever state I am, therewith to be content.
For nothing earthly, temporal, mortal, to long [for] nor to wait.
Grant me a happy life, in piety, gravity, purity,
in all things good and fair, in cheerfulness, in health, in credit,
in competency, in safety, in gentle estate, in quiet; a happy death, a death-
less happiness.
LANCELOT ANDREWES, *English minister (1555–1626)* [US PD]

A PRAYER FOR TODAY

Lord, here is where I am experiencing want in my life . . .
I know that this can lead to some discontentment, as seen in . . .
I know that this can lead me to anxious striving, as seen in . . .
I want to be a person who is content regardless of my external circumstances.
But this is hard for me because I equate contentment with having plenty and
abundance.
Let me experience my contentment in You—not in my circumstances. . . .
I affirm that my ultimate good does not rest:
in my talents, . . . *(name the talents you are prone to trust)*
in my achievements, . . . *(name the achievements you are prone to cite)*
or in my wealth, . . . *(name the wealth you are prone to rely upon)*
But it comes from Your love alone! Amen.

PRAYERS *for* RENEWAL

Lord, You require that those who have been given a trust must prove faithful.   1 CORINTHIANS 4:2

May we accept this day at your hand, O Lord,
    as a gift to be treasured,
    a life to be enjoyed,
    a trust to be kept,
    and a hope to be fulfilled;
    and all for your glory.
      STANLEY PRITCHARD, *American clergy (twentieth century) [CBP, 316]*

Lord, our lives are as if You, as a master of an estate, have gone on a long journey and entrusted us with Your property. To one You have given five talents, to another two talents, and to another one talent, all based upon each person's ability. . . . To those who use these talents well You will say,
    "Well done, good and faithful servant! You have been faithful with a few things;
    I will put you in charge of many things. Come and share in my happiness." . . .
But to the one who does not use these talents well You will say,
    "You wicked, lazy servant! . . . Take the talent from him and give it to the one who has many.
    For everyone who has will be given, and he will have an abundance.
    Whoever does not have, even what he has will be taken from him."
      MATTHEW 25:14–15, 23, 26, 28–29

Lord, everything we have, all that we are, comes from you. Our gifts, our talents, all our possibilities belong to us only because they come direct from you. Help us not to belittle these gifts of yours, not to bury them, but rather use them to make you better known to the people of our neighborhood.
      COLIN SEMPER, *Anglican clergy (1938–present day) [BTP, 35]*

A PRAYER FOR TODAY

Remind me today that all I have are gifts entrusted to me. . . .
I thank You for all You have entrusted and given to me.
I celebrate these things as gifts. . . .
Remind me to use what I have been given for more than merely my enjoyment. . . .
Remind me that I will be evaluated for how I use what I have been given. . . .
Renew my desire to prove faithful with what I have been given. Amen.

PRAYERS *of* PRAISE/ADORATION

You, Lord Almighty, have purposed, and who can thwart You?
Your hand is stretched out, and who can turn it back? ISAIAH 14:27

You, my God, are from heaven. You do whatever pleases You.
PSALM 115:3

Now, Lord, to You who are able to do immeasurably more than we can ask
or imagine, according to Your power that is at work within us, to You be
glory in the church and in Christ Jesus throughout all generations,
forever and ever! Amen. EPHESIANS 3:20

I rise today with the power of God to guide me,
the might of God to uphold me,
the wisdom of God to teach me,
the eye of God to watch over me,
the ear of God to hear me,
the word of God to give me speech,
the hand of God to protect me,
the path of God to lie before me,
the shield of God to shelter me,
the host of God to defend me against the snares of the devil and the temptations of the world,
against every man who meditates injury to me, whether far or near.
BREASTPLATE OF PATRICK, *Irish minister (c. 389–461) [EOP, 248]*

A PRAYER FOR TODAY

Lord, sometimes I have a limited view of Your power
because I see the size of the problems before me, . . .
because I have been disappointed before, . . .
because I see through my finite eyes, . . .
because I forget the powerful things You have done in the past. . . .
But today I affirm that nothing is too hard for You.
I affirm that no plan of Yours can be thwarted.
I affirm that You can do whatever You want.
I affirm that You enjoy doing immeasurably more than I can ask or imagine.
I trust in You and in Your power in these circumstances . . .
Help me to remember Your power. I praise You for Your power!
I praise You for Your willingness to do more than I can ask or imagine.
Amen.

PRAYERS *for* CHRISTLIKE CHARACTER

🌸 I will not take vengeance or bear a grudge against others, but I will love my neighbor as myself.   LEVITICUS 19:18

🌸 *God*, to be a Christian is to forgive the inexcusable,
because *You* have forgiven the inexcusable in me.
> C. S. LEWIS, *English professor at Oxford/author (1898–1963) [US]*

🌸 Jesus, *your* prayer was "Father, forgive them; they know not what they do."
A prayer born in death, writhing with pain.
A prayer risking faith, facing the sorrow.
A prayer living in hope, seeing the future. . . .

My prayer became, "God, forgive them, they know what they did."
A prayer that wrestled with injustice.
A prayer that acknowledges weakness.
A prayer that found hope in God's love.

My prayer remains, "God, forgive them; they know what they did."
Because forgiving recreates life from death.
Because forgiving cleanses the healing wound.
Because forgiving builds the bridge of freedom.
> JARED P. PINGLETON, *American psychologist (twentieth century)*
> *[CDP, 696–97]*

🌸 O Lord, give me strength to refrain from the unkind silence that is born of hardness of heart . . . and is the enemy of peace.
Give me strength to be the first to tender the healing word and the renewal of friendship,
that the bonds of *goodwill* and the flow of charity may be strengthened for the good of the brethren and the furthering of thine eternal, loving purpose.
> CECIL HUNT, *English journalist (1902–1954) [OBP, 113]*

A PRAYER FOR TODAY

Lord, I acknowledge the hurts caused me by these people . . .
But I do not want to hold on to this or seek vengeance, so I release those who have hurt me. . . .
I commit this to You and will not seek repayment through my coldness . . .
or through my words . . . or actions. . . . Rather I will seek them out to redeem this relationship with wisdom. . . . Amen.

I am not trying to win the approval of other people;
I seek to win Your approval, Lord.
If I were still trying to please people, I would not be Your servant.
GALATIANS 1:10

Father, I know now, if I never knew it before, that only in You can my restless human heart find any peace. For I began life without knowledge, but full of needs. And the turmoil of my mind, the dissatisfaction of my life all stem from trying to meet those needs with the wrong things and in the wrong places.
PETER MARSHALL, *chaplain of U.S. Senate (1902–1949) [CDP, 537]*

Christ, when I can say that I live for You, then to die is all gain.
But when I live for something else, to die is to lose it all.   **PHILIPPIANS 1:21**

Father God, when I seek ultimate fulfillment from things here, even good
things, the end is empty.
When I seek fulfillment in my appearance, the end is to appear worn down
and lose the appeal.
When I seek fulfillment in success, the end is either a need for more
success, or a nagging sense of failure.
When I seek fulfillment in my family, the end, if good, is only a taste of
eternity, and the end, if poor, will leave deep and abiding wounds.
When I seek fulfillment in acquisition, the end is that another acquires
what I acquired.
When I seek fulfillment in sexual expression, the end is an ever increasing
desire for more—or a blasé deadness.
Even when I seek fulfillment from doing good in the world, the end is that I
feel good for a short time, but there are still deeper longings within me.
When I seek approval for the good that I have done, I am doing nothing
more than trying to get others to think well of me for doing good things.
Grant that I may feel *Your* fulfillment and approval above all else.
KURT BJORKLUND, *American minister (1968–present day)*

A PRAYER FOR TODAY

Father, show me the ways that I try to fill needs with wrong things. . . .
Show me the emptiness of seeking to fill these needs in this way . . .
Show me how to seek fullness primarily in You. . . .
Show me where I am seeking approval from people instead of from You. . . .
Show me how to seek Your approval above all others. . . . Amen.

PRAYERS *of* INTERCESSION

May I offer petitions, prayers, intercessions, and thanks on behalf of all people, for kings and all those who are in authority, that all people may live peaceful and quiet lives in all godliness and reverence. This is good and acceptable in Your sight, God our Savior, for You desire all people to be saved and to come to the knowledge of the truth. 1 TIMOTHY 2:1–4

We bring before you, O Lord,
the troubles and perils of peoples and nations,
the frustration of prisoners and captives,
the anguish of the bereaved,
the needs of refugees,
the helplessness of the weak,
the despondency of the weary,
the failing powers of the aged
and the hopelessness of the starving.
O Lord, draw near to each, for the sake of Jesus Christ our Lord.
     ANSELM, *bishop of Canterbury (1033–1109)* [*BTP, 191* PD]

God of the common good, who has bound us in one bundle of life, we plead our neighbor's need.
For the nations we pray: give peace in our time.
For the workers of the world we pray: gird them and us that none may lack bread, since you have given enough for all.
For the sorrowing and the sick we pray: make their shadow the secret way of your coming.
For our friends and loved ones: befriend them in your own befriending. Amen.
     BOOK OF COMMON PRAYER [*BDD, 59* PD]

A PRAYER FOR TODAY

Lord, I pray for the difficult situations in the world that are in the news or my awareness . . .
Lord, where there is war I ask . . . where natural disasters have hit I ask . . .
for the prisoners I ask . . .
for those who have lost loved ones to disasters and wars I ask . . .
for the refugees I ask . . . for the aged I ask . . .
for those who are exhausted from their work and have no other option I ask . . .
for the hungry I ask . . .
Lord, for those who are physically sick and facing disease I ask . . .
Lord, for the part I can play in these needs I ask . . .
Lord, for those who do not have an experience of You I ask . . . Amen.

Day 230
PRAYERS *of* SURRENDER

⚜ Lord, may I not be one who merely listens to Your Word and so deceives myself. Help me to live it.   JAMES 1:22

⚜ O Lord, I place myself in your hands and dedicate myself to you.
I pledge myself to do your will in all things;
To love the Lord God with all my heart, all my soul, all my strength.
Not to kill, not to steal, not to covet, not to bear false witness, to honor all persons.
Not to do to another what I should not want done to myself.
Not to seek after pleasures.
To love fasting. To relieve the poor. To clothe the naked. To visit the sick. . . .
To help those in trouble. To console the sorrowing. To hold myself aloof from worldly ways.
To prefer nothing to the love of Christ.
Not to give way to anger. Not to foster a desire for revenge.
Not to entertain deceit in the heart. Not to make a false peace.
Not to swear, lest I swear falsely.
To speak the truth with heart and tongue.
Not to return evil for evil.
To do no injury, indeed, even to bear patiently any injury done to me.
To love my enemies. Not to curse those who curse me but rather to bless them.
To bear persecution for justice's sake.
Not to be lazy. Not to be slothful. Not to be a detractor.
To put my trust in God.
To refer the good I see in myself to God.
To refer any evil I see in myself to myself. . . .
To remember that God sees me everywhere.
To call upon Christ for defense against evil thoughts that arise in my heart.
To guard my tongue against wicked speech.
To avoid much speaking. To avoid idle talk.
Not to seek to appear clever.
To read only what is good to read. To pray often.
To ask forgiveness daily for my sins, and to seek ways to amend my life. . . .
To make peace after a quarrel, before the setting of the sun.
Never to despair of your mercy, O God of mercy.
   BENEDICT, *founder of the Benedictine monks (480–543) [EOP, 94–95]*

Reread Benedict's prayer and focus on praying personally what stood out most to you. . . .

PRAYERS *of* THANKSGIVING

🌿 Therefore, Jesus, Son of God, since You are such a great high priest who ascended into heaven, let me hold firmly to the faith I profess. For I do not have a high priest who is unable to empathize with my weakness, but in You I have One who has been tempted in every way, just as I have been— yet You did not sin. Let me then approach God's throne of grace with confidence, so that I may receive mercy and find grace to help me in my time of need.   **HEBREWS 4:14–16**

🌿 Lord Jesus, I want to express my deep gratitude that you are the High Priest of my life. . . . I am the recipient of all of your love and care because You came into the world to be one of us. In all things, You were made like unto the brethren that You might be a merciful and faithful High Priest to me!
　　　DAVID JEREMIAH, *American pastor (1941–present day) [PGA, 192]*

🌿 O God, for your love for us, warm and brooding,
　which has brought us to birth and opened our eyes
　to the wonder and beauty of creation, **we give you thanks.**
　For your love for us, compassionate and patient,
　which has carried us through our pain,
　wept beside us in our sin,
　and waited with us in our confusion, **we give you thanks.**
　For your love for us, strong and challenging,
　which has called us to risk for you,
　asked for the best in us,
　and shown us how to serve, **we give you thanks. . . .**
　　　ALI NEWELL, *Scottish minister (unknown era) [BTP, 80–81]*

A PRAYER FOR TODAY

Think about Jesus experiencing temptation, rejection, and suffering. . . .

Jesus, I thank You that You have experienced the same types of things I am experiencing.
I thank You that my emotions are not foreign to You.
Today there is no concern that I have with which You are not familiar.
Even this, the deepest of my current concerns . . .
Thank You for not asking me to face things that You were unwilling to face.
Although the particulars are different, I know that You know how it feels to be me.
Thank You that there is mercy and grace available to me. . . . Amen.

PRAYERS *of* CONFESSION

Jesus, Son of Man, You taught that whoever wants to become great must be a servant, and whoever wants to be first must be the slave of all.
For even You did not come to be served,
but to serve and to give Your life as a ransom for many.   MARK 10:44–45

Lord, I size up other people in terms of what they can do for me;
> how they can further my program,
> feed my ego,
> satisfy my needs,
> give me strategic advantage.
I exploit people, ostensibly for your sake, but really for my own sake.
Lord, I turn to you to get the inside track and obtain special favors,
> your direction for my schemes,
> your power for my projects,
> your sanction for my ambitions,
> your blank check for whatever I want.
Change me, Lord. Make me a *person* who asks of you and others, what can I do for you?
> ROBERT RAINES, *English vicar (1805–1878) [quoted in IYS, 94–95]*

For the hatred which divides nation from nation, race from race, class from class; **Father, forgive.**
For the greed which exploits the labours of *people* and lays waste to the earth; **Father, forgive.**
For our envy of the welfare and happiness of others; **Father, forgive.**
For our indifferences to the plight of the homeless and the refugee; **Father, forgive.**
For the lust which uses ignoble ends, the bodies of men and women; **Father, forgive.**
For the pride which leads us to trust in ourselves and not in God; **Father, forgive.**
> PRAYER AT THE ALTAR OF COVENTRY CATHEDRAL [*GMO, 280* PD]

A PRAYER FOR TODAY

Lord, I often do want to be served and to be first. . . .
I often use people and even try to use You for my advantage. . . .
I turn from my self-seeking. I want to live a life that gives itself away to the good of others. Today I can do this by . . .
Make me aware of the little choices I will make today between serving myself and serving others. . . . Amen.

PRAYERS *of* AFFIRMATION

I am not ashamed of the gospel of Christ, for it is Your power to salvation for everyone who believes, for the Jew first and also for the Greek. For in it Your righteousness is revealed from faith to faith, as it is written, "The just shall live by faith." **ROMANS 1:16–17**

Father, I affirm the reality of Jesus Christ
He was born in an obscure village, the child of a peasant woman. . . .
He never owned a home. Never wrote a book.
He never held an office. He never had a family.
He never went to college. He never put His foot inside a big city.
He never traveled two hundred miles from the place where He was born. . . .
When He was dead, He was laid in a borrowed grave through the pity of a friend.
Nineteen long centuries have come and gone, and today
He is the centerpiece of the human race and the leader of the column of progress. *It is not overstated to* say that
    all the armies that have ever marched,
    all the navies that were ever built, all the parliaments that ever sat,
    and all the kings that ever reigned, put together,
    have not affected the lives of humanity upon this earth as powerfully
as that one solitary life.
    "ONE SOLITARY LIFE," ANONYMOUS *[SOL, 156–57]*

You demonstrated Your own love toward us in that while we were still sinners, Christ died for us. **ROMANS 5:8**

O God, what a treasure I have in your gospel! You show me there what no therapist can do, what no government program can do, what no money can buy. Your gospel shows how you give a sinner like me a fresh start in life and a glorious destiny in eternity. And I don't have to trigger this wonderful change with my own power or virtue. I receive it with the empty hands of faith. Enlarge my understanding of your gospel. In the holy name of Christ. Amen.
    RAYMOND ORTLUND JR., *American minister (1946–present day) [PFG, 32]*

A PRAYER FOR TODAY

Father, I know that You have sent Jesus into this world.
Through Him I have been declared righteous and I am freed from sin.
I affirm that without Christ my life would be . . . and with Christ my life is . . .
He has done for me what no other could ever do.
Enlarge my appreciation and affection for Jesus and Your gospel. Amen.

PRAYERS *of* PETITION

❧ This is what You require of Your people, God:
    to fear You,
    to walk in Your ways,
    to love You,
    and to serve You with all our hearts and with all our souls.
       DEUTERONOMY 10:12

❧ Lord, direct my heart into God's love and Christ's perseverance.
    2 THESSALONIANS 3:5

❧ With all my heart, **I love Thee, O my God.**
With all my soul, **I love Thee, O my God.**
With all my mind, **I love Thee, O my God.**
With all my strength, **I love Thee, O my God.**
Above all possessions and honors, **I love Thee, O my God.**
Above all pleasures and enjoyments, **I love Thee, O my God.**
More than myself, and everything belonging to me, **I love Thee, O my God.**
More than all my relatives and friends, **I love Thee, O my God.**
More than all men and angels, **I love Thee, O my God.**
Above all created things in heaven or on earth, **I love Thee, O my God.**
Only for Thyself, **I love Thee, O my God.**
Because Thou are the sovereign Good, **I love Thee, O my God.**
Because Thou are infinitely worthy of being loved, **I love Thee, O my God.**
Because Thou are infinitely perfect, **I love Thee, O my God. . . .**
In life and in death, **I love Thee, O my God.**
In time and in eternity, **I love Thee, O my God.**
       POPE PIUS IV *(1717–1799)* [*EOP, 79* PD]

A PRAYER FOR TODAY

Pray for any special concerns that You might have. . . .

In the Bible, believers are commanded to love God. This seems odd to us because we connect love with a feeling rather than an act of the will. But to love in the Bible is more often to choose to act in love than it is to experience an emotion. As you pray the prayer of Pius, do it not to express emotion but as a choice to say "I am loving You, my God" in each description.
Lord, today I choose to love You by . . .
I ask that loving You would not merely be an act of my will.
I ask that I would also feel the emotion of being loved by You. . . .
I ask that I would feel love for You. . . .

PRAYERS *for* RENEWAL

🌸 Lord, I will not lose heart; even though my outward self is perishing,
yet my inner self is being renewed day by day.
For this momentary, light affliction (Gk.=*elathros thlipsis: a weightless trifle of
a trouble, or pressure*) is working for me a far more exceeding and
eternal weight of glory.   2 CORINTHIANS 4:16–17

🌸 I rejoice in my tribulations,
    (Gk.=*thlipsis: trouble, pressure, hardship caused by circumstances*)
knowing that tribulation produces perseverance; (Gk.=*hupomone: patient
    endurance, ability to continue*)
and perseverance, character; (Gk.=*dokime: approved through a trial, approved
    character*)
and character, hope. (Gk.=*elpis: a faithful trust in God's promises for the future
    while in tribulations*)
And hope does not disappoint, because Your love, O God, has been poured
out into my heart through the Holy Spirit whom You have given to me.
    ROMANS 5:3–5

🌸 *Lord,* let nothing disturb *me,* nothing frighten *me,*
for all things are passing; patient endurance attains all things.
One whom *You* possess lacks nothing, for *You God* alone suffice.
    TERESA OF ÁVILA, *Spanish nun (1515–1582) [EOP, 363]*

🌸 Almighty and merciful God who are the strength of the weak, . . .
the God of patience and of all consolation:
Thou knowest full well the inner weakness of our nature,
    how we tremble and quiver before pain,
      and cannot bear the cross without thy divine help and support.
Help me, then O eternal and pitying God, . . . to possess my soul in patience,
    to maintain unshaken hope in thee,
      to keep that childlike trust which feels a Father's heart . . .
so shall I be strengthened with power according to thy glorious might and
in the very depth of my suffering, to praise thee with a joyful heart.
    JOHANN HABERMANN, *German theologian (1516–1590) [EOP, 105 PD]*

A PRAYER FOR TODAY

Lord, let me not be overwhelmed by what is hard in my life. . . .
Let me be confident that through these trials I will experience You and Your
hand in hardship . . .
that through these trials my character will be approved. . . .
Let me rejoice in my tribulations. . . . Amen.

PRAYERS *of* PRAISE/ADORATION

I will proclaim Your name, O Lord, and praise Your greatness, O my God.
You are the Rock, Your works are perfect, and all Your ways are just.
You are a faithful God who does no wrong,
You are upright and just. . . .
You are our Father, our Creator,
the One who made us and formed us.   DEUTERONOMY 32:3–4, 6B

God, because You are . . .
> My Creator—I will glorify *You.*
> My Father—I will adore *You.*
> My Lord—I will worship *You.*
> My King—I will serve *You.*
> My Master—I will obey *You.*
> My Friend—I will confide in *You.*
> My Shepherd—I will follow *You.*
> My Rock—I will build on *You.*
> My Refuge—I will hide in *You.*
> My Strength—I will lean on *You.*
> My Comforter—I will turn to *You.*
> My Peace—I will rest in *You....*
> My Way—I will walk in *You.*
> My Truth—I will believe in *You.*
> My Life—I will rejoice in *You....*
> My Vine—I will abide in *You.*
> My Example—I will emulate *You....*
> My Salvation—I will hope in *You.* My Judge—I will implore *You.*
> My Vindicator—I will depend on *You.* My Redeemer—I will exult in *You.*
> JOSEPH HOPKINS, *American minister (twentieth century)* [PFH, 7–9]

A PRAYER FOR TODAY

*Add your own names or images of God from the Scriptures with your own "I will"
statements.... Which image is most compelling to you today? Why?...
Which action corresponding with the image is most compelling to you? What would it
look like to really implement that action into your life today?...*

Lord, let my worship of You in thought move me to worship of You in action by
. . . Amen.

PRAYERS *for* CHRISTLIKE CHARACTER

🌿 Christ Jesus, I will keep the pattern of sound teaching that I have heard, in the faith and love that You give.   **2 TIMOTHY 1:13**

🌿 Lord, I believe in you—increase my faith.
I trust in you—strengthen my trust.
I love you—let me love you more and more.
I am sorry for my sins—deepen my sorrow.
I worship you as my first beginning, I long for you as my last end, I praise you as my constant helper, and call on you as my loving protector.
Guide me by your wisdom, correct me with your justice, comfort me with your mercy, protect me with your power.
I offer you, Lord, my thoughts, to be fixed on you;
    my words—to have you for their theme;
    my actions—to reflect my love for you;
    my sufferings—to be endured for your greater glory.
I want to do what you ask of me—in the way you ask, for as long as you ask, because you ask it.
Help me to repent of my past sins and to resist temptation in the future. . . .
Help me to conquer anger with gentleness, greed with generosity. . . . Help me to forget myself and reach out to others.
Make me prudent in planning, courageous in taking risks. . . .
Make me patient in suffering, unassuming in prosperity.
Let my conscience be clear, my conduct without fault, my speech blameless, and my life well-ordered. . . .
Lead me safely through death to the endless joy of heaven.
Grant this through Christ our Lord. Amen.
    POPE CLEMENT XI *(1649–1721)* *[EOP, 134–35 PD]*

A PRAYER FOR TODAY

Reread the prayer of Clement XI slowly, asking the Holy Spirit to identify to you what would most please God in your life as the lines of the prayer. Think about specific situations where the character quality noted above would please God.

Lord, show me where I can . . . *(insert lines of prayer you identified)*
Show me how I can . . . *(insert lines of prayer you identified)*
Grant me the desire to . . . *(insert lines of prayer you identified)*
Lord, let me not be deceived by doing these things, thinking my standing with You rests in "works."
Let me be assured of my standing with You through Jesus Christ and act from a place of assurance, not to gain assurance. Amen.

PRAYERS *for* WISDOM/GUIDANCE

O Lord Almighty,
the sun of righteousness will rise with healing in its wings
for those who revere Your name.
They will go out and leap like calves released from the stall.
MALACHI 4:2

You are my lamp, O Lord;
You turn my darkness into light.
With Your aid, I am able to advance when the odds are against me.
With You I am able to leap over a high wall.
2 SAMUEL 2:29–30

Lord, we offer you ourselves this day
for the work you want accomplished,
for the people you want us to meet,
for the word you want to be uttered,
for the silence you want to be kept,
for the places you want us to enter,
for the new ways you want pioneered.
. . . enable us to realize your presence, at all times and in all places,
our loving Lord Jesus Christ.
MORRIS MADDOCKS, *English bishop (1928–2008) [CBP, 344]*

A PRAYER FOR TODAY

Lord, I am facing this decision today . . .
Help me not to choose based on the approval of people, but for Your honor. . . .
Help me not to choose based on financial advantages, but on spiritual advantages. . . .
Help me not to assume that I know what is best, but to seek wisdom in Your Word. . . .
Help me not to assume that earthly power is where real strength is found, but to find power in You. . . .
Help me not to assume that a past decision is still the best decision, but to seek Your guidance. . . .
Help me not to be blinded to the presence of evil as I choose . . .
Help me not to be blinded to the impact of fear as I choose . . .
Help me not to be blinded by my own ambition as I choose . . . Amen.

PRAYERS *of* INTERCESSION

To the faithful, Lord, You show Yourself faithful,
to the blameless You show Yourself blameless,
to the pure You show Yourself pure,
but to the crooked You show Yourself shrewd.
You save the humble but bring low those whose eyes are haughty. . . .
My God, You turn my darkness into light.
      PSALM 18:25–28

God of mercy, we bless you in the name of your Son, Jesus Christ,
    who ministered to all who came to him.
Give your strength to *(insert name)*, your servant, (bound by the chains of
    addiction).
Enfold *him/her* in your love and restore *him/her* to the freedom of your
    children.
Look with compassion on all those who have lost their health and freedom.
Restore to them the assurance of your unfailing mercy.
Strengthen them in the work of recovery (and help them to resist all
    temptation).
To those who care for them, grant patient understanding and a love that
    perseveres.
We ask this through Christ our Lord, Amen.
      FROM THE METHODIST BOOK OF WORSHIP *[UMW, 107]*

Lord you are a present help in trouble. Come revive, redeem, restore, . . .
    in our sadness come as joy,
    in our troubles come as peace,
    and in our weakness come as strength.
Come Lord to our aid, revive, redeem, restore us.
O Lord, open our eyes to your Presence.
Open our minds to your grace. Open our lips to your praises.
Open our hearts to your love. Open our lives to your healing.
      DAVID ADAM, *English author (twentieth century) [BTP, 105]*

A PRAYER FOR TODAY

Lord, today I pray for *(insert name)* who is caught in addictive and destructive
behavior patterns.
I ask You to show them the pathway they are on. . . .
I ask You to grant them the courage, perseverance, and resources to change.
Show me how You want me to aid them in their journey out of bondage and
into freedom. . . . Amen.

PRAYERS *of* SURRENDER

❧ Lord, remind me that if I love money, I will not be satisfied with money; and if I love abundance, I will not be satisfied with its increase.
ECCLESIASTES 5:10

❧ O God, be Thou exalted over my possessions. Nothing of earth's treasure shall seem dear unto me if only Thou art exalted in my life. . . .
Be Thou exalted above my comforts, *though* it mean the loss of bodily comforts and the carrying of heavy crosses. . . .
Be Thou exalted over my reputation. Make me ambitious to please Thee even if as a result I must sink into obscurity and my name be forgotten as a dream.
Rise, O Lord, into Thy proper place of honor, above my ambitions, above my likes and dislikes, above my family, my health and even my life itself. Let me sink that Thou mayest rise above.
A. W. TOZER, *American pastor (1898–1963) [POG, 101–102]*

❧ Jesus, help me to watch out and to be on guard against all kinds of greed; remind me that a person's life does not consist in the abundance of possessions. . . . **LUKE 12:15**

❧ Dear Teacher, teach me what life is all about.
Help me to learn that it does not consist of possessions, no matter how many, no matter how nice.
Help me to realize that the more things I selfishly accumulate, the more barns I will have to build to store them in. Help me to realize, too, that the storage fee on such things is subtracted from a life that could be rich toward you instead.
Where have I enriched myself at the expense of my soul? Where have I been a fool? Show me Lord, while there is still time to change.
Teach me that life is more than the things necessary to sustain it. Help me to learn that if life is more than food, surely it is more important than how the dining room looks; if it's more than clothes, certainly it is more important than whether there's enough closet space to hold them.
Keep me from treasuring those things, Lord.
KEN GIRE, *author (1950–present day) [MWS, 220–21]*

A PRAYER FOR TODAY

Lord, I surrender the resources I have been entrusted with and their management to You. . . .
Help me to be rich toward You by . . . Amen.

PRAYERS *of* THANKSGIVING

🌿 It is by Your grace, God, that I am what I am. 1 CORINTHIANS 15:10

🌿 You reached down from on high and took hold of me;
You drew me out of deep waters.
You delivered me from my strong enemy,
    from those who hated me, for they were stronger than I am.
        2 SAMUEL 22:17–18

🌿 Thank You Lord:
For Your sovereign control over our circumstances
For Your holy character in spite of our sinfulness
For Your commitment to us even when we wander astray
For Your Word that gives us direction
For Your love that holds us close
For Your gentle compassion in our sorrows
For Your consistent faithfulness through our highs and lows . . .
For Your understanding when we are confused
For Your Spirit that enlightens our eyes
For Your grace that removes our guilt.
        CHARLES SWINDOLL, *American pastor (1932–present day) [GOC, 121]*

🌿 May I be filled with joy, always thanking You Father, who has enabled me
to share the inheritance that belongs to God's people, who live in the light.
For You have rescued us from the dominion of darkness and brought us
into the kingdom of the Son You love. In Him we have redemption, the
forgiveness of our sins. COLOSSIANS 1:12–14

A PRAYER FOR TODAY

Lord, I tend to think that the good things in my life are a result of my talents
and hard work.
Yet Your Word teaches that You are the One who has brought good things into
my life.
It is Your grace that I am what I am. . . .
It is Your grace that I have what I have. . . .
It is Your grace that I have had the opportunities I have had. . . .
It is Your grace that I have met the people I have met. . . .
Thank You for these, your gracious gifts.
You are the author not just of good temporal gifts, but of the gift of salvation.
Thank You for Your good gift of salvation. . . .
Thank You for rescuing me from darkness. . . . Amen.

PRAYERS *of* CONFESSION

Christ Jesus, I will count myself as dead to sin but alive to God in You. I will not let sin reign in my mortal body so that I obey its evil desires. I will not offer the parts of my body to sin, as instruments of wickedness, but rather I will offer myself to God as one who has been brought from death to life. I offer the parts of my body to God as instruments of righteousness.

ROMANS 6:11–13

O Lord, open our minds to see ourselves as you see us, and from all unwillingness to know our weakness and our sin—**Good Lord, deliver us.**
From selfishness; from wishing to be the centre of attraction; from seeking admiration; from the desire to have our own way in all things; from unwillingness to listen to others; from resentment of criticism—**Good Lord, deliver us.**
From love of power, from jealousy; from taking pleasure in the weakness of others—**Good Lord, deliver us.**
From the weakness of indecision, from fear of adventure; from constant fear of what others are thinking of us; from fear of speaking what we know is truth, and doing what we know is right—**Good Lord, deliver us.** . . .
From possessiveness about material things and people; from carelessness about the needs of others; from selfish use of time and money; from all lack of generosity—**Good Lord, deliver us.**
From failure to be truthful; from pretence and acting a part; from hypocrisy; from all dishonesty with ourselves and with others—**Good Lord, deliver us.**
From impurity in word, in thought, and in action; from failure to respect the bodies and minds of ourselves and others; from any kind of addiction —**Good Lord, deliver us.**
From hatred and anger, from sarcasm; from lack of sensitivity and division in our community; from all failure to love and to forgive—**Good Lord, deliver us.**
From failure to see our sin as an affront to God; from failure to accept the forgiveness he offers—**Good Lord, deliver us.**

PETER NOTT, *Anglican bishop (1933–present day)* [*CBP, 261–62* PD]

A PRAYER FOR TODAY

Lord, reveal to me areas of my life that are sinful. . . .
Lord, I confess those areas to You now. . . .
I know that when I come to You, You will receive me, forgive me, and restore me.

PRAYERS *of* AFFIRMATION

God, You chose me in Christ, before the foundation of the world, to be
holy and blameless in Your sight.
> In love, You predestined me to be adopted as Your child through Jesus Christ,
>> according to the good pleasure of Your will,
>> to the praise of the glory of Your grace,
>> which You bestowed upon me in the One You love.   EPHESIANS 1:4–6

We see You Jesus,
>> who for a little while was made lower than the angels
>> and now is exalted with glory and honor because You suffered death
>> for us.
> By God's grace You have tasted death for everyone in the entire world.
> And it was only right that God,
> who made everything and for whom everything was made,
> should bring many people into glory.   HEBREWS 2:9–10

Lord God, I am not ashamed, because I know You, the one I have believed,
and I am persuaded and confident that You are able
to protect and safeguard that which I have given to You
for safekeeping for that day.   2 TIMOTHY 1:12

I take God the Father to be my God;
I take God the Son to be my Savior;
I take the Holy Spirit to be my Sanctifier;
I take the Word of God to be my rule;
I take the people of God to be my people;
And I do hereby and dedicate and yield my whole self to the Lord:
And I do this deliberately, freely and for ever. Amen.
> MATTHEW HENRY, *English Bible commentator (1662–1714) [EOP, 97]*
> *Prayer of affirmation taught to him by his father*

A PRAYER FOR TODAY

Lord, I affirm that salvation is Your deal from beginning to end.
In the past You chose me.
At the cross You saved me.
In the future You will lead me home.
I affirm that whatever I entrust to You, You are able to keep for that day.
Here is what I entrust to You . . . Amen.

PRAYERS *of* PETITION

⚜ Lord, impress upon me that the wounds of honest words that hurt from a
friend can be trusted. . . .
Creature comforts bring joy to the heart, and the pleasantness of one's
friends springs from the earnest counsel that is given.
I will not forsake my friends or the friends of my father. . . .
PROVERBS 27:6, 9–10

⚜ May I be an enemy to no one and the friend of what abides eternally.
May I never quarrel with those nearest me, and be reconciled quickly if
I should.
May I never plot evil against others, and if anyone plot evil against me,
may I escape unharmed and without the need to hurt anyone else.
May I love, seek, and attain only what is good.
May I desire happiness for all and harbor envy for none.
May I never find joy in the misfortune of one who has wronged me.
May I reconcile friends who are mad at each other.
May I, insofar as I can, give all necessary help to my friends and to all who
are in need.
May I never fail a friend in trouble.
May I be able to soften the pain of the grief stricken and give them
comforting words.
May I respect myself.
May I always maintain control of my emotions.
May I habituate myself to be gentle, and never angry with others because of
circumstances.
EUSEBIUS, *bishop of Caesarea (263–339)* [*EOP*, 72–73 PD]

A PRAYER FOR TODAY

Lord, I want to be the kind of friend I would want to have.
Help me to provide constancy *(to be reliable, not fickle)* to my friends by . . .
Help me to be vulnerable *(willing to share my weaknesses and struggles)* with my
friends by . . .
Help me to be honest *(speaking truth to and about them, even if it is unpleasant)* with
my friends by . . .
Help me to affirm *(expressing the good things I see in them)* my friends by . . .
Help me to sympathize and be present with my friends in their struggles. . . .
Help me to comfort my friends by feeling with them what they feel. . . .
Help me not to be the friend who gives bad advice. . . . (1 Kings 12:8–14)
Help me to be ever expanding my circle of friends. . . . Amen.

PRAYERS *for* RENEWAL

If I spend myself on behalf of the hungry and satisfy the needs of the
   oppressed,
Then my light will rise in the darkness, and my night will become like the
   noonday.
You, Lord, will guide me always;
Then You will satisfy my needs in a sun-scorched land and will strengthen
   my frame.
Then I will be like a well-watered garden, like a spring whose waters never
   fail.   ISAIAH 58:10–11

Take, Lord, and receive all my liberty, my memory, my understanding, and
all my will, all that I have and possess.
Thou hast given them to me;
to thee, O Lord, I restore them;
all things are thine, dispose of them according to thy will.
Give me thy love and thy grace, for this is enough for me.
   IGNATIUS OF LOYOLA, *Spanish hermit (1491–1556)* [*CBP, 54* PD]

Almighty God, you who have made all things for us, and us for your glory,
   sanctify our body and soul, our thoughts and our intentions,
   our words and actions, that whatsoever we shall think, or speak, or do,
   may by us be designed to the glorification of your name . . .
   and let no pride or self-seeking,
   no impure motive or unworthy purpose,
   no little ends or low imagination stain our spirit,
   or profane any of our words and actions.
But let our body be a servant to our spirit, and both body and spirit
servants of Jesus Christ.
   THOMAS Á KEMPIS, *German monk (1379–1471)* [*US* PD]

A PRAYER FOR TODAY

Lord, Your Word promises that when I give myself away in Your cause, I will
find renewal.
Yet I often try to preserve my time, my resources, and my energy rather than
being spent for others.
Help me to choose generosity by . . .
Help me to choose to be spent for others by . . .
Keep me from living for little ends. . . .
Dispose of all that I have been given for Your ends. Amen.

PRAYERS *of* PRAISE/ADORATION

Your name will be great,
O Lord Almighty, among the nations, from the rising to the setting of the sun.
In every place incense and pure offerings will be brought to Your name,
because Your name will be great among the nations.   **MALACHI 1:11**

Father God, You have exalted Jesus to the highest place,
giving Him the name that is above every name,
and at the name of Jesus every knee will bow in heaven and on earth and
under the earth,
and every tongue will confess that Jesus Christ is Lord, to Your glory.
PHILIPPIANS 2:9–11

We praise thee, O God; we acknowledge thee to be the Lord.
All the earth doth worship thee, the Father everlasting. . . .
The holy Church throughout all the world doth acknowledge thee,
the Father of an infinite majesty,
thine adorable, true, and only Son,
also the Holy Spirit, the Comforter.
Thou art the King of glory, O Christ.
Thou art the everlasting Son of the Father.
When thou tookest upon thee to deliver man,
thou didst humble thyself to be born of a Virgin.
When thou hadst overcome the sharpness of death,
thou didst open the kingdom of heaven to all believers.
Thou sittest at the right hand of God, in the glory of the Father.
We believe that thou shalt come to be our judge.
We therefore pray thee, help thy servants,
whom thou hast redeemed with thy precious blood.
"TE DEUM LAUDAMUS" [*BCP, 52–53* PD]

A PRAYER FOR TODAY

Lord, I join the company of people throughout history in praising You. . . .
I join the company of people living presently all over the world who worship
You. . . .
I join those who do not now, but who one day will worship You. . . .
I proclaim that Your name is great. . . . I declare that Your works are great. . . .
I ask that people would see Your greatness in my life and in my worship. . . .
I ask that Your greatness would be seen around the world in the lives of those
who worship You. . . .
You alone are worthy of my honor, praise, and devotion. . . . Amen.

PRAYERS *for* CHRISTLIKE CHARACTER

If I learn to speak in the tongues of men and angels, but I do not love, I am
only making noise to attract attention to myself.
If I have the gift of speaking and can understand and explain the mysteries
of faith, but I do not love, I am nothing.
If I give away all that I possess to aid the poor, and am burned for my faith,
but I do not love, I gain nothing.
Love never gives up on another.
Love cares deeply about others and expresses that concern as kindness.
Love doesn't covet another's position, possessions, or praise.
Love doesn't boast and seek acclaim for itself.
Love isn't full of itself, proud, arrogant, conceited, or puffed up.
Love isn't rude or pushy. Love isn't all about self.
Love is not easily angered, or easily upset with others. . . .
Love doesn't keep score, noting when it has been done wrong.
Love does not delight when bad things come to another. . . .
Love always protects, always trusts, and always endures.
Love will never fail.   1 CORINTHIANS 13:1–8

You, God, do not care so much about our outward actions, however sincere,
as *You do* about the heart, its motives, and especially the love for *You* that is
carried there.

Works of charity may help others, demonstrations of courage and ide-
alism may inspire others to faith and action, but these and even miracles of
faith can still flow through a life where the love of Christ has grown cold. If
I have not love, I am nothing.

I should look to my own heart, and ask how much love for You it holds.
CELTIC AIDEN READING [*CBP, 579* PD]

A PRAYER FOR TODAY

*Pray through 1 Corinthians 13 again slowly, considering each word and the ways that you
have loved—and not loved—the people in your life. . . .*
Lord, help me to rest in Your love and so be able to give love freely to those in
my life.
Help me to give love without condition and without judgment.
Help me not to presume that powerful experiences, public ministry, and per-
sonal sacrifices are substitutes for really loving people (1 Corinthians 13:1–3).
Show me where I have not been loving in recent days. . . .
Show me where I could act more lovingly in the days ahead. . . . Amen.

Lord, I do not even know what will happen tomorrow.
What is this life? A mist that appears for a little while and then vanishes.
JAMES 4:14

Dear Jesus, during this day help me quiet all the thoughts that fill my head—
> where I must go,
> whom I must see,
> and what I must do.
In their place, give me a sense of your order, your peace, and your time.
Help me to understand that you are in control, and I can trust you with my day.
Help me to realize that nothing on my to-do list is important if it is not what you want me to do.
I give all my tasks to you and trust you to bring order to them.
In these moments, dear Jesus . . . free me from the tyranny of "to do."
PATRICIA F. WILSON, *American author (twentieth century) [GSG, 346–47]*

Send, we beseech Thee, Almighty God, Thy Holy Spirit into our hearts,
that He may rule and direct us according to Thy will,
comfort us in all our temptations and afflictions,
defend us from all error, and lead us into all truth;
that we being steadfast in faith, may increase in love and in all good works,
and in the end obtain everlasting life; through Jesus Christ, Thy Son, our Lord. Amen.
COMMON SERVICE BOOK OF THE LUTHERAN CHURCH *(1917) [EOP, 112]*

Father, Give us wisdom to perceive you,
> intellect to understand you,
> diligence to seek you,
> patience to wait for you,
> eyes to behold you,
> a heart to meditate on you, and a life to proclaim you, Amen.
POPE BENEDICT *(480–543) [EOP, 14 PD]*

A PRAYER FOR TODAY

Lord, my life is full of things I must do.
Direct me to what is most important and to what is essential. . . .
As I meditate on You today, I sense . . .
My life can proclaim You today by . . .
Grant me the courage to act on what You have shown me, for this life is a mist.

PRAYERS *of* INTERCESSION

Lord, there is no one besides You to help the powerless against the powerful. Help us, O Lord our God, for we rely on You and in Your name we can stand against a mighty force. O Lord, You are our God.   2 CHRONICLES 14:11

Father God, I acknowledge that to clasp the hands in prayer is the beginning of an uprising against the disorder of the world
> RICHARD FOSTER, *American author (1942–present day) [PHH, 243]*

O God, you are our refuge.
When we are exhausted by life's efforts;
When we are bewildered by life's problems;
When we are wounded by life's sorrows:
> **We come for refuge to you.**
O God, you are our strength.
When our tasks are beyond our powers;
When our temptations are too strong for us;
When duty calls for more than we have to give to it:
> **We come for strength to you.**
O God, it is from you that all goodness comes. . . .
And now as we pray to you,
help us to believe in your love,
so that we may be certain that you will hear our prayer;
Help us to believe in your power
so that we may be certain that you are able to do for us above all that we ask or think;
All this we ask through Jesus Christ our Lord. Amen.
> WILLIAM BARCLAY, *Scottish Bible professor (1907–1978) [PCY, as quoted in GMO, 88–89]*

Almighty God, we pray that *(insert names)* may be comforted in their suffering and made whole.
When they are afraid, give them courage;
when they feel weak, grant them your strength;
when they are afflicted, afford them patience; . . .
when they are alone, move us to their side; . . .
In the name of Jesus Christ we pray. Amen.
> FROM THE METHODIST BOOK OF WORSHIP *(UMW, 101)*

A PRAYER FOR TODAY

Lord, I pray for *(insert names)* as they face . . .
I ask that they would come to You for . . . Amen.

Day 250
PRAYERS *of* SURRENDER

Now my Lord, I will revere and serve You with all faithfulness.
I will eliminate rival gods and affections. . . .
As for me and my household, we will serve You, Lord.
JOSHUA 24:14–15

Lord Jesus, I give thee my hands to do thy work.
I give thee my feet to go thy way.
I give thee my eyes to see as thou seest.
I give thee my tongue to speak thy words.
I give thee my mind that thou mayest think in me.
I give thee my spirit that thou mayest pray in me.
Above all, I give thee my heart that thou mayest love in me thy Father, and
all *people.*
I give thee my whole self that thou mayest grow in me, so that it is thee,
Lord Jesus, who live and work and pray in me. . . .
I hand over to thy care, Lord, my soul and body, my prayers and my hopes,
my health and my work,
my life and my death, my *children* and my family,
my friends and my neighbors, my country
and all *people.*
LANCELOT ANDREWES, *English minister (1555–1626)* [CBP, 49 PD]

O Lord, my best desire fulfill,
and help me to resign
life, health, and comfort, to your will,
and make your pleasure mine.
WILLIAM COWPER, *English poet/hymn writer (1731–1800)* [COS, 50 PD]

Lord, let me not live to be useless.
JOHN WESLEY, *Anglican minister (1703–1791)* [PD]

O Lord, I am yours. Do what seems good in your sight,
and give me complete resignation to your will.
DAVID LIVINGSTONE, *Scottish medical missionary (1813–1873)* [EOP, 114 PD]

A PRAYER FOR TODAY

Lord God, my aim is to be a good and faithful servant of Yours.
I surrender all of my life to You and to Your ends. . . . Amen.

PRAYERS *of* THANKSGIVING

Lord, remind me that when I experience favor with people, it is because
Your good hand is upon me. . . .
Remind me that when I experience success, it is because
Your good hand is upon me.   EZRA 7:6, 9

Let us give thanks to God our Father for all his gifts so freely bestowed on
us. For the beauty and wonder of your creation, in earth and sky and sea—
I thank you, Lord.
For all that is gracious in the lives of people, revealing the image of Christ—
I thank you, Lord.
For our daily food and drink, our homes and families, and our friends—
I thank you, Lord.
For minds to think, and hearts to love, and hands to serve—
I thank you, Lord.
For health and strength to work, and leisure to rest and play—
I thank you, Lord. . . .
Above all, we give you thanks for the great mercies and promises given to
us in Christ Jesus our Lord; to him be praise and glory . . . Amen.
      "A LITANY OF THANKSGIVING" *[BCP, 837]*

Lord, remind me that You hear my grumbling against You.
      Remind me that my grumbling is not against circumstances or people,
      but against You, Lord.   EXODUS 16:8

Father God, You are a God of goodness and grace.
Your good hand has brought so many good things into my life.
Yet I often focus on what I don't have and grumble and complain, if even
only in my mind. When I do this,
I lose sight of Your grace.
I lose sight of Your goodness. I lose sight of Your goodness to me.
Help me today to see and celebrate Your goodness to me.
      KURT BJORKLUND, *American minister (1968–present day)*

A PRAYER FOR TODAY

God, I am thankful today for the people with whom You have granted me favor
. . . *(name them)*
I am thankful for the places You have granted me success . . . *(name them)*
I acknowledge that this is a result of Your good hand upon me.
Remind me that when I grumble about people and situations, I am grumbling
against You.
Today I will choose to be thankful and to not complain. Amen.

PRAYERS *of* CONFESSION

🌣 Lord, You have spoken with a strong hand, warning me not to follow
    the way of people:
Therefore I will not be swept up in fear of what human power can do,
    and I will not fear what people fear; I will not dread it.
You call me to regard You as holy and that
You are the one I am to fear,
and You will be a sanctuary to me.
        ISAIAH 8:11–14

🌣 Forgive us God, that we have taken your creation for granted.
You have given us the run of the land, the pick of the crop
and we have squandered these resources;
distributed them unfairly, vandalized their beauty, violated their purity.
Forgive us God, that we have taken your kingdom for granted.
You have given us the seeds of faith, the fruits of the Spirit
and we have misused these resources;
displayed them rarely,
bestowed them grudgingly,
ignored them blithely.
        JEAN MORTIMER, *Salvation Army captain (twentieth century) [SAW, 1/3/11]*

🌣 Almighty and most merciful Father, whose clemency I now presume to
    implore, after a long life of carelessness and wickedness,
have mercy upon me.
I have committed many trespasses;
I have neglected many duties.
I have done what Thou hast forbidden, and left undone what Thou hast
    commanded.
Forgive, merciful Lord, my sins, . . . and enable me, by the Holy Spirit,
    to amend my life according to thy Holy Word, for Jesus Christ's sake.
        SAMUEL JOHNSON, *English writer (1709–1784) [GMO, 281]*

🌣 **Forgive me, Lord,** for those times when I have not spoken,
when I have not held out my hand
when I have not shared time, space, my life and faith.
Forgive me, Lord, for those times when I have not been a source of
friendship, joy, encouragement and grace
when I have not allowed your love to flow and a child of yours find peace.
        ANONYMOUS *[US]*

A PRAYER FOR TODAY

Ask God to reveal any areas of unconfessed sin to you. . . .
Add your own prayers of confession. . . .

PRAYERS *of* AFFIRMATION

Since I have received You and believed in Your name, You have made me Your child.
I am Your child not because of my human lineage, not because of my choice or the choice of another, but because I have been born of You.
   JOHN 1:12–13

O Lord, whatever the world may say, may we only pay attention to what you are saying to us,
and seek only your approval, which far outweighs any honor or praise that the world might bestow or withhold.
   GENERAL GORDON, *British army officer (1833–1885)* [BTP, 39 PD]

Father in heaven, you are the only one whose judgment matters in the end. What people think of us can burden or brighten our days. But it is of little account in the end. . . . Truth is all that will matter. This we have learned from your Son, Jesus. Oh, how we love his unswerving indifference to the approval of people. We praise you that he was fixed on you as the polestar of his life. What people said did not sway him to the right or the left. His compass was fixed on you. . . . Fill our minds and our mouths, O Lord, with the truth of Christ that we may speak well of him.
   JOHN PIPER, *American pastor (1946–present day)* [SJC, 69–70]

A PRAYER FOR TODAY

Lord, I am Your child (John 1:12).
I am Your friend (John 15:15).
I am justified (Romans 5:1).
I am united with You and one in Spirit (1 Corinthians 6:17).
I am bought with a price, and I belong to You (1 Corinthians 6:19–20).
I am a member of Your body (1 Corinthians 12:27).
I have been chosen by You before the world began (Ephesians 1:3–8).
I have been adopted into Your family and made an heir (Romans 8:15–17).
I am redeemed and forgiven (Colossians 1:13–14).
I am complete in You (Colossians 2:9–10).
I have direct access to the throne of grace through Jesus (Hebrews 4:14–16).
I am free from all condemnation (Romans 8:1).
I cannot be separated from the love of God (Romans 8:31–39).
I am a minister of reconciliation (2 Corinthians 5:17–21).
I am Your workmanship equipped for every good work (Ephesians 2:10).
Help me to live today in light of who I am in You. . . . Amen.
Note: Many other affirmations of who we are in Christ are found in the Bible.

PRAYERS *of* PETITION

❦ O Lord, grant us Your favor and establish the work of our hands.
   (Hebrew for *establish=konen* and means *to be firmly founded; used of
   kingdoms and buildings that will not be easily shaken.*)
   PSALM 90:17

❦ The Spirit of the Lord . . . brings good news to the poor,
   binds up the brokenhearted,
   proclaims liberty to the captives
   and the opening of the prison to those who are in chains,
   and proclaims the year of the Lord's favor
   (Hebrew for *favor=rason: acceptable and pleasing*)
   and the day of vengeance of our God. **ISAIAH 61:1–2**

❦ God of Truth, save us from a religion of mere words:
   from repeating phrases which have lost their meaning;
   from uttering empty prayers that have no soul;
   from calling Jesus "Lord, Lord," when we fail to own his sovereignty.
   FRANK COLQUHOUN, *English minister (1909–1997) [BTP, 71–72]*

❦ Save me, Lord, from the distraction of trying to impress others,
   and from the dangers of having done so.
   Help me to enjoy praise for work well done,
   and to pass it on to you.
   Teach me to learn from criticism,
   and give me the wisdom not to put myself at the centre of the universe.
   ANGELA ASHWIN, *American author (twentieth century) [BTP, 54]*

A PRAYER FOR TODAY

Father God, today I ask that Your favor would rest upon me.
I ask that Your beauty and sweetness would be evident in me and in my life.
May You establish the work of my hands, making what I do firmly founded.
Let me put my hands to doing what You would have me do.
Help me to love what You love and orient my life around what pleases You.
Bring favor and endurance to my marriage. . . .
Bring favor and endurance to my parenting. . . .
Bring favor and endurance to my work. . . .
Bring favor and endurance to my leadership. . . .
Bring favor and endurance to my ministry involvement. . . .
Bring favor and endurance to my friendships. . . .
Bring favor and endurance to my finances. . . . . Amen.

PRAYERS *for* RENEWAL

- Why is my soul downcast?
  Why am I so disturbed within myself?
  I will put my hope in You; God, I will yet praise You, my Savior and my God.
  PSALM 42:11

- Surely, You God are my salvation. I will trust and not be afraid.
  You, the Lord my Lord, are my strength and my song; You have become my salvation. **ISAIAH 12:2**

- My time is in your hands, O Lord.
  O Lord, deprive me not of your heavenly blessings.
  O Lord, deliver me from eternal torment.
  O Lord, if I have sinned in my mind or *my* thought, in word *or* deed, forgive me.
  O Lord, deliver me from every ignorance and inattention, from a petty soul and stony, hard heart.
  O Lord, deliver me from every temptation.
  O Lord, lighten my heart darkened by evil desires.
  O Lord, I, being a human being, have sinned; you, being God, forgive me in your loving kindness, for you know the weakness of my soul.
  O Lord, send down your grace to help me, that I may glorify your holy name. . . .
  O Lord, grant me tears of repentance, remembrance of death, and the sense of peace.
  O Lord, make me remember to confess my sins.
  O Lord, grant me humility, love, and obedience.
  O Lord, grant me tolerance, *benevolence*, and gentleness.
  O Lord, implant in me the root of all blessings; the reverence of you in my heart.
  O Lord, grant that I may love you with all my heart and soul, and that I may obey your will in all things. Amen.
  JOHN CHRYSOSTOM, *Greek minister (347–407)* [US, PD]

A PRAYER FOR TODAY

Lord, I bring the places of my soul where I am downcast to You. . . .
You are my hope. You are my salvation. I will hope in You.
I have no reason to fear. You are my strength.
Remind me that the confidence I have in my own abilities and goodness is misplaced.
Amen.

PRAYERS *of* PRAISE/ADORATION

I will come to You and worship.
I will bow down before You my Lord, my maker.   **PSALM 95:6**

I will guard my steps when I go to a place of worship.
I will go near to listen rather than to make a display of foolishness,
not even knowing what I do wrong.   **ECCLESIASTES 5:1**

God, You call us to worship because it is the only safe, humble, and creaturely
way in which *people* can be led to acknowledge and receive the influence of
objective Reality. . . .
Worship then is the avenue that leads *us* out of our inveterate self-occupation
into a knowledge of *You* God. . . .
Thus worship purifies, enlightens, and at last transforms, every life
submitted to its influence.
    EVELYN UNDERHILL, *English author (1875–1941) [FSC, 254]*

Our Father, we thank You that You have given us so much. . . .
Your grace does not just come in and forgive us of our sins. . . .
It changes the way in which we live in the world
and it changes the way in which we live with each other.
Please let us be like Your son who came not to be served but to serve. Amen.
    TIM KELLER, *American minister (1950–present day) [TKS, 3/10/10]*

A PRAYER FOR TODAY

Lord God, You are my maker.
I bow before You in humble adoration.
I worship You. I worship You for Your strength, Your perfections, and Your
compassions. . . .
I worship You for being great enough to forgive sins. . . .
I worship You for being greater than the problems of this world. . . .
I worship You for being the reason for hope, and joy, and purpose in a world
without much of these things.
I worship You for . . .
Amen.

PRAYERS *for* CHRISTLIKE CHARACTER

Lord, I will seek to cast off (Gk.=*apotithimi: to place or lay something down, put out of reach*)
all filthiness (Gk.=*ruparia: used for dirty clothes and for moral filth*)
and abundant wickedness (Gk.=*kakia: evil, malice, or anything out of line*)
and receive with meekness (Gk.=*proutos: to be submissive when offended*)
the implanted Word, which is able to save my soul.
I will be a doer of the Word,
not merely a hearer (Gk.=*akroates: used for listening without accountability*)
therefore deceiving myself. **JAMES 1:21–22**

Lord, help me step out of the sins and bad attitudes that have held me captive for so long. Help me know the right steps to take to remove these destructive and unworthy things from my life. You want me to be free, and I desire to be free. With Your help, I know I can be permanently set free. . . .

Today I start the process of acknowledging my sin and removing these attitudes, actions, and sins that are unworthy of the new creation I am today in Christ.
RICK RENNER, *missionary to Russia (twentieth century) [RSG, 12]*

Almighty God. Give us, we pray, the power to discern clearly right from wrong and allow all our words and actions to be governed thereby.
DWIGHT D. EISENHOWER, *American president (1890–1969) [EOP, 230]*

A PRAYER FOR TODAY

Lord, I acknowledge that I can get so used to moral compromises
that I rarely see them as filthiness and wickedness.
So today, show me where I am adorning what is filthy and wicked. . . .
Grant me a vision and a desire to adorn and take in Your Word.
Show me how my life would be different if I received Your Word with
meekness. . . .
Now help me to put away the habits and actions that are contrary to You and
Your ways.
The pride . . . the greed . . .
the covetousness . . . the judgmental attitudes . . .
the criticism . . . the selfishness . . .
the comfort seeking . . . the acclaim seeking . . .
the credit hogging . . .
the indifference . . . the independence . . .
the lust . . .
Help me to see these things for what they are and to desire Your ways. Amen.

Day 258
PRAYERS *for* WISDOM/GUIDANCE

❦ You, Lord, have made my mouth like a sharpened sword,
   in the shadow of Your hand You hide me;
   You, Lord, have made me into a polished arrow
   and concealed me in Your quiver. . . .
   I will shout for joy, with the heavens;
   and I will rejoice with the earth;
   I burst into song with the mountains!
   For You, Lord, comfort Your people,
   and You will have compassion on Your afflicted ones. ISAIAH 49:2, 13

❦ Help me, O God,
   To listen to what it is that makes my heart glad and to follow where it leads.
   May joy, not guilt,
   Your voice, not the voices of others,
   Your will, not my willfulness,
   be the guides that lead me to my vocation.
   Help me to unearth the passions of my heart that lay buried in my youth.
   And help me to go over that ground again and again until I can hold in my
   hands, hold and treasure, Your calling on my life.
        KEN GIRE, *American writer (1950–present day) [WOS, 73]*

❦ God guide me with your wisdom,
   God chastise me with your justice,
   God help me with your mercy,
   God protect me with your strength,
   God shield me with your shade,
   God fill me with your grace,
   For the sake of your anointed Son.
        GAELIC PRAYER [PD]

A PRAYER FOR TODAY

Lord, make me to see how You have made me unique. . . .
Let this lead my decisions rather than the expectations of those around me or
my culture.
Let me see the high ends to which You have created me,
ends that lead me to Your calling on my life . . .
ends that are not merely about my comfort, but about serving. . . .
Draw me to the passions that You have placed deep within me. . . .
Let Your leading of my passions guide my decisions, today and always. Amen.

PRAYERS *of* INTERCESSION

❦ Lord, it is You alone who decides who will rise and who will fall.
   PSALM 75:7

❦ We will be strong and courageous and act.
   We will not be afraid or discouraged, for You, Lord God, are with us.
   1 CHRONICLES 28:20

❦ Eternal Father, it is your joy to call men and women to serve you
      across the barriers of race and language and culture:
   Give them strength and courage, and satisfy their longing to make known
      the good news of Christ.
   When they face danger, save them from fear;
   When they are disheartened, be their friend;
   When they think they have failed, show them the cross.
   Give them peace in their hearts, and peace in their homes. . . .
   For Jesus Christ's sake.
      JOHN KINGSNORTH, *Salvation Army captain (twentieth century)*
      [SAW, 1/10/11]

A PRAYER FOR TODAY

Lord, You are the One who brings people high.
I ask that You would . . .
(Repeat the prayers for each category of people: my immediate family, my extended family, my closest friends, my coworkers, the leaders in my country, the leaders in the media, the leaders in my church, my general acquaintances, those who serve me day in and day out in various business, and those who view me with contempt.)
Draw *(insert names)* to Yourself, bringing them to spiritual salvation.
Grant *(insert names)* a sense of closeness and fellowship with You.
Inspire *(insert names)* to serve You selflessly and fully.
Give *(insert names)* a sense of what is right and good, and determination to stand
for it.
Encourage *(insert names)* where they are discouraged and scared.
Strengthen *(insert names)* when they sense their inadequacies and weaknesses.
Amen.

Day 260
PRAYERS *of* SURRENDER

🌢 If I turn away from what You have called me to do and refuse to speak of You,
Your word becomes a fire in my inner being and a fire shut up in my bones.
I am weary, I cannot hold it in; I really can't.
I hear people around me saying, "He/She is in real trouble." . . .
But You Lord are with me like a mighty warrior or a dreaded champion.
So those who persecute me will stop and not prevail.
You, Lord Almighty, are a pattern for the righteous,
and You probe hearts and minds;
Allow me to see how You act against them,
For to You alone have I committed my cause.   JEREMIAH 20:9–12

🌢 O God, enlarge my heart that it may be big enough to receive the
      greatness of your love.
Stretch my heart that it may take into it all those who with me around
      the world believe in Jesus Christ.
Stretch it that it may take into it all those who do not know him, but who
      are my responsibility because I know him.
And stretch it that it may take in all those who are not lovely in my eyes, and
      whose hands I do not want to touch; through Jesus Christ, my Savior.
      PRAYER OF UNNAMED AFRICAN CHRISTIAN [*BTP, 174* PD]

🌢 Bring me to see that what I have is there to be shared. . . .
Bring me to see that what I have is not the last word in life.
Bring me to see that ultimately my security, my peace of mind depends
not on my talents,
not on my achievements,
not on the status that goes with these,
but on knowing that all that I have gains its meaning from you.
      REX CHAPMAN, *English minister (twentieth century)* [*HBP, 103*]

A PRAYER FOR TODAY

Lord, there are times when I am disheartened
because it seems that those who are against me are prevailing. . . .
At times, when I sense this, I want to quit.
But when I feel that way, I cannot escape Your call on my life.
When I step back and look to You, I realize Your power. . . .
And I realize that You are with me. . . .
And I realize that You are for me. . . .
So I praise You today. . . . Amen.

WORKS CITED

For fast reference, the sources of prayers utilized in this book are noted at the end of the prayer with an abbreviation followed by the page number. Below are the abbreviations in alphabetical order, followed by the source information.

AC = *Authentic Christianity: From the Writings of John Stott.* Edited by Timothy Dudley-Smith. Downers Grove, IL: InterVarsity, 1995.

AGP = *A Guide to Prayer for All God's People.* Rueben P. Job and Norman Shawchuck. Nashville: Upper Room, 1990.

BCP = *Book of Common Prayer.* The Episcopal Church. New York: The Church Hymnal, 1979.

BDD = *Beyond Doubt: Faith-Building Devotions on Questions Christians Ask.* Cornelius Plantinga Jr. Grand Rapids: Eerdmans, 2002.

BHE = *Between Heaven and Earth.* Ken Gire. San Francisco: Harper, 1997.

BJD = *Begin the Journey with the Daily Office.* Peter Scazzero. Elmhurst, NY: Emotionally Healthy Spirituality, 2008.

BSP = *The Believer's School of Prayer.* Andrew Murray. Minneapolis: Bethany, 1982.

BTP = *The Book of a Thousand Prayers.* Compiled by Angela Ashwin. Grand Rapids: Zondervan, 1996.

BUP = *Book of Uncommon Prayer.* Joseph Parker. Leesburg, FL: The Great Commission Prayer League, n.d.

CBP = *The Complete Book of Christian Prayer.* Edited. New York: Continuum, 2000.

CBR = *Creative Brooding.* Robert Raines. New York: Macmillan, 1966.

CDP = *Celtic Daily Prayer. Prayers and Readings from the Northumbria Community.* New York: HarperCollins, 2002.

CH = *A Church Hymnary.* Revised edition. London: Oxford Univ. Press, 1927. Cited in *A Passion for God.* Raymond C. Ortlund Jr. See PFG

COS = *The Communion of Saints: Prayers of the Famous.* Edited by Horton Davies. Grand Rapids: Eerdmans, 1990.

CPB = *Catholic Prayer Book.* No Author. Cincinnati: St. Anthony Messenger Press, 1986.

DOG = *Days of Grace Through the Year.* Lewis B. Smedes. Downers Grove, IL: InterVarsity, 2007.

DPP = *A Diary of Private Prayer.* John Baillie. New York: Fireside, 1949.

EGA = *31 Days of Praise: Enjoying God Anew.* Ruth Myers with Warren Myers. Sisters, OR: Multnomah, 1994.

EOP = *Encyclopedia of Prayer and Praise.* Edited by Mark Water. Peabody, MA: Hendrickson, 2004.

FRC = *Concordia Commentary: Romans.* Martin H. Franzmann, St. Louis: Concordia, 1968.

FSC = *Spiritual Classics.* Edited by Richard Foster and Emilie Griffin. New York: Harper One, 2000.

GMO = *A Guide to Prayer for Ministers and Other Servants.* Rueben P. Job and Norman Shawchuck. Nashville: Upper Room, 1983.

GOC = *The Glory of Christmas.* Charles Swindoll, Max Lucado, and Charles Colson. Nashville: Nelson, 2009.

GSB = *The 52 Greatest Stories of the Bible.* Kenneth Boa and John Alan Turner. Ventura, CA: Regal, 2008.

GSG = *A Guide to Prayer for All Who Seek God.* Norman Shawchuck and Rueben P. Job. Nashville: Upper Room, 2006.

GST = *Systematic Theology.* Wayne Grudem. Grand Rapids: Zondervan, 1994.

HBP = *Harper Collins Book of Prayers.* Compiled by Robert Van de Weyer. Edison, NJ: Castle, 1997.

HCG = "How Can God Be Loving Yet Send People to Hell?" D. A. Carson video interview; at www.chrisbrauns.com/2009/11/27/d-a-carson-how-can-god-be-loving-yet-send-people-to-hell/

IGG = *If God Is Good*. Randy Alcorn. Colorado Springs: Multnomah, 2009.

IYS = *Improving Your Serve*. Charles Swindoll. Waco, TX: Word, 1981.

JFM = *Jesus Freaks: Stories of Those Who Stood for Jesus*. D.C. Talk and the Voice of Martyrs. Tulsa: Albury, 1999.

JJE = *The Journals of Jim Elliot*. Jim Elliot. Ventura, CA: Regal, 2002.

JWP = *The Prayer Book*. J.W.; full name unknown. n.p., 1859.

KCL = *Know Your Christian Life*. Sinclair Ferguson. Downers Grove, IL: Inter-Varsity, 1981.

LAV = *Life as a Vapor*. John Piper. Sisters, OR: Multnomah, 2004.

LP = *Leadership Prayers*. Richard Kriegbaum. Carol Stream, IL: Tyndale, 1998.

MG = *My God, My Glory*. Eric Milner-White. London: SPCK, n.d.

MGH = *31 Days of Prayer: Moving God's Mighty Hand*. Warren and Ruth Myers. Sisters, OR: Multnomah, 1997.

MOP = *The Meaning of Prayer*. Harry Emerson Fosdick. Nashville: Abingdon Press, 1949.

MPE = *Money, Possessions and Eternity*. Randy Alcorn. Wheaton: Tyndale, 2003.

MRG = *The Ragamuffin Gospel*. Brennan Manning. Sisters, OR: Multnomah, 2005.

MUH = *My Utmost for His Highest*. Oswald Chambers. Westwood, NJ: Barbour, 1935.

MWS = *Moments with the Savior*. Ken Gire. Grand Rapids: Zondervan, 1998.

NTW = *Not the Way It's Supposed to Be: A Breviary of Sin*. Cornelius Plantinga Jr. Grand Rapids: Eerdmans, 1995.

OBP = *The Oxford Book of Prayer*. Edited by George Appleton. New York: Oxford Press, 1985.

OHP = *Prayer*. O. Hallesby. Minneapolis: Augsburg, 1931.

PBW = *Pierced by the Word*. John Piper. Wheaton: Crossway, 2007.

PCS = *Developing a Prayer-Care-Share Lifestyle.* Various Authors. Grand Rapids: HOPE Ministries, 1999.

PCY = *Prayers for the Christian Year.* William Barclay. London: SCM Press, 1989.

PD = Public Domain

PDL = *The Private Devotions of Lancelot Andrewes.* Lancelot Andrewes. London: Suttaby.

PE = Personal e-mail. Leighton Ford, January 1, 2010.

PFG = *A Passion for God.* Raymond C. Ortlund, Jr. Wheaton: Crossway, 1994.

PFH = *Penned from the Heart*, vol. 15. Edited by Jana Carman. New Willmington, PA: Son-Rise Publications, 2010.

PGA = *Prayer, the Great Adventure.* David Jeremiah. Sisters, OR: Multnomah, 1997.

PGP = *Pearls of Great Price: 366 Daily Devotional Readings.* Joni Eareckson Tada. Grand Rapids: Zondervan, 2006.

PHH = *Prayer: Finding the Heart's True Home.* Richard Foster. San Francisco: Harper Collins, 1992.

PL = *Power Lines: Celtic Prayers About Work.* Edited by David Adam. Harrisburg, PA: Moorehouse, 1992.

POG = *The Pursuit of God.* A. W. Tozer. Camp Hill, PA: Christian, 1982.

PSH = *Praise Songs and Hymns.* Compiled by Charles Wickman. Grand Rapids: Zondervan, 1979.

RFG = *The Reason for God.* Tim Keller. New York: Dutton, 2008.

RSG = *Sparkling Gems from the Greek.* Rick Renner. Tulsa: Teach for All Nations, 2003.

SAW = Salvation Army Web Site.www.salvationarmy.org.

SJC = *Seeing and Savoring Jesus Christ.* John Piper. Wheaton: Crossway, 2001.

SOL = *Signs of Life.* David Jeremiah. Nashville: Nelson, 2007.

SSP = *Seventy Short Prayers for Use of the Young by a Clergyman's Wife.* J. W. London: Winchester Barclay, 1859.

TAL = *The Attentive Life.* Leighton Ford. Downers Grove, IL: InterVarsity, 2008.

TFG = *The Forgotten God.* Francis Chan. Colorado Springs: David C. Cook, 2009.

THF = *A Touch of His Freedom.* Charles Stanley. Grand Rapids: Zondervan, 1991.

TKS = Tim Keller. Sermons. Website: www.redeemer.com.

TTO = *The Tale of the Tardy Oxcart.* Charles Swindoll. Nashville: Nelson, 1998.

UMW = *The United Methodist Book of Worship.* Nashville: The United Methodist Publishing House, 1992.

US = Unknown Source

WJ = *Wings of Joy.* Compiled by Joan Winmill Brown. Cited in *Between Heaven and Earth.* Ken Gire. Old Tappan, NJ: Revell.

WGW = *When God Weeps.* Joni Eareckson Tada and Steven Estes. Grand Rapids: Zondervan, 1997.

WOS = *Windows of the Soul.* Ken Gire. Grand Rapid: Zondervan, 1996.

WSC = *Simply Christian: Why Christianity Makes Sense.* N. T. Wright. San Francisco: Harper, 2006.